PACIFISM AND THE JEWS

by
Evelyn Wilcock

In memory of
my father's cousin
Joseph Kaufmann 1895-1919
(J. Alan Kaye)
Jew and Pacifist
for whom it proved impossible

HAWTHORN PRESS

Evelyn Wilcock is hereby identified as author of this work in accordance with Section 77 of the Copyright, Designs and Patent Act, 1988. She asserts and gives notice of her moral right under this Act.

Published by Hawthorn Press,
Hawthorn House, 1 Lansdown Lane, Lansdown, Stroud, Gloucestershire, GL5 1BJ.

Typeset by Saxon Graphics Limited, Derby.

Cover by Patrick Roe, Glevum Graphics,
2 Honyatt Road, Gloucester.

Cover photograph is of Rev. John Harris,
reproduced by permission of the Harris family.

Printed by Cromwell Press Limited,
Broughton Gifford, Melksham, Wiltshire.

A catalogue record of this book is available from the British Library Cataloguing in Publication Data.

ISBN 1 869 890 48 5

Contents

Introduction
Non-violence in the Jewish Tradition

There is a story of Rabbi Yohanan ben Zakkai. He refused to bless the Jewish rebellion against Rome which was to cost so many lives. Instead he negotiated with the Romans, and was smuggled out of Jerusalem in a coffin. With Roman permission, he energetically re-established a religious centre at Yavneh near the coast. So an act of non-violence preserved the God and faith of Judaism after the Temple was destroyed. But to dwell on the Judaism of two thousand years ago would give a false impression. Judaism as such is not a pacifist religion. Like Christianity, it has a minority pacifist strand within it.

To speak of a pacifist strand is to say that in effect there is not one Judaism. Judaism is as varied as Christianity, displaying internal differences as great as those which separate the Eastern Orthodox Church, for example, from the Baptists. Not only are there differences within Judaism at any one time, but, like Christianity, Judaism has developed over the centuries, responding both to geographical location and to social and cultural influences. The corollary of this is that, though Judaism has a tradition of its own, one finds that in any century Judaism tends to share the preoccupations and characteristics of the Christianity of the day. So, though one might like to say 'this is Jewish', and 'this is Christian', making a clear cut division, it is not something that one can do as neatly as those would like, who say that pacifism is a Christian concept and does not belong to the Jewish tradition at all.

Jews did join in the defence of their cities from the Middle Ages onwards but they were not generally associated with war. Diderot's great eighteenth century encyclopedia attributed the survival of the Jews partly to the fact that they were not liable for military service. When the French Revolution emancipated the Jews, Jews were expected to show their gratitude by serving in the revolutionary armies along with everyone else. The Rabbis were ordered to make this clear and they probably did so most willingly. Quite apart from sharing the patriotic fervour of their countrymen, Jewish religious law obliges Jews, for their own safety, to comply with the law of any country where they may live.

As soon as there was a legal possibility of conscientious objection, individual Jews began to make out a case for Jewish pacifism, and, naturally, Jewish religious objection is based on many of the Biblical texts that will be familiar to Christians. The chapters that follow concentrate on pacifism which is more specifically Jewish and draws on a tradition which will be less familiar. The classic writers are little known today to non-orthodox Jews in peace movements. Rediscovery of these texts is an important step in understanding Jewish spirituality and sharing it with fellow pacifists.

Many pacifist Jews turned their backs on Jewish identification altogether and lived as political activists in a non-Jewish world. The international nature of the Jewish community proved that men of many nationalities could have common ground. International disputes must be solved by negotiations, not through bloodshed. The history of secular pacifism and of international bodies designed to keep peace is marked by the high number of Jews involved. Even today their Jewishness is often not pointed out. Historians are unhappy to label a Jew, to suggest that a Jewish ethical background is relevant, or to imply that Jews lacked loyalty to the countries of which they were citizens.

This book is not an exhaustive history of Jewish non-violence. It examines the ways in which some individual Jews have formulated a pacifist philosophy, how they based their pacifism on the way they saw their identity as Jews, and how their pacifism affected their lives.

Acknowledgements

In writing this book I have been helped by many people whose views do not coincide with mine but who have given me of their time and insight. My thanks are for their advice and encouragement.

I acknowledge with gratitude the help of the rabbis, all eminent in their field, who found time to talk to me, Rabbi Albert Axelrad, Rabbi I. Domb, Rabbi Louis Jacobs, Rabbi Jeremy Milgrom, Rabbi Isaac Newman and Rabbi Michael Rosen. In the United Kingdom I have been helped with material provided by Rabbi David Goldberg, Hyam Maccoby, Rabbi John Rayner, Rabbi Jonathan Romain and Rabbi Norman Solomon. From the States I have had help from Rabbi Philip Bentley, Naomi Goodman, Murray Polner, the late Rabbi Steven Schwarzschild, and the staff of the Jewish Peace Fellowship. I owe particular thanks to the family of Rev. John Harris for allowing me to use his personal papers, to the Trustees of the Imperial War Museum for allowing access to the papers of J.E. Hoare and to his family for permission to quote from them. I appreciated very much the generosity of Rabbi Irwin Zeplowitz who allowed me to make use of his unpublished thesis on Jewish attitudes to the Vietnam War. I am grateful to Belinda Part and Michael Shire for bringing information from the States and to Uri Davis and Amos Gvirtz for material from Israel. I benefitted from the professional encouragement of David Cesarani at the Wiener Library and Michael May at the I.J.A. and of Rabbi Danny Rich. It is not possible to name all the librarians who have helped but my particular thanks go to Ezra Kahn at Jews' College and Jonathan Gorsky at Yakar, to Roy Segal at Leo Baeck College, and to the librarians at Friends' House, the Wiener Library, the Hebrew Union College, and the Hebrew Community Library in Venice. To Jonathan Gorsky and to Fanny Perry, my thanks for help translating modern Hebrew.

This book would not have been completed without the encouragement, conversation and hospitality of my friends, in particular, Barbara Hudson in Oxford and Janet Unwin in London. But my thanks go above all to my husband who alone financed this research, uncomplainingly translated from German and Italian, accompanied me to libraries and corrected my spelling.

Extracts from translations of the Talmud and works of Maimonides published by Soncino Press and Yale University Press are reproduced in the Appendix by kind permission of the publishers. Inconsistencies in the spelling of Hebrew terms and Rabbinic names in the Appendix and elsewhere in this book are due to the requirement for copyright reasons to retain the transliterations used in differing sources. Most of Chapter 1 first appeared in *The Transactions of the Jewish Historical Society of England* Vol. XXX to whom my thanks are due.

Chapter 1
Rev. John Harris: Issues in Anglo-Jewish Pacifism 1914-18

John Harris, a minister at Prince's Road Synagogue in Liverpool, was probably the first person to argue that Jewish boys should have the same rights as Christians to lodge a conscientious objection to military service. Harris was an unassuming and religious man. His pacifism was personal and not political, but he raised questions about Jewish pacifism, Jewish self-censorship and the freedom of the rabbinate, which caused consternation and self-questioning in the Jewish Community and in the end cost him his job.

So great was the concern that the Chief Rabbi, Joseph Hertz, was obliged to use his influence to get Harris reinstated and Alfred Jessel KC. was brought in to mediate. Jessel was "one of earth's enviable men,"[1] an eminent barrister, and Vice President of the United Synagogue. Above all we are told that he had "an absolute genius for resolving serious difficulties into matters of tweedledee and tweedledum".[2] But this was April 1916 when Verdun dominated the headlines and the disruption and carnage of the First World War were exceeding all expectations. The task proved too much even for Jessel. It is innocent enough to claim that British legislation should apply equally to Jew and non-Jew but in the context of 1916 it brought John Harris's patriotism into question and posed a severe threat to his congregation.

From the outbreak of war in August 1914, the middle class youth of Liverpool, as elsewhere, rushed to enlist. This included the Jews. There was enormous pressure to volunteer and young men of any persuasion who refused on principle, evidently held strong convictions, either political or religious. At first religious objections were ill defined. In August 1914 not even membership of the Society of Friends was synonymous with pacifism; a number of young Quakers volunteered for active service on the grounds that this was a special case. A small nation, Belgium, had been attacked by a militarist power, Germany.[3] The principle of Quaker pacifism in all circumstances was quickly reasserted. But the debate within the Society of Friends illustrates the difference between refusal to participate in a particular war, and a religious conviction that all war was wrong. The differentiation between wars that are commanded, wars that are permitted and wars that are forbidden is central to any Torah-based discussion of Jewish pacifism.

Not all religious objections were synonymous with pacifism; the Christadelphians were not necessarily opposed to war but their religion forbade them to obey army orders from a non religious source. Again one is reminded of certain Hasidic groups who will fight only in an army commanded by the Messiah. Orthodox Judaism was not pacifist, but there were religious objections to Cohenim serving since it was contrary to the law for the priestly caste to be in contact with the dead. This problem was conveniently solved by dispensations from the Chief Rabbis on both sides in the conflict. However, it is fair to mention that the Leeds Beth Din publicly opposed the Chief Rabbi on this issue and his dispute with them was going on at the same time as he was being called on to use his influence in the Liverpool affair.

A more fundamental problem for religious Jews was the lack of Kosher food in the forces or of any provision for strict religious observance. None the less the substantial number of Jews serving (10,000 in January 1915 out of a total Jewish population of 250,000) does not seem to have been a smaller proportion than for the British population as a whole.

During the summer of 1915 there was increasing political pressure to get all eligible men into the army. Under the Derby Scheme a register of available manpower was made through a door to door canvas. Jews were involved in this (in Manchester for instance) and there was nationally an active Jewish Recruiting Committee. "England has been all she could be to Jews; Jews will be all they can be to England" was used as a rallying cry and the psalms were quoted to justify the holiness of a just war. *Blessed be the Lord, my Rock, Who teacheth my hands to war and my fingers to fight* (Psalm CX 54).

On 29 January 1915, the Jewish National Movement in Liverpool held a debate on the issue that compulsory military service was opposed to Jewish ideals, but outside Zionist circles it was widely propagated that pacifism was contrary to the Jewish religion. Herbert Samuel, Home Secretary, and a Jew with Liverpool connections, declared that a Jew could not be a C.O. on religious grounds. "Everything that is Jewish, even the fine Jewish Ideal of

Peace .... points the finger of scorn, derision and contempt at the Jewish C.O."[4] Though its original intention was to prevent and curtail hostilities, by 1916 even the Jewish Peace Society was endorsing the righteousness of the allied cause.[5]

The insatiable military demand for manpower was finally given the force of law in the Military Service Act of January 1916 which introduced conscription. Appeals against compulsory military service were to be heard by local appeal tribunals. Objections on grounds of conscience were supposedly allowed. In British law the principle of conscientious objection had been established not by pacifists but by people who had religious objections to compulsory vaccination against smallpox. Therefore in 1916 tribunals took conscientious objection to mean a religious objection, and some tribunals rejected even this. To prove that an objection was genuine, it was important for conscientious objectors to obtain a testimonial from a clergyman of their own faith. Certain 'liberal' churchmen, including William Temple, while not themselves opposing the war, gave testimonials on behalf of young men personally known to them. Harris's controversial stand was taken, he claimed, because his colleagues at Prince's Road (and one suspects elsewhere) were not willing to perform a similar service for their congregants.

In March 1916 the Government issued a directive that the Act exempted from Military Service those who were already studying for the ministry. One therefore finds Jewish theological students coming before the tribunals, along with those preparing for the Christian priesthood. The archives of the Chief Rabbi show that he was asked by the authorities to substantiate exemption claims from lists of foreign-born Hebrew teachers, most of whom came from yeshivas outside his normal jurisdiction. Evidence of other Jewish conscientious objectors is hard to find. Sometimes British Jews appeared in front of the tribunals to ask for exemption on humane grounds because they had relatives in the German or Austrian forces, or interned as aliens. A few C.O.s, Jewish by birth, were international socialists. These men were popularly regarded as archetypal Jewish pacifists, representing the whole. In fact, they had abandoned Judaism and their Jewish origin was rarely produced to support their claim, although it was used against them in some tribunals by anti-Semitic military representatives. It was easy enough to dismiss Jewish pacifism, as they did at Cardiff, with the jeer that it was Jews who had killed Christ.[6]

But here and there, as at Cardiff, there is the isolated case of a young Jew who had the courage to state a religious objection to fighting. Some of these objections were not pacifist, but rested on exemptions in *halakha* (Jewish law) set out in Deuteronomy XX. A man is excused service if he has just married and has lived with his wife for less than a year. He is excused service if he has built a new house in which he has lived for less than a year, or planted a vineyard from which he has not yet taken the harvest. From a pacifist viewpoint it may be observed that these exemptions lean towards the exclusion of young men, and are designed to ensure the birth of a new generation, and to provide for their material support. But the Bible also exempts men who are fearful or fainthearted. This final exemption of those who have no heart for war later became an important plank in the Jewish pacifist argument. But at a time when white feathers (signifying cowardice) were handed out to those who failed to volunteer to fight, exemption of the fearful was not an argument presented to tribunals in the First World War.

The exemptions in Deuteronomy are also used from time to time by Christian Fundamentalist objectors, but they are objections which postpone military service for a limited period of one year and (apart from the final exemption of the fainthearted) cannot provide for permanent exemption on grounds of conscience. However, talking to Hyam Maccoby, whose father in Sunderland pleaded the objection that he was newly married, confirms the suspicion that Jews who objected on the basis of Biblical exemptions were true pacifists, but that they could think of no other authentic Jewish way of presenting a religious objection.

Jewish cases were frequently misreported in the local press or ridiculed. Isaac Ruben aged 23 of Bangor, a boot and shoe dealer, had his case dismissed on the grounds that he had been a member of the local rifle club.[7] A friendly clergyman, Rev. John W. Graham of Walton Hall, sent *The Jewish World* a corrected account of the stand taken by Eliezar Million, a tailor. He appeared before the Salford tribunal claiming that the divine principle was in every man and that one should love all men and should not kill.[8] This Jewish universalism, the biblical notion that all men are brothers created in the likeness of God, is explored and enlarged on in the Talmud. It is one of the earliest arguments for Jewish pacifism and it has continued to be used right up to the present day by American Jews opposed to the war in Vietnam and to nuclear arms.

It was for such pacifists that Harris had volunteered to speak at tribunals. He taught Hebrew to boys preparing for their Bar Mitzvah, and would have been a natural person to turn to for a reference.[9] He argued that it was therefore proper for him as for any other religious instructor to testify to the genuine convictions of his former students.

His insistence on this right shows that there were Jewish conscientious objectors connected with the Prince's Road synagogue, even though it has so far been impossible to identify more than a handful. Few tribunal records have survived and Liverpool local newspapers cannot help because the tribunal there initially withheld names of objectors, and heard many conscience cases *in camera*. The task of 'uncovering' Jewish conscientious objectors of British descent is not helped by the wishful-thinking at the time that they simply did not exist. The Chief Rabbi felt unable to make any public statement recognising a religious basis for Jewish pacifism. On the contrary, a letter from him was in circulation endorsing the war effort. As a result, tribunals, at Stockport for instance, refused to recognise any plea based on Judaism.[10] The body of religious pacifist opinion was Christian, and often claimed a distinction between the teaching of Jesus (non resistance) and the earlier Jewish code of retribution. Individual Christian pacifists were not free of anti-Semitism. In the circumstances some Jewish C.O.s denied that they were Jewish by religion. Other Jews who openly practised their religion in detention would not admit they were pacifists, lest the authorities should further hinder their religious observances. This extract from a prison diary kept by a Christian objector, a courageous young public school boy from Repton, does much to explain their caution:

> Billeus is a heavily built chap of unmistakeably Jewish features. His conduct too unfortunately looks fishy though I have no doubt about him as the others have. He will not class himself as a C.O. except to us until he is sent to the Jewish battalion at Plymouth. .... He has a real pleasure: strict observance of his religious rites and prohibitions – food – going short of food or providing it himself. With phylacteries on wrist and forehead in the morning he stands calmly humming, refusing to budge from

his standing place in spite of being bullied once actually by the sergeant of the guard.[11]

Anti foreign feeling was widespread during the early years of this century, and prejudice was constantly reinforced both in the press and in popular literature. A surviving pacifist who had Jewish friends recalled that the anti-German feeling of the period was virtually synonymous with anti-Jewish feeling,[12] an impression confirmed by press reporting of antisemitic racial harassment. Many Jews did indeed come from Germany. But others were from Eastern Europe and Russia, Britain's ally in the war. After the sinking of the Lusitania in May 1915, German (i.e. German-Jewish) property was attacked and shops with German names broken into in violent demonstrations in Liverpool. It is a notable coincidence that one of the businesses which suffered, Kaufmann's, shared the original name of a Liverpool Jewish family with a pacifist son. There was a noticeable delay in preventative action by the police who were so quick to control Labour or pacifist demonstrations.

Although both the well-meaning Liberal Press in Liverpool and the Jewish establishment denied that there was any link between anti-German and anti-Jewish sentiment, Jews who served in the forces knew otherwise. In May 1916 Captain Neville Laski reported to the Board of Deputies that in the Army the prevalent view was that all foreigners were Jews.[13] Not surprisingly, when Jewish chaplains did at last contact serving men they discovered that some had enlisted as C of E.[14] Rabbi Adler explained that this was in error. But it was more likely a way to avoid anti-Semitism.

Harris's stand epitomises the dilemma of British Jews. He associated the Synagogue with pacifism; thus he laid it open to the suspicion of pro-German sentiment. The embarrassment to his colleagues and congregation shows that then, as now, assimilated immigrant groups found themselves trapped by their insecure position in society into being more Roman than the Romans.

It was not the first time Harris had been in trouble with his congregation for being un-British. In 1898 he had been reprimanded for supporting Herzl and political Zionism. On that occasion Harris wrote demanding that he should have full liberty of action outside his duties in connection with the synagogue.[15] On that occasion too he was at odds with the Minister, Friedeberg.

Unfortunately for Harris, his Liverpool congregation consisted of those Liverpool Jews who regarded themselves as most British and who therefore distanced themselves from Zionism. It is hard to appreciate that in the 1890s even the Chief Rabbi, Adler, was anti-Zionist. As for the Jewish establishment in Liverpool, they had secured their social status in Liverpool society, and had assimilated without sacrificing their religious identity; they dispatched their sons to public schools such as Uppingham and Clifton. The last thing they wanted was to give the impression of divided loyalties. They were exclusively British.

In 1874 the Liverpool Old Hebrew congregation had built a fine new synagogue away from the city centre; "The finest in England," the Jewish Chronicle called it. According to Kokosalakis' study of the Liverpool Jewish Community[16,] the Old Hebrew Congregation was controlled by an élite of about thirty families, who were free members. Prince's Road then was not the depressed Toxteth of today but a smart residential district close to the parks where successful businessmen and cottonbrokers had their houses. There the congregation adopted progressive, anglicised forms of worship which disassociated them still further from more recent waves of Jewish immigrants[17] and from aspirations for a Homeland in Palestine.

In 1914 Zionism and pacifism did not necessarily go hand in hand. Its emphasis on international Jewry certainly influenced a section of Jewish opinion. Dr. Gaster, the Haham, leader of the Sephardic community, deplored a conflict which set Jew fighting Jew. Yet militant Zionists fought enthusiastically for the British in Palestine. Jewish recruiting in both the German and the Allied Forces was deliberately encouraged by the promise of Jewish self-government in Palestine. The Jewish Community contributed willingly to the British war effort and shared the general anti-German hysteria. War loving German Jews were un-Jewish, declared *The Jewish Chronicle* in February 1916, the same month that it closed its Roll of Honour for those who had volunteered to fight on the Allied side. It was constantly maintained that anti-Semitism was exclusively German and did not (officially) exist in Britain.

The subsequent history of the Holocaust should not deceive us. Although at the outbreak of war German Jews were barred from the judiciary, the civil service and university posts, they were an assimilated population and were resolutely included in the German war effort. Israel Cohen returned from Rühleben and reported that there were 60,000 Jews serving in the German army.[18] In America the Jewish Press was not anti-German and there was a marked Jewish element within the peace organisations which opposed entry on the Allied side.

It seemed to many British Jews too that it was Britain's ally, Russia, which was most anti-Semitic. The authorities allowed repeated pogroms both in Russia and in Russian-controlled Poland. The war on the Eastern front savaged the Pale of Settlement; reversals were blamed on the Jews, culminating in mass expulsions and the banning of Hebrew in July 1915. In Russia Jews were not conscripted on an equal basis with other groups, a sign that they were not full citizens.

As a result, British born sons of non-naturalised Russian Jews were not conscripted into the British Forces under the 1916 Act. This actually created anti-Semitism because it looked as if Russian Jews were excused service. Even their internment failed to satisfy public opinion and they were next threatened with deportation to join the Russian forces, an alarming prospect for men who had come to Britain for political asylum. This problem of "friendly" aliens dragged on and was resolved only by the Russian withdrawal from the war after the Revolution of 1917. Then in the final wave of recruitment, Jews who had not been able to afford naturalisation were enlisted with the promise that for those with proper residence and language qualifications, active service would confer British nationality without fee after a time lapse of three months.

Enemy aliens were a different matter, and the illogical extremes of their internment sometimes created discrepancies within families. German-born sons of naturalised parents were not eligible to serve in the British forces. But British-born sons of the non-naturalised were. *The Liverpool Daily Post* records the tribunal appearance of a young man whose father was born in Germany, who had arrived in Liverpool at the age of three, but had never been naturalised and who had therefore been interned. The son, British-born, applied for exemption which was refused. The tribunal none the less also refused to set his father free.[19]

It was not possible for interned Jews to practise their religion, but the Jewish press was careful not to criticise the government on so sensitive an issue. The Board of Deputies announced that internment was not a Jewish Question.[20] Rev. Harris evidently disagreed. He was involved, along with other Jewish ministers, in visiting internment centres with gifts of Matzos, and pressing for the supply of Kosher food.

One sees that the military authorities were truly confused by their simultaneous desire to enforce universal conscription and to exclude alien elements from the British forces. Whether foreign born Jews were subject to the Military Service Acts and/or whether there should be a separate Jewish Regiment were questions fiercely argued in the Jewish Press at the time. It seemed as if the right to enlist was an important element of non-discrimination, and it is this issue, along with radical immigrant opposition to the war, which has been most discussed by Jewish historians since.

But John Harris was notably different from the Russian emigré Jews who failed to identify with the Allied war effort. To them he appeared incongruously English. He had a black dog. He was *"der reb mit hund"*.[21] Harris was born in London in 1866, the son of a British minister, Raphael Harris, who had been Chazan at Bayswater Synagogue. This qualified John Harris to hold a specially endowed Braham Readership at the Liverpool Prince's Road Synagogue. The post could not be given to Rev. Joseph Polack, Minister at Prince's Road from 1882-1890, who had not been so lucky in his birth.

Harris himself was no outsider in the congregation. His father had been a Minister at the synagogue before him and when Polack's departure enabled an appointment to be made, Harris became reader in 1894 and later Secretary. Perhaps it was the Englishness of his background and education, together with the apparent security of his appointment that gave Harris the confidence to speak out against conscription in much the same terms as any other Englishman.

His superior, the Minister of the Synagogue, Rev. Samuel Friedeberg, had a different interpretation of Englishness. He was "a keen advocate of patriotic service, and (has) continually urged young men to join the army and has held special military services at the Synagogue."[22] He was Honorary Chaplain to Jewish soldiers serving in the area and was photographed with them.[23] The synagogue was therefore closely identified with the war effort and in 1916 the crux of the matter was that Friedeberg had refused a tribunal testimonial to a pacifist. The pacifist, H. Endbinder, was an ex-member of his congregation, a fellow Freemason, a draper from Ellesmere Port on the other side of the Mersey. When taken to task for this by *The Jewish Chronicle*, Friedeberg justified his refusal by explaining that although he knew Endbinder, he had no knowledge at all of his pacifist views and was therefore not in a position to testify on his behalf or on behalf of any pacifist who applied to him.[24] Instead Endbinder had to turn for a character reference to a Christian clergyman, Rev. Arthur Price. This was what offended John Harris.

He wrote to *The Jewish World*, 22 March 1916:

> It is because respect has been denied to the Jewish Conscientious Objector, that I have entered this controversy. In the opinion of the Conscientious Objector, Jewish or otherwise, and in my own opinion, all war is wrong. My reading of my religion does not prevent me from holding that view. It strengthens me therein.
>
> I would not suggest for one moment that it is the view of the majority of English Jews. None the less, as a Jewish Minister, I claim my right of perfect freedom to hold and express my conscientious convictions and to assist those who hold similar convictions.

Yet Harris's attempt to provide Jewish testimony for Jewish objectors was blocked. An "official" of the synagogue ignored the convention of keeping differences of opinion within the Community by giving an interview to the non-Jewish press. *The Liverpool Express* on 11 March reported that Harris was a conscientious objector and had 'shown sympathy with men who sought to escape military service on these grounds.' The Committee had therefore decided to dismiss the minister. They stated that they had no objection to Harris himself holding a conscientious objection. They took exception to his using his position as a Jewish minister to appear before tribunals and lay it down as a Jewish Doctrine that it was wrong to take up arms in support of the country. It is interesting that the Synagogue Committee could not accept Harris's argument that young Jews needed testimony from a minister of their own religion.

The irony is that Temple thought it was impossible for clergy in the established Church to oppose the war (as Harris had done and was apparently permitted to do). Yet they did testify before tribunals by virtue of their office. Gore, the liberal Bishop of Oxford, used his position both to give written testimony on behalf of objectors and to mount public campaigns against their ill-treatment by the military and by tribunals. Harris's protest brought a noticeable shift of emphasis within the Jewish press. *The Jewish World* suggested that, by refusing character references, Friedeberg was impeding the work of the tribunals set up by Parliament.[25] *The Jewish Chronicle* wondered how it could be an offence for a Jew to do what the government had recognised.[26] "It seems that only a gentile is allowed to have a conscience," wrote L. Bennett from Liverpool. "Is a Jew supposed to be without one?"[27] Encouraged by sympathy in London, 62 members and seat holders met with the Senior Warden Mr A.M. Jackson on 5 April to support Harris. The affair had split the community and become embarrassingly public. Behind the scenes, senior members of the Conference of Jewish Ministers were unhappy to see a Minister's freedom of action so circumscribed by his congregation and were pressing Dr. Hertz to intervene. Mr Jessel stepped in as a peacemaker.

Thanks to the mediation of Mr Jessel, on Sunday 9 April the sub-committee of the Synagogue, what would elsewhere be called the executive, met with Harris and a lawyer friend, Price. The negotiations appeared to succeed and the dismissal was withdrawn. In return Harris undertook not to use his official position to preach pacifism or vouch for conscientious objectors. Friedeberg regarded this as total withdrawal. However, as Harris saw it, he agreed only that pacifism was not the view of the governing body or the majority of the congregation; he agreed not to appear before tribunals because he had been persuaded that his doing so would not benefit the C.O.s.

This compromise proved purely cosmetic. Lionel Collins, President of the Congregation and apparently Harris's main contact, had correctly assessed the situation: the views of the two Ministers could not be reconciled and Harris had virtually no support within his own congregation.[28] The sub-committee which reinstated Harris only controlled his post as Braham Reader. His position as Registrar and Secretary was in the hands of the select committee, what would elsewhere be called the council. It met a week later on Saturday 15 April. Harris was not present, but when the minute books were handed to him as Secretary, he found to his dismay that notes had been added to the sub-committee minutes after he and Price had left the meeting. These notes attributed the "extreme unpleasantness" entirely to Harris's obstinacy in refusing six weeks earlier to give assurances which he had now conceded regarding his attitude to conscientious objectors. Harris was unwilling to accept this partial record of events and he resigned precipitously, much to Jessel's disapproval. The resignation was accepted by the sub-committee on 19 April. The effect of Jessel's intervention had been to transform a dismissal into a resignation. The Committee had shifted the onus onto Harris. From outside Liverpool it appeared ungentlemanly and (oddly enough) un-English.[29] *The Jewish World* remarked that calm and deliberate action seemed incompatible with the very atmosphere of this congregation.

But that is to ignore the substance of the dispute. Whatever the official version, it is clear that Harris was doing more than upholding the rights of congregants to a conscientious objection. He was himself a pacifist and was publicly putting the case for Jewish pacifism. On 19 February, 1916, he had preached a sermon at Prince's Road which questioned the basic assumption that the Jewish religion could not be pacifist. When preaching, Harris was careful not to impose his views on his congregation. He acknowledged Elijah's exploits with fire and sword. None the less he used the teaching of both Elijah and Elisha to link pacifism with the Jewish tradition. He reinforced his argument with biblical quotations and post-biblical midrash. Again and again he reminds one of the contemporary Israeli peace movement. He is particularly critical of racial hatred. His sermon is subtitled 'a plea for tolerance'. It calls for a variety of religious practice within Judaism and for love of one's fellow men.[30] "What strange paradox is this?" he asks " that makes the Jew the least tolerant of men? Have we not suffered enough because the world would not recognise the sanctity of the human conscience."

Up to that time the Jewish press had treated pacifism with scant respect. During April writers began to distinguish between the Jewish religion which did not necessarily justify pacifism, and the individual Jewish conscience which might. The eminent Quaker, Edward Grubb, argued in February that Quaker beliefs on war could equally well be shared by Jews.[31]

Harris was in touch with British pacifist circles, beleaguered though they were. He received moral support from at least one non-Jewish minister in Liverpool. Stanley Mellor, minister of Hope Street Church (whose journalist brother William was a prominent socialist C.O.) wrote to *The Jewish Chronicle* in support of Harris. Perhaps while visiting internment camps Harris had met members of the Society of Friends. Their Emergency War Victims Relief Committee had been active on behalf of interned aliens and their families. Edward Grubb was National Treasurer of the No-Conscription Fellowship.

The NCF was the self-help anti-conscription organisation which offered contact and moral support to conscientious objectors both socialist and religious. It campaigned against the abuse of C.O.s, and was at great pains not to be identified with any pro-German sympathies. Harris's attempt to organise a separate support organisation for Jewish pacifists came to nothing, even his well-wishers recognised that opinion in the community was against them and that it was not politically expedient. However, the NCF included Jewish members, both in Liverpool and elsewhere. Joseph Hoare's diary mentions a fellow C.O, Bak, member of Willesden No Conscription Fellowship, a Jew by birth and by religion. Because *The Tribunal*, the NCF journal, suggested a mode of defence for Christian C.O.s in front of aggressive tribunals, *The Jewish World*, tongue-in-cheek, put forward a set of similar coherent answers for Jews.

But in Liverpool the NCF was regarded as a subversive organisation which coached defendants to out-argue the tribunals. Herbert Samuel, the Home Secretary, accused the NCF of manufacturing conscientious objectors.[32] It was said to be no coincidence that five days after Harris attended an NCF meeting, there came the incident of the altered minutes. The Anglo-Jewish community in Liverpool could never accept that the NCF was proper company for a minister to keep. Alderman Cohen said that he would not call Harris a friend nor attend the synagogue.[33]

Status within the British hierarchy was extremely significant to the Jews of the Prince's Road Synagogue but their respect for the élitist structure should not be taken as deference. In Liverpool, as in Manchester,[34] the Jews were part of the élitist structure. The community leaders were integrated and identified with the civic leadership. Louis Cohen, founder of Lewis's Store, had been Lord

Mayor in 1899. There were Montagu and Samuel family connections with the peerage. Herbert Samuel had become Home Secretary in the Liberal government largely through defending the passage of the Military Service Act and it was his task now to enforce conscription, (though it was not a party matter since the majority of Jewish M.P.s were Conservatives). The tribunals were heavily weighted by the local commercial, political and military leadership whose support for the war and for conscription dominated the hearings. The Lord Mayor of Liverpool (who annually with the corporation attended a welfare service at Prince's Road Synagogue) presided over the county Appeal Tribunal for Lancashire. The Anglo-Jewish community were flattered that a high profile role was played by Major de Rothschild as Military Representative at the City of London Appeal Tribunal.

Tribunals were supposed to have labour representatives and to reflect the opinion of society at large, but in fact most had no members who were not wholeheartedly in support of the war effort. In the Liverpool area there seem to have been one or two maverick representatives of pacifism, but they were rapidly ousted from office on the grounds that it was not right for a man whose own son was a C.O. to send other men's sons to the trenches.[35]

By this stage in the war people knew that the Army was not a path to glory but a likely one-way ticket to death. Some of the congregation had already lost relatives killed in the war. Friedeberg's own son was approaching military age and was to serve from the following Autumn, as George Frampton. (In November 1916 Friedeberg finally followed many members of his congregation and rid himself of his too Germanic name.) In all, 113 men from the synagogue served in the war and Harris's sons were not among them. Hugh Harris, who had had his 18th birthday the previous September, was already a pacifist. He worked for the Friends' War Victims Relief Committee and was one of twenty-three Jewish pacifists in the Home Office Work Centre on Dartmoor in November 1917.[36] Thirteen men from the congregation died and it cannot have helped matters that one of the Polack boys, B.J. Polack of the Worcester Regiment, then aged 25, was reported killed in Mesopotamia in the week of 21 April, at the time of the fracas over Harris's pacifism. Tragically Polack lost another son, Ernest, three months later.

The personal resentments involved were not appreciated by the London Jews who now condemned the Liverpool congregation for dismissing their Minister without compensation. The Liverpool congregation did not take kindly to religious direction from the authorities in London.[37] The tensions are clearly revealed by the question of financial provision for Harris and for his family. In May, alongside the appeal for an honorarium for Harris, there was also another (said to have been previously planned) to benefit Friedeberg after 25 years service. On June 16 a bitter meeting of free members turned down for a second time the proposal to give a grant to Harris. None the less there was a certain sympathy for Harris both inside and outside Liverpool. Gaster, the *Haham*, a fellow-Zionist, sent a letter of appreciation on 5 June applauding Harris's conception of the duties incumbent on a Jewish Minister in these critical times, and recognising the wider implications of the affair. "We Jews have obtained our position by our claim for liberty of conscience and it will be safeguarded only so long as this liberty of conscience will be respected by others." He and several prominent figures contributed to a fund which was set up to make some provision for Harris. It was never officially endorsed by his synagogue. His furniture was sold up for less than he had hoped and he wrote wretchedly to his friends seeking any employment he could find, teaching or secretarial.[38]

Although this seemed harsh at the time, there is no evidence that the Jews were harder on Harris than a Christian congregation would have been. Mr Dunn Kaye, a Minister of the United Methodist Church, appeared before Walton-on-Thames Tribunal on behalf of his son. He "said he had been mobbed in London as a pro-German and had lost his Living."[39] Yet Harris continued in employment. In 1916 he eventually stepped in as acting minister at Hammersmith Synagogue and Headmaster of Poland Street Hebrew and Religious Classes. After the First World War when rabbis returned from being military chaplains, Harris was from 1919-25 Minister of the new Ealing and Acton Associate Synagogue. Thereafter he served from 1926 on the Welfare Committee of the United Synagogues. He was the Honorary Secretary of the Jewish Peace Society and his son Hugh followed in his footsteps as a campaigning Jewish pacifist.

In 1916 (a letter from Hugh Harris puts the date at 1918), John Harris published *Lex Talionis and the Jewish Law of Mercy* in support of his beliefs, but it was a slim booklet, moderate in tone and hardly likely to cause a stir. Perhaps significantly it was privately printed for the Jewish Peace Society at the Pelican Press under Francis Meynell, an ardent young Roman Catholic pacifist and moving spirit in the Catholic Guild of the Pope's Peace. The Peace movement provides a mirror image of the inter-denominational co-operation on the military side. There the YMCA worked closely with the Jewish army chaplains, provided facilities for Jewish services and in turn received funding from Jewish contributors. What is interesting about Harris is not that he was an Anglo-Jew but that Anglo-Jewry was itself split, with a small minority of pacifists reflecting the split in English opinion.

The Liberal Jews, the most English of all Jews, seemed in public to be most conventionally loyal and completely untouched by arguments of conscience. In private it may have been a different matter. Lily Montagu, a founder of Liberal Judaism, was cousin of Herbert Samuel, the Home Secretary. She was a radical and gifted teacher and the first Jewish woman to preach a sermon in Britain. When Hugh Harris appeared before the Paddington Tribunal in October 1916, she was one of the people who provided him with a testimonial.

> Mr Hugh Harris belongs to a family whom I have known for very many years, and for whom I have the greatest esteem. ....
>
> I feel convinced that he is a high minded youth, who has a very proper sense of his responsibility, and no desire whatever to shirk his duty, I have very much sympathy with his point of view.
>
> He has gathered, as I myself have done, from the study of the scriptures and from Jewish teaching, that the evils of the world cannot be overcome by physical force.
>
> It seems to us that by refusing to take part in war itself, or in any movement in support of war, we are humbly testifying to our faith, in the unity of God, as expressed in the unity of man.[40]

Her words are generous and, in the circumstances, courageous. The survival of letters in the Harris archives reveals her commitment, and Harris's relationship with the theological reformers in Anglo-Jewry.

Up to 1914 Harris had not been regarded as a marginal Jew. He came from a family respected in the ministry. One must not be misled by his lack of Rabbinic title. The Old Hebrew Congregation at Prince's Road did not have a Minister who held a Rabbinical degree until 1949. Harris carried out all the duties of a minister and since the start of the century he had contributed sermons both signed and unsigned to *The Jewish Chronicle*. Nor should we picture him as cut off from developments in Jewish thought. At the time of this controversy *The Jewish Chronicle* published an article by Rabbi Stephen Wise who was at the time still active in the American peace movement. It also published a significant extended essay by Mordecai Kaplan packed with the Reconstructionist ideas that are now famous. Presumably Harris wrote the sort of book he did because American-style Jewish philosophy was inappropriate to the English situation. His book provides a scholarly argument for a pacifist evolution of Jewish law. But it is set out very simply, in the style of other English religious pacifist pamphlets. It is addressed to Jews and Christians alike. He wants to dispel the idea that Christians are natural pacifists and Jews are not. He points out that the Jewish law of an eye for an eye established the principle that a penalty should never exceed the wrong suffered. Over the centuries money values had been replaced by physical punishment. Fines provided reparation, a substitution reaffirmed by Maimonides. Harris suggests that by the beginning of the Christian Era the Pharisees wished to abrogate even the death penalty for murder. He concludes "Of the loving and humane spirit that underlies Judaism the evidence is overwhelming." Unlike some Jewish pacifists Harris does not claim that this is anything special to the Jewish people or to the covenant. "In that it does not claim to be different from other religions. Love is one of the elemental virtues, like honesty or chastity, common to all faiths.. and can be exercised by those who are unattached to any of the recognised creeds." The book is completed by a series of quotations on Peace and Brotherhood. Again Harris pleads for the love and tolerance of foreigners. There is to be no notion of revenge. He quotes from Deuteronomy XXIII 7: *Thou shalt not abhor an Egyptian because thou wast a stranger in his land.* He argues for something other than Nationalism, whether that nationalism be British or Jewish.

If one finds the book slightly disappointing, coming as it did from a man who had sacrificed his home and livelihood to his beliefs, the clue lies perhaps in his view of the spiritual role of Judaism. In 1902 he had made an unfavourable comparison between the worldliness of his congregation and the spiritual regeneration of Christian chapel-goers in neighbouring Wales. It was not on theoretical grounds that he took his stand but on the carrying out of his ministry, testifying for men whose dissent would lead to court-martial and prison. He may have under-estimated the risks he took. In the words of a sermon he published in 1902, "We are not hampered by anti-Semitism or persecution, we have outgrown our ghetto prejudices and are free to exercise our religious advantages without let or hindrance."[41] What his uncle, Morris Harris, condemned as an obsession and meddling in politics,[42] John Harris saw purely in terms of religion. There is a letter from him in *The Jewish Chronicle*, May 12. 1916: "For my part I am an avowed pacifist. I believe intensely in the paramount duty of returning good for evil, and in the final and certain victory of love and love alone over hatred and prejudice."

Yet the Anglo-Jewish community in Liverpool felt perhaps justifiably that their own sons were defending British liberties against what was generally regarded as German militarism, and against the anti-Semitism which had brought many of their families to England in the first place. Their reluctant participation in the war was therefore all the more fervent. This is not a case of Jews pretending to be Englishmen; their loyalty to the Empire was genuine. One is reminded of Michael Marrus' study of the Frenchness of French Jews at the turn of the century.[43] Anglo-Jewry did not have to choose between British nationalism and their Jewish identity. The two were synonymous. Citizenship of the British Empire conferred the additional privilege of being a British Jew. Grateful for Englishness they found themselves committed to a perhaps excessive constitutional conformity.

The past sixty years has done little to alter the situation. In the States there has been a Jewish pacifist tradition which has not extended to Britain. The Jewish Peace Society revived in the twenties but then the horrors of Hitler and the Holocaust made Jewish pacifism almost a contradiction in terms during the second world war. Even John Harris found to his intense regret that he was forced by events to abandon pacifism.

"The cry of the tortured and persecuted victims of the Nazis has been too bitter to deny to them what appears to be the only solution of their sufferings and the only alternative to their extermination," he wrote to Victor Gollancz on 14 June 1943.

Yet Harris did make a difference. As a pacifist, he succeeded in persuading his Christian contacts that Jews could be religious pacifists too. In Britain, the Fellowship of Reconciliation is still exclusively Christian but internationally it has become a multi-faith organisation. In the States, in France and now in Israel it provides support and affiliation for Jewish religious pacifists, whose pacifism has much in common with that of Harris.

As an English Jew, Harris established a precedent. He dissented from national policy in war-time both as a Jew and as an Englishman without being charged under the Defence of the Realm Act, or abandoning his own very English identity.

Finally as a Minister, he forced the Community to debate in public and in very British terms some of the on-going problems of Judaism. How far is a Minister bound to reflect the moral views of the congregation which employs him? Should his priority be the safety of the Jewish people, or is it his duty to preach his religion as his conscience dictates?

In the Diaspora museum in Tel Aviv there is a quotation on the wall from Rabbi Salanter which may serve as an epitaph for Harris. "The Rabbi whose community does not disagree with him is not really a Rabbi, and a Rabbi who fears his community is not really a man."

Chapter 2
The War-Time of Judah Magnes
Jewish pacifism in the United States
1917-20

While John Harris re-adjusted to the relative safety of obscurity, on the other side of the Atlantic one of the most charismatic and publicity-conscious Rabbis of New York was about to take a public stand as an uncompromising pacifist. This time there could be no back room diplomacy or fudging the issue. Judah Magnes, Californian, all-American Jew, was to argue the religious case for Jewish pacifism and play a dominant role in the national peace movement.

Many who came into contact with Judah Magnes found themselves captivated. "Sunny, enthusiastic and decisive," one of his friends, Henrietta Szold, described him.[1] He had an open and personal charm which was irresistible. He was, in a way, the spoiled child of American Jewry, beloved by all and the enemy of none.

From 1914 to 1917 there was nothing untoward about his being a pacifist in New York. A large body of opinion was opposed to America entering the First World War. For the Jews especially there were cogent arguments against intervention. The United States was an immigrant society with a strong German element. Most of the Jews who had arrived in the early and middle decades of the nineteenth century were part of this German immigration, and many still had warm cultural and family links with Germany. In Germany too lay the roots of Reform Judaism which was already dominant in the United States. German Jewish opinion was understandably anti-interventionist.

The much larger and more recently arrived Russian Jewish population also opposed entry. They had only recently escaped from the Tsarist regime. Their concern for the persecuted Jews still in Russian hands was shared by the American Jewish élite and, thanks largely to the oratory of Magnes, large sums were raised for relief. If America entered on the Allied side, Jews might lose the freedom to protest about the maltreatment of Jewish communities

in the East. An editorial in *The American Hebrew* complained that
Jews in England were not free to criticise Russia.[2]

The peace movement in the States had different roots from that
in Britain. In America in the period leading up to 1917, a pacifist
was anyone who advocated international co-operation for peace.
The American Peace Society was part of a general, progressive
alliance which hoped for a settlement of the war in Europe. Jewish
leaders, as representatives of a trans-national community, also
hoped for peace through negotiation rather than intervention.

Two Reform rabbis emerged as spokesmen for the peace
movement at this time: Emil Hirsch of Chicago's Sinai Temple and
Stephen Wise in New York. In the Autumn of 1914 Lillian Wald
(Jewish herself) and Jane Adams called a meeting of twenty-six
social reformers at the Henry Street Nurses' Settlement. Those
invited included Rev. John Haynes Holmes, Unitarian Pastor of the
Church of the Messiah, New York, who was to write movingly on
Jewish Pacifism in the Second World War, and Rabbi Stephen
Wise. Rabbi Wise like the others became active in the peace
movement primarily because he was a social reformer. He had been
commissioner for child labor as Rabbi in Portland, Oregon. In 1907
he founded the Free Synagogue in New York, an independent
pulpit which gave him the liberty to speak out on social issues, and
to set up social welfare programs. Wise was always convinced that
the struggle for Jewish rights made it imperative for Jews to press
for justice for all. From 1909 onwards he signed petitions in
support of the National Association for the Advancement of
Coloured People. Discussing the relationship between pulpit and
politics in his autobiography, he explains, "For me the supreme
declaration of our Hebrew Bible was and remains 'Justice, Justice
shalt thou pursue' – whether it be easy or hard, whether it be justice
to white or black, Jew or Christian."[3]

The peace issue came into this category. The U.S. draft system
was selective and had always fallen heavily on the working class,
men who did not have money to pay a commutation fee or hire a
substitute to fight in their place. During the Civil War, the Draft
Act caused uprisings in Ohio and Illinois which were put down by
Federal troops. In New York City mobs stormed draft offices and a
thousand civilians were killed or injured in the riots which followed.
In the post Civil War period, a concern for the under-privileged
went hand in hand with opposition to war. Social reformers

believed that military expenditure squandered finite resources which were needed for public welfare. In 1914-1916, Rabbi Wise and his colleagues were "anti-preparedness", lest an arms build-up should make war more likely. It was on these grounds that Wise emerged as a spokesman for the American Union Against Militarism, which was founded in April 1916. Although he spoke as a social reformer, he represented all sides of American Jewish opinion, not just the OstJuden, the poor, but the wealthy establishment. A significant number of Jewish businessmen were involved in the New York Peace Society 1913-14.

The American peace movement, and Stephen Wise with it, gave full support to democrat President Woodrow Wilson in his campaign for re-election in the Autumn of 1916. The President had kept America out of the war and was sympathetic to the welfare and civil rights causes in which Wise was active. In reality peace was no longer possible. America had already abandoned neutrality. The ties between the States and Britain were strong, and Wilson personally was Anglophile. The supply of munitions and loans to France and Britain meant that German submarines imposing a naval blockade now turned on the American ships that were supplying the Allies. Although Wilson was re-elected on a "He Kept Us Out of the War" pacifist vote, his victory was narrow (277 electoral votes to 254). President Wilson now presented war and not peace as the moral imperative.

> To fight thus for the ultimate peace of the world and for the liberation of its people, the German peoples included. .... The world must be made safe for democracy.[4]

Jewish opinion in general and Rabbi Wise in particular responded to the religious tone in which the President justified his decision to declare war. In April 1917, the American Peace Society, the Church Peace Union and the World Peace Foundation, all supported Congress and the decision to fight on the Allied side. Jewish religious opinion followed suit. Yet Judah Magnes was unmoved and continued to address mass meetings, a seemingly illogical pacifist, lending dignity and intellectual glamour to a cause which otherwise might have seemed lost before it had begun.

To be a Jew in the Diaspora is always in one sense to be a dissenter. Jews follow a minority religion and, by doing so, to a greater or lesser extent fail to comply with the prevailing culture.

To be a pacifist Jew is to take dissent a step further, dissenting even from the main body of dissenters. For it must be emphasised that no large section of the American Jewish community remained pacifist in the war situation.

In February 1917 when United States' diplomatic relations with Germany were broken, *The American Hebrew* pointed out that Jews had been neutral because there were Jews fighting on both sides in the conflict. Since Wilson himself had been neutral at that stage, Jewish neutrality had been pro-American. "Of all the immigrants coming to these shores, the Jews have brought with them no ties with any foreign governments of nations that hindered them from becoming part and parcel of America. .... It is natural that American Israel is pro-American, undivided, ready for any sacrifices the American people may be called upon to make for the sake of American rights, for the sake of justice, liberty and equality."[5] The rival *Jewish Chronicle* under its German editor Strauss was accused of pro-German propaganda.

In March 1917 the Russian revolution removed all obstacles to Jewish support for the Allied cause. It was welcomed as the liberation of the Jews and the Passover Haggadah that year was augmented with thanks for the freeing of the Jews from Russian bondage.

The American Jewish establishment were already committed to the war effort. Like Wise, they saw themselves first and foremost as loyal American citizens benefiting from the religious liberties of the constitution. They were sensitive too to latent anti-Semitism in American society, which had been exacerbated by prejudice against the large, newly arrived population of East European Jews with their radical politics and unfamiliar culture. Stephen Wise shared the establishment view and supported the war.

Wise is often represented as a Jewish pacifist. This he had never been. In a sermon in 1911 he had reminded his congregation that he was not for "peace at any price"[6] and in early 1917 his support for the President did not waver. "By February 1917," he recalled, "I had become convinced that President Wilson had kept the U.S. out of the war as a result of high statesmanship and infinite patience, but that the time had come for the American people to understand that it might be our destiny to have part in the struggle to avert the enthronement of the law of might over the nations."[7] Wise resigned from the Union against Militarism in

February/March 1917, declaring himself in favour of a war against Prussianism.

His defection was a bombshell to his fellow pacifists but it reflected a fundamental uncertainty within the movement. Radical dissent from the war would make it impossible to promote effective social action and many reformers argued like Wise, that the success of specific welfare programmes was more important than opposing the war. For Wise those causes included Zionism; it was he who had initiated and then led local and national American Zionist organisations. If Jews antagonised the Administration, the Zionist cause was unlikely to prosper.

Wise's apparent turnabout reflects a profound logic in the Jewish attitude to war. Jews may oppose the declaration of war, but once that same war is in progress, its successful pursuit and conclusion may be essential to the well-being of the Jewish people. The same principle explained shifts of attitude in the Israeli Peace Movement during the invasion of the Lebanon in 1982.

Wise's view of his rabbinic responsibility made identification with the Presidency inevitable. Roland Marchand points out that "Catholic prelates were intent upon establishing the American character of the Catholic church and its compatibility with American political institutions." Leaders such as Cardinal Gibbons therefore disassociated themselves from the peace movement as soon as it involved opposition to the U.S. government.[8] The rabbinate were in a similar position; indeed their congregants had more to lose: their complete identification as Americans was now in question. Dr. Joseph Silberman, President of the Eastern Council of Reform Rabbis wrote, "Pacifism, hitherto borne with patience, now becomes intolerable."[9] The war was seen as "a holy cause." Jews should volunteer to fight. An editorial in *The American Hebrew* blamed radicalism for causing anti-Semitism.[10]

Surveys of prejudice suggest that a major cause of anti-Semitism is the underlying suspicion that Jews have a divided loyalty. War is a crucial event; Jews cannot afford to be accused of working against the patriotic interests of the host community.[11] It is not surprising that Jewish law has advocated or indeed ordered Jews to comply with the law of the state where they happen to be resident. To be a Jewish pacifist, to have a conscientious objection to conscription in war time, demands a sense of security in one's country of abode.

Harris had this in England, and Judah Magnes certainly had in the States.

Magnes was born on 5 July, 1877, in San Francisco, and when he was five years old his family moved to Oakland, California, where he went to school. The photographs show a strikingly handsome boy. He was an admired eldest son, and in that well-integrated community he shone at school, moreover he shone in fields where his Jewishness was irrelevant. He edited the school journal and was pitcher in the baseball team. His attachment to things American never left him; throughout his life he continued to play baseball on 4 July, the day before his birthday. Growing up in a district free from prejudice and achieving such personal success, gave Magnes a confidence in himself and in his own judgement which might later seem misplaced. But, crucially, it gave him the confidence as an American to take undisguised delight in his own ethnic and ethical inheritance as a Jew.

At the age of seventeen he entered Cincinnati's Hebrew Union College, the Reform Seminary, where he was the first graduate born West of the Mississippi. Magnes seems always in some way to have been unique, even to have sought out uniqueness. He constantly questioned the views of his religious superiors. His home background may have encouraged this non-conformity. His father was not orthodox, but he came from Poland, and transmitted to Judah the relaxed Hasidic influence of his grandfather. Magnes' mother came from a more traditional orthodox, German Jewish family, well-established department store owners. Magnes spent a lifetime attempting to reconcile these two Jewish traditions in his own thinking. Another example of non-conformity came from his rabbis back home: the orthodox Oakland 1st Hebrew Congregation to which the family belonged became Reform, and he was later taught and sponsored by Rabbi Jacob Voorsanger of San Francisco's Temple Emanu-el. Magnes' Judaism remained both all-questioning and all-embracing.

During the Spanish American War of 1898 when Magnes was twenty-one years old, he was strongly in favour of arbitration. He wrote to his parents that war was 'unrighteous'. "Where are your good Christian ministers with 'Peace on earth and good will towards men'? I am ashamed of Rabbi (Marcus) Friedlander (Minister of

Oakland 1st Hebrew Congregation) that he should class himself among the 'fighting parsons'. What a contradiction in terms."[12]

Magnes did not accept that being a Jew entailed giving unquestioning support to each and every American administration. A Jewish life had to be governed by ethics and conscience. In 1900 (in a college magazine article and in his maiden sermon) Magnes ridiculed the extreme patriotism of the Reform Jews. Like Harris, he saw with despair that assimilated Jews were less religious than their Christian neighbours. Integration into American society seemed to spell the death of their Jewishness. The college was anti-Zionist. Magnes suggested that Palestine was the only alternative to this Jewish 'death'.

Even as a rabbinical student Magnes was grappling with the problems inherent in Reform Judaism. Reform had questioned and discarded the dispassionate halakhic foundation of traditional, orthodox Judaism. But in the States as elsewhere this had been replaced by an equally dispassionate modernising rationalism. Magnes, before his time, was looking for more, and unlikely for a Reform Rabbi, he found it among the OstJuden of Berlin.

"How they cling to life and to hope and what a fine intellectuality they all have, and what a tremendous spiritual power is in them," he wrote to his family on 7 November 1901.[13] In Berlin, Magnes met fellow students who managed to combine a liberal and universal interpretation of their religion with a devotion to the distinctiveness of Jewish culture. It was this Jewishness which had been bleached out of Reform Judaism, resulting, as Magnes saw it, in a lack of self-confidence and ethnic pride among his fellow Jews in America. He had disassociated himself from mainstream American Jewry long before the First World War.

In 1905 Magnes left the academic world of his college to take up a post at Temple Israel in Brooklyn. Like Harris he found that his Zionism led to trouble. He had to resign after only two years, accused of proving "too active in Zionism and too conservative in Judaism". His appointment as Assistant Minister at Temple Emanu-El in New York, the premier temple of Reform Judaism, came to a similar abrupt end when he was dismissed for preaching a characteristically outspoken sermon at Passover, 24 April 1910.

The word conservative was applied to Magnes in a particular Jewish sense. Magnes' conservatism lay in his desire to restore the authentic Jewish identity to Jewish American life. The conservatism of his middle class congregants lay in resisting any such disruption of their lives as integrated Americans. They had little Jewish or religious education and based their Jewish identity on good works and an upright life, very much in the liberal protestant tradition. The balance between the two views remains precarious to this day and it is important to point out that the Reform congregants were not, as Magnes maintained, devoid of spirituality. By discarding much outmoded ritual and folksy tradition, Reform could claim to have restored the spiritual foundations of Judaism. Ethics rather than ethnicity was the keynote of their services just as it is the key to Magnes' pacifism.

Magnes in this sense remained a Reform Jew in spite of himself. It was not practical for a Jewish leader to preach pacifism after America entered the war, but Magnes became a vigorous campaigning pacifist. What is more he saw this as his moral duty as a Jew. "The fact that we are at war cannot make us abhor war the less," he declared.[14] Like Harris, he lost his job because of his views and yet, recognising this failure, he still asked. "Would it not have been a disgrace to the Jewish people had no one, particularly no Jewish teacher of religion (and he means no Rabbi) – taken the pacifist and radical stand?"[15]

Magnes had not previously emerged as a pacifist leader. His energies had been devoted to mitigating the effects of the war on the Jewish communities in Europe. Magnes' failure to accommodate, which had destroyed his position within every congregation to which he was appointed, proved a strength when it came to visible popular leadership. On 4 December 1904, 100,000 Jews demonstrated against pogroms in Russia and Magnes was at their head. His gifted oratory lent itself to successful fund-raising for the cause. Magnes played a major part in Jewish Relief and in the summer of 1916 he went on a four month mission to Poland on behalf of the Jewish Agency. This experience influenced his attitude to the conflict. The Russian authorities refused to issue him with a passport for entry. He could get no access to Jewish settlements under their control.[16] The German authorities were very different. They gave him every assistance in channelling funds to the war zone. Magnes had always felt at home with German Jews and his complaints about the Russians led to inevitable accusations that he was pro-German. Communal leader Louis Marshall and Rabbi Stephen Wise were both of Central European origin. It was easier for them than for Magnes to regard German autocracy as the real enemy. But Magnes was not pro-German. He condemned German militarism as strongly as any other. He was a self-declared pacifist.

Unlike Harris, Magnes did not take Christian pacifism as common ground. He placed less emphasis than Harris on the Jewish biblical sources which have provided much-loved texts for Christian pacifists also. Because Magnes' main concern as a Reform Rabbi was with the character of Judaism and of Jewish integrity in a multi-racial, multi-cultural society, he framed his pacifism in particularly Jewish terms. That is not to say he did not have Christian pacifist friends and colleagues. He did, and he must have known Quakers as neighbours at his house in Nantucket. But he had a profound sense of his own identity as a Jew. One could say that, if Jewish pacifism did not exist, Judah Magnes was about to invent it.

He wrote no great theological work. But his sermons, the speeches he chose to print, and the contents of his notebooks and correspondence show that for many years Magnes struggled to give an authentic Jewish expression of the pacifist position and, in doing so, he not only proposed a pacifist philosophy but ignored none of the associated problems.

He based his pacifism on two things: the Jewish law and the Jewish People. He began with Jewish respect for life, the over-riding prohibition against spilling blood.[17] In Judaism the law is always over-ridden if a life is at risk. For instance work is forbidden on the Sabbath but a Jewish doctor may save a man's life. However, there are three things which are forbidden under any circumstances: idolatry, incest and the spilling of blood. "The blood is the soul. ...." Even the slaughtering of animals for food, has been surrounded with religious sanctions [for Jews]." So it was hardly surprising that the Jewish people should believe there were better ways than the spilling of blood as a solution to conflict between peoples. Classic Judaism regarded blood as the life, the soul. Magnes' pacifism is based on this extreme, Torah-based reverence for life. Addressing radical Jewish workers in 1917, he took it for granted that Jews could not consent to fight. There should be a religious outcry from the Jewish people against the war. Was it cowardice, he asked, Was it fear of death? Yes. It was right to abhor death. "Is not our whole Jewish instinct towards life?" he asked.

He summed it up in Chicago, in 1920,

> I abhor bloodshed. I believe that human life and human personality are sacred, and that human life may not be taken at any time. I do not believe in war between one people and another, and I did not believe in this past war, and I do not believe in the next.

But life alone was not sufficient argument. He explained,

> Biological reason, the desire of any people to perpetuate itself, is a sufficient reason for its struggle to maintain its life and ways of living, ... yet the Jewish people, the *Am ha Safer*, the people of the book, have always searched out .... the spiritual justification for the existence of the Jewish people.

In the New York election campaign of 1917, he put it this way:

> This hatred of all the arts of soldiering, this repugnance for war, this abhorrence of blood spilling that has characterised the Jewish masses is nothing more nor less than a continuance of the great Jewish tradition which exalted the spiritual life of Jacob and condemned the brute force of Esau.[18]

A journal entry of 2 October, 1917, deals directly with the subject of Jews and pacifism. He believes that pacifism represents the heart and soul of the Jewish people. The Jewish experience has led to a hatred of war. "How many religions and philosophies and ideals and patriotisms have we not seen justify the slaughter of men! We look upon the madness, the lust after blood, horrified, yet detached, with wisdom... sated with it through our long experience." Jewish experience for Magnes was that of the Diaspora. It is a unique experience because it is unattached to temporal power, to national governments. The Jews are different. "We have called ourselves a kingdom of priests and holy people – the priests were to guard the truth and to pursue peace."[19]

Magnes recalled with pride that from the time of the Exodus the Jewish people had always resisted tyrannical regimes. He insinuated that this resistance came from the spirit, from learning and from a long tradition. His underlying rationale, laid out with great clarity in the introduction to his published war time speeches, is that armed defence is a short term solution at best and that war of any kind between people generates such hate and disorder that in the end it defeats its purpose.

In 1917-21 the problem of self-defence did not loom large for an American citizen, nor for most Jews. The Jews at that point had no territory to defend and their separate spirit had survived centuries of persecution without any organised use of force. Arming the Jews would appear to contradict Magnes' pacifism. But in 1906 Magnes was associated with the American Jewish Defence Association which channelled funds to Jewish communities in Russia and provided arms for self-defence against pogroms. Certainly Magnes was always deeply troubled when defenceless Jews were attacked simply because they were Jews. He later faced similar dilemmas in Palestine, but, like many American pacifists, Magnes never saw the citizen's personal right to defend himself in the same light as the waging of war.

In any state or culture the definition of 'pacifist' is closely related to the prevailing legal definition. A conscientious objector in American law need object only to participation in war. Both Jewish and American law strictly limit the use of violence in personal self-defence and in particular the taking of life. Yet both to some extent recognise the right of the individual to self-defence. Jewish law is commonly (but not universally) interpreted as ordering a Jew to resist an armed pursuer. The American constitution allows a citizen to carry arms for self-defence. British law does not allow every citizen the right to carry arms and British definitions of pacifist tend to exclude the use of any violence whatever in any situation.

Magnes does not regard pacifism as total non-resistance. Resistance and eventual triumph will come through the power of the Jewish spirit which Magnes sees as both specifically Jewish and as universal. As a Jewish spirit it is what binds Jews together, no matter where they may live. It creates an international, para-national fellowship which is an example to other men. Magnes realises how sensitive is this point. Anti-Semitism then as now always harped on the existence of a worldwide Jewish conspiracy. Magnes dismisses the conspiracy theory as a fiction and a libel. The reality of Jewish international feeling is quite different, and indeed it exists. Only ghetto cowardice would persuade Jews to deny it.

But for Magnes the international brotherhood which prohibits Jew fighting against Jew is not particular to Jews. It is an example to all men and is to be shared by the righteous of all nations. The Jews are a chosen people and different only in that they are elected to preach the fatherhood of one God and the brotherhood of man. Magnes takes Hasidic particularism and enlarges it to American proportions. Here again Jewish philosophy of the most traditional kind is given a new vitality by Magnes.

His universalist train of thought is revealed in a bitter attack on Reform Judaism. Reform Judaism had (rightly in Magnes' eyes) rejected Jewish particularism and had preached universal brotherhood, preached it but not practised it. They had supported the war and the American government. The revolutionary doctrine of Reform Judaism required revolutionaries to put it into practice and revolutionaries the Reform Jews of America were certainly not. Magnes contested "their claim to be bearers of the living Jewish spirit". The orthodox rabbinate were no better; they were not in touch with the Jewish people. It was the people themselves, the Jewish masses, who had a mission to the rest of mankind. .... The Jewish mission, a spiritual force, expresses itself not through ecclesiastical forms alone, but through all the ways and hopes of life – religious, moral, artistic, political, social.

Therefore the freedom of the Jews depended on the freedom of all peoples. And conversely the Jews had a special moral mission to insist on peace among all peoples.[20]

Magnes then deals with the accusation that to be pacifist provokes anti-Semitism. Anti-Semitism, he reasons, is not a consequence of pacifism. There was anti-Semitism in America before the war and it cannot be affected by more patriotism and heroism in the trenches.

> As long as the Jews remain a distinctive people; as long as they give evidence of original, independent thought; as long as they achieve conquests of the spirit and in material ways among populations numerically and physically their masters; as long as the status of the Jews among the nations is abnormal; so long, among other reasons, will there be anti-Semitism. There will never be a complete disappearance of anti-Semitism any more than that any other people that is active, creative can produce spiritual values without stirring up enmities.[21]

The insistence on spiritual values inevitably leads to anti-Semitism. But to abandon spiritual values is tantamount to abandoning Judaism.

For Wise there was a choice: what was best for the Jewish people and Zionist prospects in a particular set of circumstances? For Magnes there was no choice, only a religious compulsion to speak for peace regardless of the consequences.

Peace and the prayers for peace are at the centre of Jewish liturgy. Those who would like to avoid the pacifist implications of this remind us that *shalom* in Hebrew is not the same as its English, or Roman equivalent. It is not *pax* in a negative sense, the absence of conflict. *Shalom* means wholeness, completeness or fulfilment. They seem to see *shalom* as something which may be achieved through war. For Magnes and for most of us *shalom* holds its Hebrew meanings but also has the accepted meaning of 'peace' with which it has always been translated.

"Seek peace and pursue it", the psalm tells us. *Shalom* involves the effort to bring together. In moving from the prohibitory aspect of pacifism, the abhorrence of bloodshed, to the positive need for the Jewish people to be an example, Magnes departs both from the passive Christian doctrine of nonviolence, and from the so-called passivity of the Jewish Diaspora. The refusal to take part in war is negative, he said at a meeting in New York in 1921. It must go coupled with a positive political, economic and spiritual program to use the world's ressources to meet the needs of humanity.[22] Peace for Magnes is peace in the Jewish sense, not just an absence of warfare but a completeness; the pacifist spirit is not passive but creative. Peace can only be achieved by the creation of justice, the elimination of fear, the establishment of liberty for all peoples.

As a Jewish leader, Magnes spent a life-time taking political and social initiatives, first in the States and later in Palestine. It won him few friends but his failures remind us that his Judaism is of this world. "It is in this world, the world we live in, that justice and righteousness and peace and love must be pursued and that the kingdom of heaven is to be established here and now upon this earth."[23]

One of the strengths of Magnes' pacifism and all later American Jewish pacifism is its pragmatic basis. His conscientious objection is based on a practical analysis of war, its devastation and the risks it creates for the future. Religious Jewish pacifism demands political application.

On Good Friday, 6 April 1917, America declared war. The same month Rabbi Magnes took the chair at a meeting of representatives of peace groups: the American Conference for Democracy and Terms of Peace. Their talks resulted in a series of major rallies and led to the formation of the People's Council for Peace and Freedom (first tentatively set up in May and then formally constituted in September 1917). In spite of its name, the Council was initially a loosely grouped alliance, which sought a rapid negotiated end to the war, opposed conscription, and deplored the loss of democratic rights of free speech.

Pacifism had taken on a new meaning, both legally and emotionally. Conscientious objection was soon defined by the Selective Service Law of May 18, 1917, which required men between 21 and 30 years old to register for service.

The law was modelled on the 1864 Act which had controlled conscription in the North during the Civil War. During the Civil War it provided for exemption from military service on payment of a fine. There was noncombatant duty for members of religious denominations opposed to bearing arms. These denominations were Christian: the Quakers, the Plymouth Brethren and the Mennonite Churches, along with the peace sects, the Seventh Day Adventists and Jehovah's Witnesses. Objectors from religious sects were given recognition on June 30. The Quakers had a strong reforming interest in government policy, but the other groups took no stand except on war. All conscientious objectors had to justify their stand before a draft board and no one was exempted from noncombatant service.

When Carnegi helped fund the Church Peace Union in 1914 he had insisted that Jews (one Rabbi and one layman) should be included. But (Marchand points out) participation by non-Protestants faded.[24] The Selective Service Act made no provision for non-Christian pacifists, nor for individuals without religious affiliation who had a conscientious objection to war. Rufus Jones and Edward Evans tried to get the government to accept the non-denominational Fellowship of Reconciliation as a religious organisation under the meaning of the Act but they had no support from the clergy in general. There was no legal recognition of Jewish religious pacifism.

Registration day was 5 June. Unfortunately for the immigrant minorities new legislation made opposition to conscription synonymous with treason. In an editorial on June 10, 1917, *The New York Times* claimed that the Selective Draft Act gave "a long and sorely needed means of disciplining a certain insolent foreign element in this nation." On 15 June the Espionage Act became law. It included a clause making it an offence to "wilfully cause or attempt to cause insubordination, disloyalty, mutiny or refusal of duty in the military or naval forces of the United States", or to "wilfully obstruct the recruiting or enlistment service of the United States." The punishment was a fine of not more than $10,000 dollars or imprisonment for not more than 20 years or both. It is no wonder that the Jewish Community was alarmed by the role Rabbi Magnes was playing.

On 31 May he addressed a meeting of about four hundred people at the Garden Theatre, Madison Avenue. The rally was preparing to send Eugene Debs as a delegate to the Stockholm peace conference, and Magnes urged a separate peace. The same month Judah Magnes was interrogated by the Department of Justice. *The American Israelite* took pains to stress that Magnes represented only a small part of the Jewish Community, even in New York, and that part of which American Jewry has the least reason to be proud:

> What to us decent Jewish citizens is particularly disheartening about this disloyal demonstration is that it should be presided over by Judah Magnes .... Dr. Magnes has not only offended against the proprieties but done that which will tend to discredit his co-religionists in the eyes of their fellow Americans. That all Jews should be blamed for what is said or done by one of them is of course hideously unjust, but such is the way of the world .... it therefore behoves each Jew to be doubly careful and especially Jewish leaders.[25]

Magnes' career had by 1917 given him a prominent role as a Jewish leader. He had helped establish, and then administered, the New York *Kehillah*, a communal organisation which presented a Jewish response to problems such as Jewish crime or anti-Semitism. The educational and welfare functions of the *Kehillah* were financed and to some extent controlled by the New York Jewish establishment to whom Magnes was linked both by background and by his marriage to the sister-in-law of lawyer, Louis Marshall. But unlike some of his influential friends, Magnes perceived the *Kehillah* in terms of the social and spiritual needs of the new immigrant community. His campaigning for peace was an extension of his role as a patrician Rabbi who spoke for the people.

The *Kehillah* brought him into friendly contact with the socialism of Eastern European immigrants. As Chairman, Magnes arbitrated in labor disputes between the Jewish clothing Unions and their Jewish bosses. In its early stages the People's Council included moderate socialists such as John Reed and New York intellectuals like Max Eastman, editor of *The Masses*. Leaders of organised labor were also involved and they included Jews: J.B. Salutsky, one of the leaders of the People's Council, was Secretary of the Jewish Socialist Federation and editor of its journal *Naye Velt*. Magnes' language and concepts as he speaks of the Jewish masses and the freedom of all peoples are not far removed from those of his socialist colleagues.

Special steps had to be taken to disassociate the New York *Kehillah* from the peace movement. On 2 June Magnes was asked to stay away from the *Kehillah* meeting being held at Temple Ansche Chesed in Harlem. Its Rabbi, Jacob Kohn, who was said to have been a close friend of Magnes for years, stressed that this "was not making an attack on him but (they) wished only to prevent anyone getting the impression from Dr. Magnes' appearance that the Kehillah was a pacifist organisation."[26]

Magnes' socialism presents historians with a problem. His critique of capitalism squandering the earth's scarce resources for profit has a modern ring. But from a later perspective he is flawed by his uncritical acclaim for the Russian revolution. His faith in nascent Russian democracy later proved naïve. He opposed American intervention against the new Bolshevik regime in Russia and the blocking of Jewish American relief supplies to areas under Russian revolutionary control. He predicted that the long term results of American policy would be disastrous. His idealism was unrealistic, but perhaps his practical objections were not.

In political terms Magnes could be called 'a Red'. John Reed and other eminent Soviet sympathisers served on the same peace committees. Yet it is unhelpful to draw a veil over this aspect of Magnes' thinking. His support for the Revolution was a logical extension of his concept of the People which also underlined his pacifism. What concerned Magnes was the rights of the People, *ha am*. War, as he saw it, was the work of governments, and was an outrage against the people. Within Russia the Jews were just one of a number of peoples and their rights depended on the freedom of all peoples within Russia, the very people who had thrown off the yoke of Tsarist government.

That was why Magnes was so ready to identify the Jewish people with "the people", the proletariat of socialist theory. He never associates the people, whether Jewish or otherwise, with government. Jewish people had no Jewish government, nor had the Russian or Polish people a share in the government of the Tsars. He failed to appreciate that as Americans, American Jews were certainly involved in the electoral process and had a government to which they were committed.

Magnes took the religious concept of the Jewish people, *ha am*, and gave it political weight by using it to signify Jewish ethnic identity in the broadest sense, with all its "variety, conflict, adaptability and different kinds of creative force." [27] He recognised that American liberties related to individuals. Jewish freedom therefore depended on individual freedoms which were being curtailed by a government engaged in war.[28]

But Magnes' pacifism took priority over his socialism. He condemned violence used by the left as strongly as he condemned it in the hands of the right. He condemned violence used by the great powers on behalf of Jews in Palestine, as firmly as he condemned its use by anti-Semites.

The original intention of the United States Espionage law may have been to control Espionage, but by August it was being openly used to punish opposition to the draft. The freedom of the press was severely curtailed; it was illegal to send anything critical of the United States government or armed forces through the post. On 27 September, 1917, *The American Israelite* explained that they were unable to comment on a address given by Judah Magnes at the First American Conference for Democracy and Terms of Peace. If they commented, that issue of the paper would probably not be sent through the mails.

The government arrested many socialist opponents of conscription, particularly those who belonged to the International Workers of the World. In the 1912 election the socialist candidate,

Eugene Debs, had got nearly one million votes. He was now sentenced to ten years' imprisonment under the Espionage act. In effect Socialism itself became treasonable. On 25 October, 1917, *The American Israelite* warned that Russian Jews who supported socialism were "playing with fire".

The following spring the Sedition Act made it an offence to "utter, print, write or publish anything disloyal to the government or armed forces of the United States." For Judah Magnes and other religious pacifists the issue of liberty became inseparable from their right to oppose conscription. Much later during the Vietnam war one finds opponents of the draft again campaigning for American liberties.

By equating pacifism with espionage, the Acts provoked a crisis of identity for the Jews of America. Rabbi Isidore Koplowitz wrote in *The American Israelite* of 31 May that universal military service was a Mosaic institution and he supported his case with passages from Numbers and Deuteronomy on the raising and control of Israelite forces, and with the halakhic exemptions from military service given in Deuteronomy XX. Many writers stressed that Judaism was a religion only and had nothing to do with war. The idea of a special Jewish regiment was anathema. "Jews can and must serve the Republic as American citizens only."

> Our little Jewish soldier
> With his heart both loyal and true,
> He answers to the call
> Of the Red, the White and Blue.
>
> With his canteen strung behind him
> And his spirits in good cheer
> The bugle is sounding "Forward"
> To our Jewish volunteer.

The certainty gives way to a painful and touching confusion.

> Our boy is now awakened
> And is anxious to the front to go,
> There to help give battle
> To the world's un-Christian foe.[29]

What does it mean in a Christian society to assert an identity that is not Christian? At what stage does being un-American become un-Christian? The Mosaic law on military service was constantly reiterated in the Jewish press.

Burton J. Hendrick wrote to *The American Hebrew* of 3 August that Jews made up 6 per cent of the regular U.S. forces although they were only 2 per cent of the population. Jewish opinion in America was as patriotic as that in Britain. In this solidly American mood, the Central Conference of American Rabbis voted against Zionism on 6 July. The American identity of the Jewish community was taken for granted both by the community and by the majority of their fellow Americans. One German was lynched during the war, but he was not a Jew. Jews were prominent in the war-time administration. A Jew, Julius Kahn of California, a Republican, was used by the Democrat president to see his Army Administration Bill through Congress in May 1917.

Reform Jews who had abandoned Jewish ritual were punctilious in adopting American civil rituals like saluting the flag. Some of the Jewish patriotic ceremonies had a religious content, for example at Rockdale Avenue Temple in Cincinnati where we are told that "despite inclement weather about 1,000 people were present to sing patriotic songs and raise the flag. .... Our beloved country is at war, and at times like these, it is right that we renew our faith in God and invoke his help and his guidance."[30]

Pacifism was automatically identified with the enemy, Germany. When Mayor Thompson of Chicago ordered his Police Chief, Herman F. Schuettler, to allow the People's Council free speech in September, *The Chicago Tribune* ran a headline "BY GRACE OF BURGOMEISTER BILL." Its reports exaggerated the foreign accents of the participants, the cries of "vot you dinks" in the hotel bar. Judah Magnes provided the keynote speech at this controversial meeting and 26,000 copies were distributed nationwide. Speaking in entirely secular terms, Magnes pressed for a peace conference. He discussed the Russian revolution and the concept of a world made safe for democracy. Some Jews accused *The Chicago Tribune* of anti-Semitism [31] but on this occasion Magnes was identified neither as a Jew nor as a religious leader, only as "the peace prophet." He was referred to not as Rabbi but as as Dr. Magnes, Chairman of the New York constituent meeting of the Council. He spoke in respectable company with Senator Works and Congressman William B. Mason of Illinois.

Troops were sent to Chicago to prevent the meeting and on October 6 another meeting of the Council was broken up in

Cincinnati. Senator John Works of California withdrew from the People's Council at this stage because it had become too socialist.

Yet for all its socialist leanings, the People's Council was primarily a peace organisation and as peace went out of fashion it gradually lost its grassroots support. By Spring 1918 almost every Union supported the war. Eastern European socialist Jews who had opposed the authority of the Tsar were equally suspicious of authority in America whether it was that of the employers or of Gompers in the American Federation of Labor. Magnes had mistaken their political idealism for pacifism; Jewish workers were not natural pacifists. After March 1917 they supported the Allies, hoping that the defeat of Germany would help the Russian socialists. When the Soviets made a separate peace, Jewish support for the Allies did not falter. On the contrary, the Balfour Declaration in November 1917 and the revival of the clothing industry with the government as a major customer swung popular Jewish opinion behind the war. The American Federation of Labor supported the war. Its leader, Samuel Gompers, was profiled on the children's page of *The American Hebrew* as the model of Jewish patriotism, a national leader who was playing a vital part on the Council of National Defence.[32] In October the Jewish Socialist League of America issued a proclamation of loyalty.

In the autumn Morris Hillquit who was both a Jew and a pacifist stood for election as Mayor of New York. His campaign had no hope of success. It distracted the energies of Magnes and the Council leaders and left their organisation $9,000 in debt. Worst of all, it gave the press (*The New York Tribune* for instance) the opportunity for a virulent campaign of anti-Semitism. *The American Hebrew* deplored the "creation of a Jewish issue in America".[33] Two weeks later it stressed that Bolshevik Jews were not religious Jews, and not connected with any specific Jewish activity. None the less on December 13 it reported that *The Chicago Tribune* claimed that the Bolshevik leaders were all Jews.

The climate of opinion had changed. Americans as a whole were determined to shoulder the responsibility of fighting. Even the pacifist David Starr Jordan began to speak in support of the administration. Anti-German hysteria swept the country and posed a particular threat to the Jews because of the confusion between espionage and pacifism. Jewish ties with Germany or Russia now seemed equally alien. On August 2, 1917, a letter from *The*

Brooklyn Daily Eagle was quoted which makes the situation of Jewish pacifists only too clear. It deplored the American objector. "He is uniformly contemptible. If he is American, born of Revolutionary stock, he is a coward; if Russian or German Jew, he is a paid spy."

It is therefore important to notice that, just as John Harris in England fits the English tradition of religious pacifism which is simply a refusal to engage in war, Magnes' pacifism has much in common with other American pacifism. His thought is similar to that of David Starr Jordan, a fellow Californian who was president of Stanford University and a scientist. As an academic, Jordan believed in marshalling his facts. His pacifist arguments depended on rationality and detailed research. He was a biologist and believed that war was detrimental to the human race, just as Magnes believed it was detrimental to the interests of people anywhere. Jordan insisted that war was undemocratic in its origins and results, and Jordan also believed that pacifists should concentrate their efforts on propaganda and public speaking. American pacifists were not afraid to deal with the nitty gritty of peace negotiations and the practical business of politics. Magnes' pragmatism was not simply Jewish but also American. There had been talks in July at the Hague on treatment of prisoners of war. Why had there not been talks on ending the war he asked in Chicago in September 1917.[34] His attention to detail is characteristic of American pacifism.

Magnes did not regard the libertarian and egalitarian ideals of radicals and Zionists as un-American. Like many American pacifists after him, he clung to a vision of the true America, America of the Declaration of Independence and of the Constitution. The press had said, "the world must be made safe for democracy", but Magnes noted wryly that the stifling of comment and criticism was not democratic. There is something affronted in his description of the Madison Garden theatre ringed round with troops.

In addition to the large force of police inside, troops with fixed bayonets were stationed in an unbroken line on the surrounding sidewalks. At each corner of the Garden block there was also a wagon containing a machine gun and a great searchlight pointed towards the exits. A group of recruits in uniform occupied seats opposite the speakers' stand and endeavoured to shout the meeting down.

He continued:

> To make the entire world safe for democracy may take a very, very long time. What particular part of the world then do we refer to, and what degree of safety do we require, and what degree of democracy will satisfy us? The United States is declaring that she does not want conquest or dominion but does she expect Germany to be exactly like the United States? Are we to dictate forms of economic as well as political life, and is the degree of democracy to be determined by our own standards?[35]

His questions are as pertinent to U.S. policy in the 1960s, 70s or 80s, as to the First World War. They reveal a fundamental difference between Magnes' pacifism and that of John Harris. The American peace movement had gone beyond religious quietism. It was provocatively critical of every sphere of government policy and questioned the legitimacy of the administration itself. Magnes' estrangement from the Jewish community and his emergence as a leader in the arena of American politics was in a sense complete.

It is rare for historical works on conscientious objection in the United States in the First World War to identify an objector as a Jew. Christian historians deal predominantly with Christian preoccupations. Rabbi Magnes receives little attention, except as an unrepresentative figure who became somewhat naïvely caught up on the radical fringe of the People's Council. There is a determination on the part of Jews and Christians alike to deny that the Jewish voice was heard on the side of the pacifists during the First World War. Yet Jewish religious pacifism existed in the States as well as in Britain.

Each year the American Reform Rabbis (who far outnumbered the orthodox) met at a Central Conference (Central Conference of American Rabbis, or CCAR) and in 1917 the Conference (28 June – 4 July) was asked to clarify its attitude towards Jewish conscientious objection. Seven rabbis tabled a resolution explaining that rabbis had been approached by "Jewish young men objecting

to being drafted for military service and basing their objection on
religious grounds."

Only ten of 113 rabbis felt there could be Jewish religious
grounds for objection. Magnes was not present and Stephen Wise
recorded no dissenting opinion:

> While the mission of Israel is Peace and its constant endeavour
> and prayer are for peace and Brotherhood among men, yet
> when one's country is at war in behalf of righteousness and
> humanity, the individual Jew who claims this hope of Judaism
> as a ground of exemption from military service, does so only as
> an individual, in as much as historic Judaism emphasises
> patriotism as a duty, as well as the ideal of Peace.

Martin Zielonka, who had proposed the original motion, offered a
significant explanation of his negative vote. He explained that he
was not a pacifist; he supported the war. His Temple was used as a
registration place. "But believing in all this as firmly and honestly as
I do, I still believe that we as Jews should protect the honest and
sincere conscientious objector who places his objection on a
religious ground. I believe that the 8th verse of Deuteronomy XX
can be and ought to be interpreted in this way."[36]

Zielonka was tackling a basic question. Can Judaism allow a
minority opinion to coexist with that of the majority? Can there be
more than one correct response to any question about the will of
God? Both Harris and Magnes had in very different ways argued
that pacifism was integral to the Jewish religion. They suggested
there was no choice about it, for them or for any other correct
interpreter of Judaism.

But governments allow the right of conscience by which an
individual citizen has the right to refuse to fight, on an unspoken
assumption that only a very small minority will do so. Governments
need to be assured that the defence of the state will be unaffected.
Indeed much conscience legislation has been drafted to facilitate
the waging of war. Vociferous and illegal conscientious objection in
Britain during the First World War absorbed a disproportionate
amount of parliamentary time. Experience shows that the Christian
pacifists speak only for a small minority of Christians. Can one

assume that a Jew may also refuse to fight on the grounds of personal conscience without speaking for all Jews?

The issue is vital in terms of practical policy and legislation. But is a difficult problem to overcome in Judaism where the Law is paramount and where conscience can exist only as an amplification of the Law. Zielonka has to find a way to suggest that Judaism is capable of providing a variety of responses to a moral or ethical problem: the question of war.

Deuteronomy XX verse 8 commands that when the officers speak to the people before going to war they shall ask whether any man is fearful and fainthearted? If he is, "Let him go and return unto his house lest his brethren's heart melt as his heart." Zielonka suggested that the mental condition of recruits, as well as their physical defects, should be taken into account by the government.

If the pacifist is classified in biblical language as a man who has no heart for war, then this commandment could provide for Jewish conscientious objection. It is a solution, and it is one that will be returned to.

However, in the circumstances of 1917 it was not a position the Reform rabbis felt able to adopt. Quite apart from the religious and political issues involved, they knew the profound feelings of their congregations. The young pacifist Rabbi Harold Reinhart in Baton Rouge received a letter from his sister urging him to hang national and service flags in his synagogue, as his congregation wished. Her equally peace-loving husband, Samuel Cohon, had done so in his Chicago synagogue; it was not politic to do anything else.

Service flags, bearing a star for every congregant on active service, were paid for by congregation members, often as a tribute to their own sons, and were presented at a religious ceremony that might include a sermon from the rabbi and a loyal address from the donor. Rabbi Cohon had been one of the ten who had supported the Conference motion on conscientious objectors. Even he found it impossible to withstand this synagogue-based integration of Judaism and civil religion. "Of course," Irma Cohon wrote, "the great burden upon our hearts is the struggle towards peace. .... But even in this, one must fight out his severest battles in the secret places of his own heart; and be sane and cautious about public utterances — not that one should compromise his principles .... but that it is utterly stupid to recklessly throw away one's liberty or one's life without accomplishing anything thereby. There are only a few people whose voice and work at present can count."[37] The personal correspondence of a few individual Rabbis shows their private religious convictions that war was wrong and supports the conclusion that Magnes' sudden stand on pacifism was also a religious one.[38]

It is not easy to establish the place of conscience in Jewish religious thought. Often observance of the law and the interests of the People seem to dictate a course of action, leaving no choice. The soul-searching of the individual is stifled by the very same religious tradition which inspires it. Magnes confessed his own agonising:

> I can well understand when people say .... it is the primary purpose of a "good Jew" to say or do nothing that might in any way imperil the life or the safety of any Jew, or the political and social standing of any Jewish group. This is a consideration which every good Jew must reckon with, and because of it I personally have held off from saying many a thing which my own Jewish conscience urged.
>
> Nevertheless, occasions do arise when a "good Jew" with a "Jewish conscience" decides the conflict within him by speaking out the truth as he sees it. Each time I have done this, particularly within recent years, I have gone through the tortures of the damned; and whereas .... I am thoroughly convinced that the Jewish position means nothing if this is not possible to Jewish individuals, I have not ceased to ask myself the question daily if I have been a "good Jew".[39]

It was as a religious pacifist that Magnes persisted. The radical peace movement had been dispersed by calculated Government policy and by the swing of popular feeling behind the war. Religious leaders now took over from the socialists, speaking out mainly on the issue of civil liberties and on behalf of religious pacifists suffering in army detention. Christian pacifist groups were formed throughout the States. In California in June 1917 members of 14 different religious denominations formed a group called Christian Pacifists. They met with opposition every bit as intense as the socialists. Many ministers were dismissed for preaching against the war. In Los Angeles a police raid ended in the arrest and jailing of three Christian ministers, Robert Whitaker, Floyd Harding and Harold Storey October. They were later released on bail.

Many university teachers were reprimanded or dismissed for anti-war attitudes, either real or imagined.[40] Scott Nearing 'resigned' from Toledo University. In the circumstances it is amazing that the Hebrew Union College, Cincinnati, voted by a majority of one vote not to dismiss their Professor of History, Dr. Deutsch, who was accused of pro-German sympathies after a raid of Federal detectives on the People's Council. The College asked him to sever his connection with the Council "for the reason that the government of the United States had pronounced this association as inimical to the welfare of the country in the present crisis." He did as requested, with this statement: "My belief in the ideal of universal peace has been the only motive for my connection with the People's Council. The pronouncement of the government condemning this organisation as disloyal is to me a final decision which I dutifully and unreservedly accept."[41] One third of all the college students were now serving with the colours. Gotthard Deutsch was censored in his absence.

It is difficult to discern whether or not Dr. Deutsch was a pacifist. But he was not alone in being forced to leave the Council. Henrietta Szold was also forced to resign, by Brandeis and Wise among others. Her pacifism is made clear in a letter. "I am afraid you have to bracket me with Dr. Magnes and Miss Wald. I am anti-war, and anti-this-war, and anti-all-war. .... My position for me is the essence of my religious and philosophical make-up."[42]

Neither the American government, the Christian churches, the Jewish religious authorities nor the vast majority of Jews recognised any Jewish religious basis for pacifism.

On 19 December Baker ordered that men who had personal scruples against the war should be recognised as C.O.s. On March 20, 1918, an executive order from President Wilson recognised as conscientious objectors, firstly those who belonged to a religious sect and had been certified by their local draft board, and secondly, those conscientiously opposed to war for other than religious reasons, but who had no certificates. There was no total exemption. All were to go to noncombatant service.

There was great pressure on objectors to serve normally. 20,873 arrived at camps with certificates. Only 3,989 eventually refused military duties. Freedom of conscience therefore became an

important issue for the peace movement leadership, especially for
Magnes, the rabbi, whose constituents had no religious right to a
conscientious objection. Magnes visited objectors in prison and
publicised their ill-treatment as prisoners of con'science. At some
camps the ill-treatment was notorious. Fifteen objectors were
mistreated on 5 September at Camp Funston. Major Frank S.
White Jnr, judge advocate at the camp, described the troublesome
prisoners there as non-religious socialist objectors, "proven to be
pro-German, who did not believe in the Deity".[43] Captain Buckley
referred to "those of Jewish birth" as "damn kikes". The prisoners
were further insulted by being given raw rations of pork and beans.
The infringement of dietary laws would have been insignificant to
non-observant Jewish radicals. One must conclude that there were
probably religious Jewish objectors.

Norman Thomas, in his book *The Conscientious Objector in
America* published in 1923, describes movingly how Rabbi Magnes
went with Mr Codma of Boston to Governor's Island to inspect the
treatment of prisoners there. He saw Hutterians in solitary
confinement, shackled in standing position to the bars of the
opening in the door. Magnes reported minutely on their
incarceration in small cells, completely in the dark, without outer
clothing, fed only on water and 2 slices of bread 3 times a day. He
wrote to Secretary of War Baker on 27 August, 1918, and as a
result in December Baker modified the conditions and gave up the
manacling of pacifists.

In another scrap of reporting we learn from Thomas that there
was an orthodox Jew, Gelerter, imprisoned with the Molokans in
Fort Leavenworth, a notorious jail, and enduring the same
treatment. There was again a difficulty over diet: the Jewish
prisoners complained of being given vegetables and bread baked in
tins greased with lard. Evan Thomas and other prisoners struck on
their behalf. By January 1920 there were only two extremist
objectors left in Alcatraz. One was Philip Grosser, whom Clark
Getts describes as having a sense of humour, enough to lie awake at
nights and play with the rats in the dungeons. Thomas, in a
different light, described him as "an aggressive and determined
political objector of the Jewish race." These men finally agreed to

work only when they felt they were going mad, after being confined in cages where they could not sit, lie down nor turn.

The liberty for which Magnes campaigned is not nebulous. It is a practical emancipation in which Jews will be free to explore and develop their own cultural identity. His Zionism depends more on freedom of economic and spiritual development within territories than on actual actual boundary lines.

> Nations must be permitted to be themselves, to think their own thoughts, to speak their own language, to develop their own national and spiritual cultures without let or hindrance. White peoples and black and brown, occidental and oriental, small and great, they must be free to nurture the intimate things of the spirit unshackled – their religion, their literature, their art, their ways of living and of thought.[44]

Magnes' vision of a multi-cultural, multi racial world provided American Jewish pacifism with another important plank in its argument. The Jews are not superior but bearers of a message for all humanity. He condemns the social theory of superior and inferior races; he condemns imperialism, the spiritual theory that man – or, as they call it, "human nature" – is incapable of creating a new social order except through warfare or exploitation.[45]

The war was for democracy and so was Judaism. On the face of it in 1919 Magnes was still the high-flying rabbi with the ear of the establishment. Stephen Wise was the 'ordinary' man's rabbi, the Minister who spent his summer vacation of 1917 working incognito as an unskilled labourer in a Connecticut shipyard. But in effect their wartime roles had reversed their positions.

Stephen Wise's influence and judgement were vindicated. Thus he was able to persuade President Wilson rather belatedly (August 31, 1918) to issue an endorsement of the Balfour Declaration. Wise had re-organised and revitalised the American Zionist movement and gained access to government. Eventually he went to Paris as a leader of the American Jewish delegation to the Peace Conference, a proud friend of the President.

Magnes had forfeited his position and his influence in the Jewish Community. His eminence made his dissent all the more reprehensible. "Dr. Magnes has been honored beyond the common by his co-religionists and it would seem to the man in the street that he owes them some return. .... Unfortunately his position in the estimation of the people is so high that his capacity for doing harm is great."[46] According to *The American Israelite* Magnes had destroyed "his possibility of giving further good service to mankind and Judaism".

Magnes had paid a personal price as well. He and his family were obliged to move house because of his pacifist activities, first leaving New York for Connecticut and then, forced out by hostile neighbours, moving again to Chappaqua. In 1919 the press once again took up the false claim that he was a German spy. War hysteria was so high that he had been unable to bring any action for libel. His name was blackened by malicious innuendo. In December 1918 the Assistant Attorney General of New York who was investigating German propaganda had asserted that intercepted messages proved that Magnes had worked with German officials. *The New York Times* reported that he had been served with a subpoena to report to the Attorney General's office and say what he knew of American bolsheviki (sic) and that Dr. Magnes had subsequently spent all day at the office, leaving after 6 p.m. The aspersion was unfounded, and the newspaper withdrew it next day. Magnes had been ill in hospital since December 1 and had not been subpoenaed at all.[47]

Although Magnes still headed the *Kehillah* the role of that organisation had changed. The war had Americanised the Jews and the idea of the *Kehillah* as a separate community waned. Their efforts now centred on Jewish education or became subsumed in the broader aims of Mordecai Kaplan for a diverse and continuing expression of Jewish community in the Diaspora. Magnes himself was not an acceptable leader.[48]

Stephen Wise attacked his colleague from the pulpit, repeatedly accusing Magnes of Bolshevism and Prussianism and calling for his resignation. Mordecai Kaplan agreed. In June 1920 Magnes complied and tendered his resignation. Though the murder of his colleague Israel Friedlander in the Ukraine[49] led Magnes to postpone his retirement for another two years, Magnes' career in the United States was at an end.

That he left was a severe loss to both the American community and to himself. Yet many of the causes he argued, and his pride in a distinctive American Jewish identity, turned out to presage future trends, movements which, joined with Zionism, succeeded in revitalising Judaism just as Magnes hoped and urged. His stand on Jewish rights to plead a pacifist case in front of Draft boards also bore fruit.

Perhaps Magnes himself never gave himself full credit. Isolated and ignored, he reprinted a few of his speeches in the hope that somewhere someone would listen. For his warning was clear:

> The world has just passed through a war, the consequences of which cannot be foreseen, but which even now has torn apart the world's social structure. Transportation, exchange, the supply of coal and fuel and of raw materials, everything is broken down; and literally millions of human beings are now suffering hunger and are being ravaged by disease, by pogroms and by the anarchy which our wise masters have created and which they seem not to be able to control. Peace treaties have been made which for savagery, hypocrisy, ineffectiveness know no equal in history. The western world is falling apart. Throughout the belligerent lands, with the possible exception of America and Japan, the masses of the people are asking themselves what has been the meaning of this catastrophe. They want to know who has led them into it, and what fundamental causes are responsible for it.[50]

His rabbinic disquiet over both the war and the ensuing Peace Settlement reveal an insight and a foreboding to which the post-Holocaust world has no answer.

Chapter 3
Theory and Practice: Hans Köhn and Enzo Sereni
Secular Pacifism in the Mandate

In early 1917 British armies advanced into Palestine and on 9 December General Allenby entered Jerusalem. Thus four hundred years of Turkish rule were brought to an end and the inhabitants of Palestine had a new master. 1917 was hardly a year of British triumph; the slaughter on the Western Front continued on such a scale that the word holocaust was used to describe it. Zev Jabotinsky, the Revisionist Zionist, had already seized the opportunity to offer Jewish reinforcements. In 1915 his Zion Mule Corps provided the first military presence that was specifically Jewish, but it was officered by British, and was no more than a small transport corps for the Gallipoli campaign. Undismayed, Jabotinsky continued to press for a Jewish legion. The idea encountered opposition both from the British government and the Jewish community. Jews were eager to fight, but to fight as Englishmen. Eventually in late 1917 the 38th battalion of the Royal Fusiliers, the so-called Judean Regiment, was set up. The battalion attracted only a few hundred volunteers in London. The majority of Judeans were Jewish conscripts directed to that regiment.

In Palestine there was a problem not of loyalties but of ideology. Labour leaders including Ben Gurion helped recruit volunteers to the 39th and 40th battalions but the idea of a Jewish Legion was hard for socialist settlers. Most were more in sympathy with the ideas of A.D. Gordon than of Jabotinsky. Gordon extolled the virtue of manual labour through which the Jewish people were to be transformed. Photographs taken in Palestine, like those from the early collectives of Soviet Russia or from German Youth camps show gleaming young bodies bringing the harvest home. Jews' new-found physical strength was to cultivate the Land, not to kill for it. When the agricultural workers' organisation rallied to send volunteers to join the Jewish Legion in August 1918 a ploughwoman voiced the doubts of many. She questioned the alien military spirit which had been introduced into Zionist life. She called it "a new form of assimilation". A heroic death and military glory were not part of the Jewish tradition. Jabotinsky emphasised the need for unquestioning obedience to a superior officer. With remarkable foresight she disagreed. "'Yes sir' is the darkness out of which light will never be born," she declared. But in the end, she acquiesced in their going.[1]

The Jewish legions numbered 5,000 men, roughly one sixth of the British army of occupation. They did not arrive from Egypt until December 1918, and by April 1919 only three or four hundred men remained. The Jewish Legion had been disbanded. Jabotinsky failed to establish a Zionist army.

Under Turkish rule the Jews had lived like any other settlers without an autonomous force to guard themselves or their property. The massacres which took place from time to time are evidence of their defencelessness. When the Balfour Declaration offered an officially recognised homeland in Palestine even Jews who had not previously been Zionist found it hard to turn down the opportunity. With land to defend there might be a need for Jews to take up arms.

Even with Palestine in view, Zionism had never been a military undertaking. Zionist after Zionist, Hess, Herzl, Pinsker, Ahad Ha-Am, had stressed the ethical and spiritual mission of the Jewish people. The land was to be reclaimed through settlement and development, not through conquest. Jews were not necessarily pictured as the majority community in Palestine, nor as having secular self-government, let alone constituting a sovereign state. It is not true that Zionist thinkers ignored the Arab inhabitants of Palestine; writer after writer emphasised their presence. What European Zionists did not envisage was the conflict which ensued from the concurrent development of Jewish and Arab nationalism.

Early Zionists did not define 'people' or 'nation' in late twentieth century terms. The empires of the eighteenth and nineteenth centuries had been multi-national. The Romanovs and Hapsburgs had ruled a conglomeration of peoples. Those peoples began to express their allegiance to separate national identities, but it was not a foregone conclusion that each nationality should aspire to its own separate state. Marxist theory and the Leninist Russian Revolution had upset existing ideas of what constituted a state. Marx suggested that if the peoples of the world were to rise in unison, then the state itself, a symbol of oppression, might wither away. He even suggested that this Messianic age might be predetermined: it might come about not by force of arms, but by the inevitable growth of true class consciousness. Zionists, eschewing war, understandably believed in the natural growth of Jewish consciousness and self-confidence in Palestine. One historian has said that Yiddish had virtually no military vocabulary.[2] Jews were not soldiers.

In the Versailles settlement Great Britain was given mandatory power in Palestine. Jews in Palestine now found themselves dependent on Britain for defence and many (particularly the British and Americans) were content, believing that the Balfour Declaration initiated a British policy favourable to a Jewish homeland in Palestine. But there is another perspective: Britain was an Empire terrified of Russian-inspired revolution. The Jewish settlers from Central and Eastern Europe were radical socialists and the co-operative farms or kibbutzim which they established were a practical expression of those same socialist ideals. British government allied itself more naturally with the Arab élite who represented a hierarchical and seemingly stable status quo. Political contact between Arab, European and Jew was multi-faceted. Both Weizmann, for the Zionist Federation, and the British sought the support of Emir Faisal of Syria in order to limit French influence and achieve their own political objectives.

The 1920s and early thirties were the years when pacifist organisations grew in those countries which had won the war. The Jewish Peace Society flourished in England and the American Reform rabbinate affiliated with peace organisations in the States, both expressive of the general war weariness and desire for peace. In Palestine there was no such cohesive Jewish peace movement. Peace-loving though the settlement was, it depended on British protection. If British help was not forthcoming, farms had to resort to self-defence against Arab attack.

The *Haganah* or illegal defence force which followed the disbanding of the Jewish Legion was a very different concept. It was not a strategic military force but was to defend settlements which in themselves had no strategic importance. In theory all Jews in Palestine wanted peace, but pacifism in day to day terms might be synonymous with suicide. Settlers were allowed shot guns which they bought for themselves.[3] This spontaneous and voluntary arming of the inhabitants has had a lasting effect on pacifism and conscientious objection in Israel. The existence of settlements on properly purchased land was not seen as a *casus belli* or provocation. The defence of properly purchased land was therefore justified, aggression was not. The *Haganah* policy of minimum force known as *havlaga* (self-restraint) became official Zionist policy in the 1930s. Even so, on an unofficial basis it was evaded by more extreme groups who were prepared to carry out reprisals, take preventive action or, in the view of some historians, provoke trouble.[4] As there was no conscription, so there was no provision for Jewish conscientious objection. In a community defended by volunteer units, those who refused to carry arms or were unwilling to join the more militant underground armies were individuals taking decisions on a personal basis.

Since both socialist Zionism and religious Judaism tended towards pacifism, it is not surprising that this yearning for peace produced lone individuals whose refusal to bear arms became the stuff of legend. One Israeli told me how before the 1905 revolution his father had enlisted for four years with the Tsar's army to learn defence. Later he was detailed by his socialist revolutionary group to assassinate the local chief of police. The contradiction between faith and politics must have remained. When his intended victim did not pass at the expected hour, the young revolutionary took it as a sign from God. He threw his gun in the river and never used arms again.

Another story tells how the charismatic writer, J.C. Brenner, returned to his Kibbutz during a period of Arab attacks and deliberately went out unarmed to walk in the orchards near Jaffa. It was May Day, a significant date, legend recalls. In fact Brenner was killed on May 2nd 1921 during disturbances that were a severe shock to the Jewish socialist settlers because they followed Arab attacks on a May Day procession in Jaffa. The death toll overall was 95 people, with 219 seriously injured, and the British eventually brought in cavalry and aeroplanes to defend Petah Tikva. Who is to say that Brenner, faced with the dismaying prospect of general violence between Jew and Arab, might not have preferred to die? Yet these stories of Jewish pacifism in Palestine are not substantiated. It is the pattern of secular pacifism in the Mandate that it failed to hold up where the Jewish interest or Jewish lives were at stake.

The newly established British presence was expected to contain the political situation and maintain order. But the previous year in the Spring of 1920 there had been widespread Palestinian agitation for union with the new Arab kingdom in Syria. The British could neither control Palestinian demonstrations in Jerusalem nor prevent attacks on Jewish settlements. Faced with physical attack, the Jewish farmers would attempt to defend themselves or, if that failed, would seek shelter in some larger nearby settlement until the British army or the police arrived. Arab Jewish dialogue and co-operation was not limited to so-called 'Peace' circles. Jewish and Arab farmers co-operated in defending farms and livestock against Bedouin raiders. Jews employed Arab guards. Contrary to the hopes of the Utopian socialist settlers, communal life did not provide the network of mutual relationships that would ensure peace. Community identity was strongly forged among these pioneers in an unpropitious terrain. There was a united response when the group was threatened either by Arab attack, or even by potential new members. The stronger the sense of community the less likely there was to be a non-violent response. There is a central problem of consent and dissent in Judaism. The Jew may question the 'secular' nationalism of others, but his own duty to identify with his community is a 'religious' one. The individual Jew can take the pacifist position only if he can formulate a pacifism which confirms his identity as a Jew. Pacifism may entail re-examining the nature of Jewish identity and in particular what it means to identify with the Jewish People.

Hans Köhn had been a convinced Zionist before the First World War made him a pacifist as well. He was born in 1891 and when he was seventeen he became a member of a Zionist student circle in Prague, the Bar Kochba Association, to which the young Martin Buber lectured and to which Franz Kafka also belonged. Bar Kochba led an abortive Jewish revolt against the Romans in 135CE and his name has become synonymous with suicidal military heroism.[5] Yet in Köhn's autobiography he said, "In my time the Bar Kochba Association opposed the military spirit and Messianic expectations that its name suggested. Its emphasis was on cultural values and ethical duties."[6] …. "The Zionism championed by me since 1909 was at no time political," he wrote. "I and a group of my friends regarded Zionism as a moral-cum-spiritual movement within which we could realise our most fundamental human convictions: our pacifism, liberalism and humanism."[7]

What is one to make of this claim to pacifism? Köhn and his friend Robert Weltsch joined the Prague Legion immediately war was declared in 1914. Jewish pacifism has a certain uniqueness. Some Jews (and Köhn is a good example) have an insurmountable objection to Jews fighting as Jews, less objection to the idea of Diaspora Jews as patriots defending their various homelands. Yet the First World War made a pacifist of Köhn. Köhn's life is an impressive intellectual development as he repeatedly analysed his own assumptions. Nor was this just a philosophical exercise; it was experiential. Köhn joined the army as a Czech in order to identify with Czechs rather than with the Austrian ruling class. He found himself, as a Czech, despised by the Germans for whom the Czechs were fighting. Next, as a prisoner of the Russians during the Revolution, he saw with dismay how the Muscovite socialists despised their own Oriental minorities. Finally, back in Prague after the war, he found himself, a Jew, rejected by his fellow Czechs in the new nation state to which they had all aspired.

The First World War made Köhn mistrust nationalism and this was to become the subject of his life's work. He particularly disliked late nineteenth century romantic nationalism, characterised, as he saw it, in German youth: an exaggerated self-esteem, an impassioned appeal to heroism, to the spirit of self-sacrifice and to a rejection of the comfortable bourgeois life. Köhn saw that this came uncomfortably close to the aspirations of some of the Zionists. Jews were aping Germans. The German people also believed that they had a mission to realise the ideal national community. The German people, like the Jews, felt that they had managed to preserve their national identity through centuries of suffering. The growth of all nationalism, whether German, Jewish or Arab, was founded on a notion of blood, destiny and an organic folk community. He recalled that Alexander the Great "recognised that inter-marriage of Greek and Barbarian was the only way of establishing peace and harmony among different peoples".[8] It is startling to find a Jewish philosopher recommending inter-marriage as a means to peace. Implied is the idea that any sort of social exclusivity, including that practised by orthodox Jews, may in itself be conducive to intolerance and to war. Köhn's critique of nationalism did not spare the Jews. Peace was incompatible with national aspirations. Individual egoism when taken over by groups was inexcusable nationalism.

His experiences in Russia as a prisoner of war first under the Tsar and then through the revolution convinced Köhn that nationalism was linked to territory and both were linked to war. His devotion to the Zionist cause for which he worked from the war's end until 1929 was an expression of his new political credo, a non-territorial identity. Being a Zionist Jew, he was no longer a Czech, he was above national boundaries, a cosmopolitan indeed.

Explaining his pacifism in Jewish terms he wrote, "It has often been argued that we (Jews) could not unreservedly sponsor pacifism or ethical politics among the European peoples, since this would result in our being regarded as aliens and traitors. Zion was to be the place where we would be able to realise our humanitarian aspirations."[9] Yet the realities of Palestine were very far from this. He appreciated Buber's concern for Jewish/Arab dialogue, but that was a side issue. "I am not concerned about Ishmael – only Isaac – us." He was not concerned with Arabs but with the Jews, their Jewishness and humane values. "As a Jew, as a human being, as a Jewish human being – two qualities which in me are inseparable and parallel – I am a pacifist, an anti-imperialist, and what in America is called a radical."

"The world events of 1917-20 which focused my attention on history also made me a pacifist." Köhn's pacifism was the child of Jewish emancipation within the Austrian Empire. His education and the European culture he imbibed was in itself an emancipation which exposed him to men from other backgrounds who took ideas as seriously as the Jews. Among them were pacifists: some were Christian, but there were others whose faith in the goodness of human nature was based on what Köhn called "descriptive empirical psychology". Köhn made a conscious decision in favour of rationalism and empiricism.

Köhn moved physically from country to country in order to live both as a Jew and pacifist. Between 1921 and 1922 he initiated the *Jüdische Gesellschaft für Internationale Verständigung*, the Jewish Society for International Understanding, whose members included celebrated names: Martin Buber, the theologian, Chaim Bialik, most famous of Israeli national poets, and Robert Weltsch, Köhn's school friend and fellow historian.[10] It was a noteworthy though perhaps premature attempt to interest Jews as Jews not just in the neutrality of peace but in the positive encouragement of mutual respect between nations. After the war Köhn was Secretary to the Zionist Delegation to the Peace Conference and found himself working for the World Zionist Organisation, first in Paris and then from 1921-25 in London. He was living and working as a Jew but in both places he encountered socialist Christian pacifists, in particular Charles Péguy and George Lansbury, the British Labour Party leader whose social circle overlapped with that of John Harris. Köhn recalled, "I followed a rather lonely path, as my conscience and my naturally limited understanding of the situation dictated."[11]

It is easy to say that because Köhn was a pacifist, he was no longer speaking as a Jew. This is not so. It was at this period of his life that Köhn wrote widely on Jewish subjects. He wrote in German on Buber's thought, and in French on Jewish humanism. He did not agree with the British Liberal Jewish universalism adopted by Claude Montefiore. Being a Jew does effect a man's citizenship of a particular country because Judaism, as humanist nationalism, proposes a moral law for all people.[12] For Köhn Judaism was a humanism, based on totally valuing every human being. "War represents the extreme case in which Kant's maxim to treat each man as an end in himself, and Seneca's words '*Homo homine res sacra*' (Man is a sacred object to man) cannot even be postulated."

His view of a Jew , as a man with a conscience, a man to whom history is "not predictable, nor a court of justice"' is not everyone's idea of Judaism. The Jewish religious concept is of God's special historical purpose for the Jewish people. Köhn always put the individual first, the nation second. Nationalism looks to the past to emphasise blood or race, he insisted. The emphasis should be on the future and on emancipation.

Some of Köhn's writing is startling for his time. He wrote with sympathy of his mother stuck at home by convention, and of the overworked maid, Marenka. "Thanks to her I know that illiterate Africans and Arabs may be wiser and better persons than those European university graduates who regard such backward peoples as 'uncivilised'."

When the finance office of the Zionist Organisation moved to Jerusalem in 1925 Köhn moved with it. In Palestine he could easily have slipped into the local habit of regarding the Arabs as less equal than the Jews, but he never did. "The ruling classes have never attributed human dignity to peoples in revolt, nor did they ever for a moment believe that the life of one of the subject people could be equal to the life of one of their own class or race." For Köhn no man or woman was less than fully human. Jews who regarded Arabs as inferiors were not true Zionists.

The growth of Arab nationalism in Palestine had begun to interest Köhn while he was a prisoner in Irkutsk, Siberia, and he had written on it in the local Zionist paper *Yevreyskaya Zhizn* (*Jewish Life*) in 1919. He quoted Ahad Ha-Am who had opposed a boycott of Arab labour, "Apart from the political danger, I cannot put up with the idea that our brethren are morally capable of behaving in such a way to men of another people. If it is so now, what will be our relations to others if in truth we shall achieve 'at the end of time' power in *Eretz Israel* (Palestine)? If this be the 'Messiah' I do not wish to see his coming."[13] Köhn maintained that Herzl too in his last novel *Altneuland* looked to a new society in which Arab prospered as well as Jew.

Arriving in Palestine and facing this predicament, Köhn supported the formation of *Brith Shalom* in 1925. In spite of its name, *Brith Shalom* (The Peace Association) was not a pacifist organisation. Its founders, veteran Zionist settlers, aspired to work out a mutually acceptable political solution. They suggested a bi-national state in which neither Arab nor Jew would dominate.[14] Its statutes state unambiguously the object of the Association:

> to arrive at an understanding between Jews and Arabs as to the form of their mutual social relations in Palestine on the basis of absolute political equality of two culturally autonomous peoples, and to determine the lines of their co-operation for the development of the country.[15]

Pacifists were involved in *Brith Shalom* because it had pacific intentions, to encourage friendly relations between Jews and Arabs. It was the forerunner of many non-pacifist peace movements which aspired to foster good relations with Arabs. It's programme was primarily educational, that of increasing Jewish/Arab knowledge and appreciation of each other's history and culture. Their hopes were not realistic. Seventy students enrolled in May 1926 for its first courses in Arabic, but there was little Arab response and the World Zionist Organisation could not accept any solution which limited Jewish settlement or accepted parity with the Arabs. The organisation petered out in 1933.

In 1929 the Arab riots brought matters to a head. The Jews were saved by British armed intervention. Köhn is perceptive and blazingly honest in his analysis. The act of settling the land could in itself be aggressive. An Arab attack could be viewed as a justified war in self-defence. There is a situation in which each of two sides views the other as aggressor and sees its own recourse to arms as justified by doctrines of self-defence.

But Köhn goes further. As pacifist, he points out the difference between calling for peace when one has the advantage and calling for peace regardless of one's own superiority . "We would gladly make peace if we were strong." In other words everyone accepts a victorious peace – a peace whereby the opponent does what we want. Naturally each party wants peace on the condition that he can obtain what he considers essential. True pacifists in the First World War rebelled against this attitude. "I would be glad if we also had a few such pacifists among our ranks. If only the Jews could show such courage in their own affairs as was demonstrated, for example, by the English pacifists in the World War."[16]

He had seen nationalism in the Russian Revolution in Siberia, he saw it in his home country Czechoslovakia where the new Czech government "identified the new state with a single ethnic, linguistic group, at the expense of the others", and he recognised the same nationalism at work in Palestine.

In his *History of Nationalism in the East*, 1928,[17] Köhn pays tribute to the modernisation of Palestine under the Mandate, the improvement of roads, posts, telephones and the Jerusalem water supply. He does not stereotype. He recognises a variety of cultures among both Jews (religious, international, Sephardic, etc.) and Arabs (effendi, fellahin, Bedou etc.). Pluralism and individuality was the keynote of the Mandate. Köhn did not blame the British Government for the tragic situation, but blamed the spirit of extreme nationalism among the peoples of Palestine. In a poetic lament Köhn speaks of

Eretz Israel, the object of (Jews') dreams and longings, the refuge of their souls for two thousand years, a land where history had stood still, the salvation awaited by so many generations. Unfortunately certain facts had barely penetrated

Jewish consciousness: that the country was not altogether a barren desert. .... Finally standing at the gates of their country, ... Jews were genuinely amazed and understandably indignant suddenly to find it occupied by aliens who disputed their right to it.[18]

Köhn's position, though European, is similar to that of Magnes, the American. Colonial peoples threaten the imperialist powers. "We pretend to be innocent victims. Of course the Arabs attacked us in August. Since they have no armies, they could not obey the rules of war." Köhn saw that the Jews depended on British arms. Instead there should have been a response of peace.

Zionists saw the Jewish situation as unique, Köhn did not. The events of 1929 were too much for Köhn, who refused to depart from his pacifist stand. "Zionism will either be peaceful or it will be without me. Zionism is *not* Judaism," he wrote to Martin Buber in 1929. (Mendes Florh, in whose book *A Land for Two Peoples* these documents are reprinted, remarks that Buber's reply to Köhn is not yet available.) But Buber did not agree with Köhn's opposition to the bayonets of the *Haganah* defence force. He referred to Köhn's moral doctrinarism; Köhn was living in an Ivory Tower.

For his part, Köhn had gone further than modern critics would dare in criticising Buber. He underlined the similarities between Buber's thought and that of the German nationalists whose cultural background Buber shared. Köhn argues that the clear, dispassionate thinking of the enlightenment gave way to a romanticised notion of the individual rooted in his own people. Buber had concocted a seductive, Jewish version of German nationalism.

Köhn questioned Buber's concept of what is natural and Buber's equation of what is natural with what is right. It could be suggested, as did Buber or Gandhi, that it is natural for people to live together in small groups, co-operating naturally, and that a natural inter-group co-operation will follow, providing they enter into a reciprocal relationship and neither group threatens the other. On the other hand it could be argued that it is natural for individuals and groups to compete for land and for resources for survival. In *The Europeanisation of the Orient*, 1937, Köhn extended this line of thought which is not a common one among pacifists and is just as pertinent today. Romanticism was the danger, whether it was a mystical devotion to the state as in Germany or Turkey, or whether it was traditional religion such as Islam which was to blame for backwardness. He criticised Gandhi whose opposition to industrialisation was no less a Romanticist nationalist return to the past.[19] Köhn believed that Western and Jewish rationalism, industrialism and individualism brought higher living standards, modern literacy and equality of the sexes to societies which had not known them before. He looked for the emergence of a more unified world. Köhn saw Judaism and the enlightenment as over-riding the basic instincts of man, a civilising humanistic force for peace in the world.

Painfully he parted company with Zionism. Looking to the future, he eventually opted for the life of a political philosopher, writing and teaching in the United States, a pluralistic, multi-ethnic society.

How difficult it is to balance the realisation of Zionism with general ethical considerations. It left me rather depressed. Is Zionism really to end up as shallow chauvinism? Is it impossible to provide the ever-growing number of Jews in Palestine with a field of activity without oppressing the Arabs?

Arthur Ruppin, founder of *Brith Shalom*, agonised over the problem that defeated Köhn.[20] Was it possible to be a pacifist and also a Zionist? Already involved in *Brith Shalom* was an impassioned Italian Zionist who answered in the affirmative.

Arriving in Tel Aviv at certain times of year, when there has been a sprinkling of rain, one looks out on an Italianate landscape. Slim pencils of cypress trees reach for the blue sky. There are familiar vines and olive trees. Beyond the green fields one glimpses a cluster of red tiled roofs. It is siesta time. There is a dusty calm. The stones are warm to touch. This is the world of the Mediterranean and it is hardly surprising that Enzo Sereni felt at home in it. He did not come like Köhn from a chilly northern capital to an office job. Sereni meant to work the land; by doing manual work alongside working men he would realise himself both as a man and a Jew. The earth he came to work was not unlike that he had left behind in the Roman countryside.

Working the Land was an important part of Zionist philosophy. The third wave of settlers, the 3rd *Aliyah*, 1920-22, were largely agricultural pioneers from Russia. They were fleeing the Revolution which left them no room to be Jews, but they brought with them many of the socialist ideals which had inspired it. Their ideas of social equality and social justice were part and parcel of the secular Jewish identity which drew them to Palestine. There were perhaps only 22,000 of these socialist settlers but their influence was out of all proportion to their numbers, and their belief in the brotherhood of man coincided with that of Magnes. These people were the only Jews who in a practical democratic sense attempted to put into practice the Judaism he preached.

Magnes' ideal of the Jewish people hardly matched the continued settlement in the Mandate period. The 4th and 5th *Aliyahs* between 1923 and 1939 brought a Jewish urban middle class and 60,000 refugees from Hitler's Germany. Their interests were material and pragmatic. They laid the economic foundation of the future Jewish state but there is no denying that they brought with them the quasi-colonial attitudes of their countries of origin. Implicit in all Jewish agricultural and industrial enterprise in the Jewish homeland was the conviction that benefits accrued also to the Arab population. It is apparent, for instance, in Albert Einstein's *About Zionism*, published by Soncino Press in 1930. Socialist agricultural settlers pointed to improved agricultural methods, and medical care for neighbouring Arab settlements. Jewish expectations of Arab gratitude and co-operation were high and this sustained a certain form of benevolent pacifism.

Enzo Sereni arrived in 1927 as part of this Zionist emigration. He was born in Rome on 27 April, 1905, and grew up in the cultured, assimilated world of Italian Judaism. His father, Samuel Sereni, was Professor of Medicine at Rome and private doctor to King Victor Emanuel. The Italian life of school, university, a Ph.D., and military service overlay an unobtrusive, religious Jewish existence. To his fellow Jews in Palestine Sereni always seemed like an Italian. His socialism certainly had the hallmarks of Italian socialism but it was a socialism which was informed and transformed by Sereni's Jewish consciousness.

The Serenis traced their family back to the time of the second temple. Like Magnes, Sereni came to socialism from the professional class, to lead the people. Sereni's communist brother,

Emilio, later became a deputy in the Italian senate. But socialist though he was, Sereni could not be neatly classified as an Italian Marxist because in Judaism he had a religion. After his bar mitzvah, Sereni wrote in his diary about his belief in God, and this easy-going faith remained with him, even though he spent most of his working life with secular Jews on the Kibbutz of Givat Brenner which he had helped establish. Before leaving for Palestine he had translated a history of ancient Hebrew literature for publication in Turin. In his thirties he was the only member of the kibbutz who attended synagogue at Yom Kippur and actually fasted.[21] It was an informal, personal, Italian version of Judaism in which conscience played a large part. Sereni often emphasised the role of Judaism in providing a religious conscience for the world. It was this ethical identity which established the Jews as a people, different from others, with their own history and identity as a nation.

In keeping with Italian political philosophy, for Sereni the nation is a living thing:

> This quality of being a Zionist essentially implies a duty, that of living together, communal life. Becoming a Zionist means realising that we are not unconnected men without links with the past and the future but, to use an old image, links in a chain, parts of a whole, members, St. Paul would have said, of the mystical body of the Jewish nation. The consciousness of this duty implies above all understanding that we are not on our own today, that the problem of our culture, that is, of our life, will be resolved through our people.[22]

The theories of Benedetto Croce on the spirit of history and of Giovanni Gentile influenced the young Sereni, just as they influenced the thought of both Mussolini and the Italian Communists. Judaism was not just a religious fact but a national act.

Italian Judaism is Orthodox but is outward looking and pluralistic. "Judaism is not considered by me to be a matter of class or organisation. There is no need for a specific programme. When we restore to Judaism all the qualities which belong to it," he wrote aged 17, "we will feel that the nation of Israel is so great that there is no need to be afraid when one encounters the most divergent aims within it."[23]

The rise of Mussolini in 1922 initially made little difference to the Jews of Italy, some of whom were active within the Fascist movement.[24] But Fascism would not countenance Zionist loyalties and it destroyed the possibility of achieving socialism within Italian society. In 1923 Enzo went to the Zionist Congress in Karlsbad and was bowled over when he heard Weizmann speak. He wrote, "I hereby continue to become a Jew – a new man is born and moving inside me." [25]

Sereni made no attempt to divide his new character as a Zionist from his character as Italian. His debt to the language and culture of Italy was undeniable. He remained as proud of being an educated Italian as he was of being a Jew. "We will continue to live as a modern people, as Jews in the Diaspora," he wrote. But then, he pointed out, Italian thought was much coloured by the legacy of Judaism. Jewish monotheism had become the common property of Europe. Yet for those who were Jews there remained a special tension, a different purpose in life. Denying Judaism is the uprooting of the flower.

In *Dal Profondo* (1926) he explained his rather tortuous search for a way of beginning to live as a Jew as well as a modern Italian. No one should imply that the study of Judaism involves abandoning the preoccupations normal to any young man. Judaism is not something finished and static which can be learned. It is a question of one's own personal development. Sereni explained that his attitude towards religion was a Jewish attitude but at the same time it was also inescapably the attitude of the modern man that he was. "Zionism is making Israel a fact in the world; for the first time it makes it possible for the whole of life with all its problems to be lived by Jews as Jews. Jewish culture is at every moment revealed as a necessity of one's life." But it was not a formula for existence. "Question after question has to be struggled with by each individual drawing on the depth of his own conscience. The answer which can only be arrived at by living must come to each man from within himself."[26] Sereni is emphatic about the role of the individual conscience in Judaism.

When Köhn or Buber spoke of the Jewish nation they meant the entire Jewish people, endowing the Jews with a national identity which owed much to mid nineteenth century nationalism, "A people like to the nations." When Sereni spoke of the Jewish people it was not a nation he had in mind so much as a complete society. He explains this most fully in *La Questione Ebraica*, written in 1939 at a moment of appalling tension after the November Pogrom in Germany and the shock of Mussolini's legislation against the Jews in November 1938. None the less, it probably presents a fair picture of Sereni's Zionism.

Sereni starts by urging Jews to take the initiative over the Jewish question. It is no good deploring anti-Semitism. Jews have to identify its causes and then they can decide what to do about it. German Jews before 1933 and Italian Jews before September 1938 had refused to believe that there was a Jewish problem. "It seemed to them that thanks to assimilation ... they had become an organic part of the people among whom they lived." But the result of assimilation was that being a Jew "lacked a positive intellectual and moral content. It was reduced to physical elements of dissent and to certain Jewish predispositions and characteristics." Non-Jews "were instinctively repelled by the haste with which the Jews were willing to throw away their own background, forget their own history and appropriate somebody else's in which they had no roots."

Sereni analysed the question in Marxist terms. Jews had been accepted in non-Jewish societies only where they had an economic function. Sereni was well aware that the Jewish class structure as he saw it did not fit the Marxist pattern. Concentrating on the Jewish societies he knew best, those of Western Europe, he described the Jewish class structure as the reverse of normal, an upside-down pyramid which lacked a working class base. Assimilators had wrongly thought they could resolve the Jewish problem by changing Jewish culture, reforming and modernising religious belief and eliminating the ideological differences between Israel and other peoples. Sereni believed that the Jewish problem could be resolved by changing the economic and social conditions in which the Jews found themselves, and that Zionism would transform the Jewish situation and Jewish consciousness by creating a new national community resting on a normal social basis. Normality involved Jews becoming workers at the primary levels of production.[27]

Sereni's prescription must be understood in the light of his time and of his Italian background. His attitudes and his approach have something in common with those of Antonio Gramsci, one of the seminal thinkers of Eurocommunism, and a founder of the Italian Communist Party which included Sereni's younger brother, Emilio. Southern Italy was rural and undeveloped. Large landowners exploited the peasants. The industrial conditions for revolutionary seizure of power by the workers did not exist in Italy. Gramsci extended Marxist theory to cover peasants and landowners. He replaced the mechanistic system with a socialism that was national and popular.

The problems Sereni found in Palestine were reminiscent of Italy: there was similar under-development and rural exploitation. Sereni had a good understanding of the political opportunities which could be created by unions, strikes and workers' control. The Moscow-controlled Comintern was anti-Zionist, condemned Jewish settlement in Palestine and advocated Jewish co-operatives within the Soviet Union. Sereni ignored the Soviet line and insisted on the Zionist right to a legitimate Jewish socialism in Palestine. The struggle against British Imperialism in the Middle East could be pursued without becoming a communist war against Israel.

Zionism offered the opportunity to Jews as Jews to create a new society. But only by peaceful means. "To build our nation, to live as Jews, without blows and without any dispersal of the soul." Sereni analysed the class structure and economic pressures in Palestine. There could be no peace where there was unemployment, where Jew and Arab competed for jobs, where Arab pay rates undercut the Jews. Sereni denounced the political control of businessmen, whether Arabs or Jews, and of the Jewish petit bourgeoisie which was building up the urban economy for profit.[28]

Peaceful solutions had to come from a properly educated working class. Sereni deplored the low level of culture and political debate on the Kibbutz as well as among the Arabs. He would walk around Givat Brenner with a book in his hand, urging his fellow workers to do the same, so that no moment would be wasted. When they were not working in the fields, they should be studying. Sereni had wanted to become a worker and had begged an old Yemenite to teach him how to work in the orange groves. But, like Gramsci, Sereni argued that the ignorance of the workers laid them open to exploitation. If working men were to control agriculture and industry, the workers had to become experts.

Italian socialism was not state oriented. It was based on the idea of workers' councils. In each factory or farm the workers were to take decisions. Similar ideas in England were advocated by the Guild Socialists who were also pacifists. Workers' control was the only way to prevent public ownership becoming bureaucratic and depersonalized. Sereni's key word is *convivenza*, living together. On Kibbutz Brenner he wanted decisions to be taken by secret ballot, not imposed by the pressure of majority opinion in an open vote.[29] Natural agreement would come only from free debate. The experimental techniques of social psychology have now provided more formal insights into the dynamics of group interaction, the tendency to arrive at a consensus and the consequent social control exercised in small groups.[30] Sereni was drawing conclusions from his own experience.

The more abstract and distant the 'group' the greater the risk that the individual would be sacrificed to it as individuals were sacrificed to dictatorships in wartime. "Even in the life of the kibbutz here, it has always seemed to me that one of the principal duties of every right thinking person who really aspires to create a society of completely free men, is the defence of the interests of the individual against the possible violence of public opinion and the pressure of 'overwhelming necessity'." [31]

Like other Italian socialists he idealised Labour, whether in the factory or on the farm. He took seriously his own need to do farm work and resisted the constant tendency to relegate him to the office as secretary or Kibbutz fund-raiser, or even to send him out to the Diaspora to recruit new settlers. But Sereni never saw the Jewish workers as acting for themselves alone. They had an identity of concern and purpose with that of Arab workers in Palestine. Both Jewish and Arab workers were exploited by a landowning and employing class whether the Arab effendis or the Jewish capitalists. Class interest cut across the ethnic division: Jew and Arab. So socialism was to heal the rift between the two communities.

Italian socialism was not monolithic or state-imposed. It was based on groupings of workers in their work places, on people's councils which could become the foundations of true democracy. Workers' councils might regulate employment in Palestine and establish a common cause between Arab and Jew. Sereni opposed the Legislative Council which would be dominated by reactionary Arabs but he was eager to instigate a joint struggle with the Arab workers for better conditions. In 1927 the 3rd Conference of the *Histadruth* (Trade Union Movement) passed a resolution in favour of a joint union of Jewish and Arab workers, The Palestine Labour League (*Brit Poale Eretz Israel*). In 1930 Sereni was active in an initiative from *Brith Shalom* to set up a Jewish-Arab workers'

Union, *Achvat Poalim*. The British reaction was to ban it on security grounds.

Sereni admitted that the First World War had made him anti-British. He analysed the historical background to the Jewish/Arab problem. The commission of enquiry into the Arab attack on Jaffa of May 1921 found the Arabs responsible but the British had responded by stopping Jewish immigration. Sereni accused the British of colluding with the Arab ruling class and landowners against the Jews and against their own Arab peasantry. It was Arabs who had complained to the authorities that during the demonstrations at Haifa "certain Arabs under the guidance of Jews openly flew red flags." Jewish colonies were accused of being typical examples of communistic villages in Red Russia, and Jewish socialists of infecting the Arab peasantry with Bolshevism.[32]

The Union's slogan 'From national separation to international unity! From the estrangement of nations to the fraternity of the workers!' must have filled the authorities with alarm. According to Sereni, it was the British interest to keep Arab and Jew divided and that was why the union was banned.

Yet the communism practised by Sereni was pacifist. If the new revolutionary socialist society was to be achieved, the Jews must not use violence against their Arab brothers. Socialism was not a danger. On the contrary, it was the only way to secure peace. He predicted that a capitalist Jewish state could not survive; it would become the equivalent of a colonial regime. So the original Zionist conception had to be developed. A Jewish state could not exist except as a bi-national state in which each nation would have autonomous control over its own internal policies. Independence had to be based on co-operation between the Arab and Jewish workers.[33]

Sereni was intensely attached to Kibbutz Givat Brenner and was its guiding light for many years, yet during the Arab attacks of 1938, he refused to carry firearms in its defence. He kept open his Arab contacts, probably sympathised with Arab opposition to partition plans which had provoked the riots, and he objected to the British armed presence in the area. He never identified Jews and Arabs as oppressor and oppressed. He regarded the Jewish settlement in Palestine as irreversible, a development which benefited all in the land and which the Arabs could not prevent. Yet the Jewish State in Palestine was not going to exist in a vacuum as some Zionists imagined. Any Jewish state would be set in an Arab sea and therefore peace with the Arabs and an identity of purpose were essential to its well-being. In Bible commentary, Hagar's son, Ishmael, is regarded as ancestor of the Arab peoples. As personal testimony, Sereni called his second child, born in 1927, Hagar, to symbolise fraternity with the Arabs.

Even among the socialists it was only isolated individuals like Sereni who resisted the pressure to conform; he was conspicuous because he refused to touch a rifle. His eccentricity seems to have stimulated some debate. Was pacifism naive? Was he a dreamer? Did he believe in miracles that he would risk his life going unarmed, wandering about outside at night or keeping in touch with his Arab friends? No, the reply comes in a simple Zionist reader, Enzo had good reasons for his pacifism; he was a disciple of Gandhi. Enzo understood human nature. His Arab contacts received him with respect. They had no need to use their knives, since he came with empty hands, without a sword, exchanging trust for trust.[34]

As a dedicated Zionist, much of Sereni's career was spent in Germany, Italy and the United States encouraging immigration. He failed to inspire a mass movement not only in numeric terms but because his idealism did not reflect social reality. Givat Brenner was not economically viable; it depended on contributions from Italy. There was a shortage of accommodation. People lived in tents or three to a room. There was conflict between the wealthier German and Italian Jews and those from Lithuania. When the kibbutz took in young people escaping from Nazism, the residents themselves were reluctant to take in the parents of the young volunteers. They had not the resources to resettle all the Jews who might have escaped from Hitler. Sereni blamed the European Jews for failing to take up the Palestine option. But it was hardly on offer. In the crisis of 1933 there was no Zionist machinery in Palestine to absorb German Jews.

Hitler's abuse of the Jews did not alter Sereni's pacifist convictions. He supported Chamberlain and the Munich agreement in September 1938, anything that might prevent a war. But with the fall of France his resolution broke.

The terrible days of May in France forced me to the long and thoughtful sequence of reasoning which has made me question many things which which seemed sacred to me for years. .... I do not deny anything in the past: the profound and sincere hatred of war and of the stupid belief that violence can rule the world and decide its fate, or bring peace and security to anyone still seems valid to me. It still seems to me right to believe in the absolute value of human life as the supreme good which must not be sacrificed to any other.[35]

One wonders what Sereni meant when he warned about the pressure of "overwhelming necessity"; his renunciation of pacifism was by no means inevitable. In 1942 Henrietta Szold was similarly asked whether young people of the Youth Aliyah should take up arms and fight on the British side. She replied, "There are Jews who believe that if [Palestine] is captured today by our enemy, the whole Jewish people would be so injured by the loss that it could not recover. My personal faith is otherwise." She could not advise the young people to fight even if the enemy came from North Africa onto Palestinian soil.[36] Yet Sereni never fully supported war. He wrote to his children towards the end of 1942: "Our war is not against the Germans, our war is not against any people. We are all today at war against Fascism and Nazism. We must struggle to the end against such ideologies. .... But a war like ours cannot and must not be accompanied by hate."[37]

In 1940 he enlisted in the British Intelligence Service. He assisted in the evacuation of Crete and began to re-educate Italian prisoners of war in Suez. In November 1941 he was arrested; he went on hunger strike, gained his release, and returned to the imperative task of helping Jews. He took arms to Jews in Iraq and blamed himself bitterly for the crime of omission, that he had failed to foresee the Holocaust and had welcomed anything that might postpone the war.

He returned to Italy in May 1944, not on a family visit this time, but dropped by parachute to gather intelligence and contact partisans. The drop miscarried. Sereni was arrested by the Germans. He was a prisoner in Dachau and eventually died under torture on 18 November 1944 at the age of thirty-nine.

He had seen the way Jews were damaged by persecution, the difficulty of responding to the other man's distress. After the war, when it is all over, "Will we know how to love the human flotsam?" he asked.

Sereni's pacifism has been neglected. His biographers both in Israel and outside prefer to emphasise his Zionist fervour. His willingness to help the war against Hitler has even been used to endorse armed resistance against all racial oppression. The legend of the hero, Enzo Sereni, is needed to stand for much else.

Golda Meir, a remarkable figure in the Labour movement and later Prime Minister of Israel, wrote, "You cannot say about Enzo: he was one of those who... There was nobody like him. He was different. There was a feeling that he did not tell everything, that there were things on his mind which he could not reveal yet, that he wanted first of all to struggle with them alone, by himself."[38] It is a telling comment. Sereni was concerned with our role as individuals in society. We are inevitably part of our society. Sereni understood the opportunities of action on a social level, but "individuals should never be sacrificed to the collective".[39] There had to be a gradual process of learning to live together. But no one must deny himself, each had to bring "his full intellect, to enrich the life of the community with all his modern experience."[40]

The extreme pragmatism of his Italian socialism enabled Sereni to cope with the day-to-day problems of life on a struggling kibbutz. His pacifism was also something that affected his life and social relationships. Sereni knew from experience how hard it was to resist majority pressure; everyone needs to feel part of the group, even if that entails carrying a gun with one's friends. Sereni points out the danger of the group swamping the individual. Zionist and Jew through and through, the way he lived, as well as what he wrote, insist on every individual Jew acting upon his own conscience within the Jewish society Sereni helped to create.

Chapter 4
The Holy Inheritance
Kabbala, Hasidism and the Guardians
of the City

Coming out of the Damascus gate of Jerusalem and skirting the Arab *suq* where patient donkeys wait loaded to carry supplies into the old walled city, one may walk up the sun-beaten hill to enter another old city. As one wanders into the shade of Mea Shearim, one finds oneself in an enclosed world of tiny shops and yeshivas. The clothes of its people mark its boundary; for they are *Haredim*, strictly observant, traditional, Orthodox Jews. Even the passer-by is asked to become part of the community by respecting its ways. One is asked not to take photographs and to come modestly dressed. The women of Mea Shearim wear their blouses buttoned to the neck, long sleeves, skirts and thick stockings cover them to wrist and ankle; their heads are hidden in scarves, hair or shaved heads covered with berets or wigs. The little girls are covered too: even in the heat of Israel, their legs are in thick stockings. But their hair is tightly braided, Polish fashion, and, were it not for the vivid colour of sunlit Jerusalem, one could imagine these children have come to life from an old photograph. The men, walking quickly alone, or deep in conversation, are equally encased. They wear black; their coats and hats are reminiscent of another century and another land.

But these outdated clothes which catch the eye are no more than symbols. Like the clothes of the Amish people in America, they denote an inner timelessness, for this is Judaism which has dispensed with externals. It is a Judaism of the spirit and of the eternal. This community, more than any other, is detached from the material and from the temporal. Life is centred instead on *Torah*, on the Law.

There was a profound reason why Magnes, radical as he was, turned to the authority of the Law to justify his idealism. Unlike Christianity, Judaism is based on the meticulous observation of a set of laws, the *halakha*, which is "The Path". Six hundred and thirteen commandments regulate every aspect of life and thus provide a bridge between the material and the spiritual. These detailed commands should never be mistaken as an end in themselves. Just as the dress of the people of Mea Shearim represents a spiritual aspiration, so observation of *halakha* reminds one constantly of one's spiritual identity as a Jew.

Orthodox Judaism is fundamentalist. The law or Torah is the direct word of God, and this means not only the rules given to Moses at Sinai, or even the complete Bible. Torah includes a mass of oral and written material in the Talmud, the original core of which was collected together between about 200B.C.E. and 200CE. This law is not, as is sometimes thought, fixed or rigid. Even in the Talmud it is subject to debate and adaptation. Minority opinions are faithfully recorded. The debate, the elaboration and the commentaries continued to be produced in various countries through the centuries wherever there were Jewish communities. This development and exploration of religious questions makes Judaism what it is, a tradition that is still alive and developing and one which allows for and indeed creates its own diversity.

Classic Judaism both allows for and encourages dissent in the public arena. In the medieval *Gates of Repentance* by R. Jonah of Gerona who was born in 1200, we read about individual responsibility. "The Creator has blown into my nostrils a living soul, wisdom of heart and the gift of reason", or, "A man must learn to observe men, to understand them, and to discriminate between what is crooked and perverse and what is just."[1]

In *The Third Gate of Repentance*, Gerondi includes the sin of standing by while some wrong is taking place. "The sixth category [of sinner] consists of those who are in a position to protest but do not do so, in whose mouths there is no rebuke; who do not sharpen their eyes against evil deeds, nor pay heed to them." He quotes the Talmud on communal responsibility: "All those who are in a position to reprove the members of their household and do not do so are accountable for the sins of the members of their household; those who are in a position to reprove the people of their city, and do not do so, are held accountable for the sins of the people of their city."[2] He then provides a charming discussion of why there is a moral obligation to protest, even when there is little chance of success. "The seventh category consists of those who see the people of their place to be stiff-necked, but who say in their hearts, 'Perhaps they will not listen if I tell them the truth and fill my mouth with rebuke.' And so he will hold his tongue and bear his transgression because of not having attempted to reprove and give warning. Perhaps if he had bestirred their spirits, they would have awakened from the sleep of their foolishness and their error would not have remained with them." Futile protest is contrary to the law, but Gerondi's conclusion seems to be that although God may know that it is useless to protest in a given situation, no man can be sure of this. The sin of remaining silent remains a sin. "Although these men are perfectly righteous and have fulfilled the Torah, they should have protested and did not."[3]

The traditional Jew justifies a course of action by resorting to the law and interpreting it. Biblical law includes detailed regulations for the waging of war[4] and since wars are authorised by God there is no place for conscientious objection to military service.

The Bible does not classify wars except to differentiate between those with cities that belong to nations close at hand and those which are very far away.[5] But, drawing on the historical evidence in the Bible, the Rabbis of the Talmud began to classify wars: there were wars which were commanded, wars which were permitted and wars which were forbidden.[6]

Obligatory wars (*milchemet mitzvah*) were to be fought against peoples who no longer exist: against Amalek who had attacked the Israelites in the desert, and against the seven Canaanite tribes. Other tribes were definitely excluded, some of them by name, Amnon, Moab, Edom and Aram. Ancient Israel went to war on the direct order of God in specific historical situations.

"Permitted" wars, (*milchemet reshut*) were to be fought only against the declared enemies of Israel. They had to be sanctioned by the Sanhedrin of 71, following direction from God as relayed by the high priest wearing his breastplate in the Temple. In other words, major obstacles were put in the way of waging any war. In the USA and some other parts of the world local Jewish communities refer to the buildings where they pray as "temples", rather than as synagogues, a word from the Greek. This modern usage should not be confused with the Temple in traditional law. In rabbinic literature "Temple" refers specifically to the sanctuary in Jerusalem. Now Jews have neither Temple nor high priest, nor apparently any direct command from God, there is no longer a war that is permitted.

Mainstream Jewish opinion now justifies war by using these categories: wars that are commanded and wars that are optional. Some authorities argue that there is no longer any optional war, either for Israel or for other countries (who have been forbidden to conquer each other's land), but that there is a third category of obligatory war which still operates: the war of self-defence to preserve the Jewish people.[7] It follows that there is an obligation to defend the State of Israel. Others argue that optional wars are still possible both for Israel and for the countries of the Diaspora when these wars have a pre-emptive purpose, a first strike to prevent an attack. Jewish military involvement and self-defence over the centuries is marshalled as evidence of the legitimate precedents for collective self-defence.[8]

The legal arguments bear little relation to the complex reality of actual political situations with which they purport to deal. They presuppose a world divided into fixed territories, each legitimately occupied by one nation. Each nation is seen as a separate and static population without claims on its neighbours. Wars themselves are regarded as classifiable, since they must be classified before a decision can be taken whether it is permissible to fight them.

The current religious debate on war and peace in Jewish law is more concerned with finding legal and moral justification for Jewish military activity than with voicing objections to it. But the classification of wars has a bearing on whether or not Jewish law can recognise valid exemptions from military service. The exemptions in Deuteronomy XX cited by some British conscientious objectors in World War One (the man newly married, or he who has built a new house or planted a new vineyard, or the man who is fainthearted) applied only in permitted wars. In wars that were commanded by God there were no exemptions whatsoever.[9]

This was explained by Maimonides, the classic Jewish philosopher, (1135 -1204), who was the great codifier and rationaliser of Jewish law. In his *Mishnah Torah* he took the Talmudic material of intricate rabbinic debate and reorganised it topic by topic. It is Maimonides who emphasises that peace must be always be offered before proceeding with war. But the manuscripts differ on his attitude to war itself. In his book on the commandments Maimonides identified the 613 commandments, positive and negative, which were actually binding on an observant Jew. He added a postscript: "Now since all these matters are known to most people, every Positive or Negative Command pertaining to the ... obligatory and non-obligatory war, it will not be necessary for me to say concerning them: 'This commandment applies only during the existence of the Sanctuary,' since this is clear on the basis of what we have mentioned." He was saying that without the Temple there could be no war at all.[10]

Orthodox Jews in peace movements argue that wars are no longer either commanded or permitted; this position removes the need to fit Jewish law to actual war situations. The arguments are self-evidently on a religious plane. Both Jewish and Mennonite commentators have regarded the Exodus as evidence that God Himself fights for the Jewish people.[11] Jews are not entitled to make war on their own behalf. The participation of God is not purely mythological. It was a real operational factor: the Jerusalem Talmud makes it plain that the Jewish tradition gave more weight to the psychological element in successful warfare than to military superiority. Terror seems central. Israel shall not fear for the Eternal marches with them. The enemy shall fear thunder and lightning from Heaven. He troubles them with great terror.[12] It is God fighting on the side of Israel who renders its soldiers fearless and therefore invincible. At the same time the participation of the God of Israel, the Lord of Hosts (Armies), as He is referred to in the Bible and in the daily prayers[13,] fills the enemy with terror.

Traditional Torah teaching goes even further than this in its subtlety of interpretation. Laws are considered in light of their context. Deductions are made from the juxtaposition of passages. The commandments regulating military campaigns cannot be taken in isolation. They are followed by one of the most famous rules. If a man is found lying dead between two cities, and no one knows who is responsible, then the nearest Jewish city (though apparently innocent) must none the less sacrifice a heifer to atone for his death. Why? asked the Rabbis. Why follow the rules on war with this rule which obliges Jews to take responsibility for a death which was not their fault? It is to impress upon us the value of life, that we must take responsibility for each life lost, in war as well as peace. We must not shift the blame onto the people of another city.

Whatever the regulations for war in the Bible, the Rabbis of the Talmud reinterpreted texts to infer that there was to be no waging of war in our *galut*, the exile. In exile all regulations concerning war became inoperative. It is because of this that religious arguments about whether or not war is permitted are often assumed to hinge entirely on whether Israel is recognised as a Jewish state. This is an over-simplification. Questions of war and peace in Judaism go well beyond technicalities; they pose ethical problems for every Jew whatever his religious outlook. It is a mistake to try to divide Jewish tradition neatly into the legal and the mystical. Maimonides, the great medieval legalist, was a man of enormous spiritual depth and awareness, and conversely the mystic teachings of the Kabbalists or Hasids are never free of structure or law. Orthodox religious opposition to war rests on the law but also on the idea of what constitutes the Holy life.

Many *Haredim* and Hasidic Jews in Israel support the state and would not call themselves pacifist. None the less their communities are unlikely to serve in the army. Women are excused military service if it would interfere with their religious life. This is the only point at which Israeli law recognises personal conscience, a religious objection to military service. For men there is a more formal condition of exemption. Orthodox men are excused service if they devote their days to Torah study within a *yeshiva*, (a religious study group). Thus Israeli law excuses some ardent religious Zionists from defending the State. The State itself recognises that waging war may not be concomitant with leading a fully observant Jewish life. This way of life involves a painstaking, traditional observance of Jewish law, and yet it also draws on the mystical notion that the only duty of a Jew is to lead a holy life, to study Torah, and give charity. The Hasidic Jew is not withdrawing from life; in prayer he plays an active role in the realisation of God's purpose, for by living in this way man will restore the unity of God's presence on earth.

This raises one of the central questions in Judaism, and in formulating Jewish pacifism. Is the law enough or is there more? This is addressed by the contemporary scholar Rabbi Aaron Lichtenstein who has spoken out for moderation in Israel.[14] Rabbi Abaye said that the whole of Torah is for the purpose of promoting peace. The implication is that peace itself must have an ethical value beyond the law. The Din, the judgement of the law, is only ethic clothed in a legal mantle. Leviticus tells us, "You shall be Holy for Holy am I, the Lord your God."[15] We are to walk in God's ways. But how can we know what God's ways are, since God is unknowable? Rabbi Louis Jacobs, another contemporary scholar, suggests that the complicated symbolism of the Kabbala and of Hasidism which followed were an attempt to bridge this gap between the God we can't know and the God-like life we have to somehow lead.[16]

Maimonides confronted the impossibility of describing God. He could define only what God was not. Kabalists agreed that God, *Ein Sof*, was unknown and unknowable. But they departed from the rational and instead used Talmudic symbolism and mystical interpretations of biblical texts to explore the nature of God. They emphasised the close presence in the world of God's spirit, the *Shekhinah*. Many of their ideas about the nature of God and creation were formulated in the *Zohar, the Book of Splendour*, put together by Moses de Leon between about 1275 and 1285. The mysteries in this book were so profound that it was said one could not be initiated before the age of forty. The Holy life of study and prayer was reserved for a few.

Israeli law, like Kabbala, recognises that some Jews lead a holier life than others. The *Nefesh* or soul is in every human being and is derived from God. But there are also two other levels of spirit, *Ruah* and *Neshamah* which are only present in one who is spiritually aware. Kabbala was a mystery never intended for the whole of the Jewish community. The fall of Adam destroyed the spiritual perfection of the world and the task of human existence is to restore the original harmony, the original Unity of God's presence of earth. This Holy life has a social function. It also has an internal one. It re-establishes the relationship between the individual and the ten *Sefirot*, the aspects or emanations of God. By praying we change inner spiritual realities. Redemption is something that has to be struggled for; every man is battling against the powers of evil. But through meditation, the Kabbalist is also hoping to achieve that ecstatic religious experience which through ascending levels will reveal more and more of the nature of God.

The Kabbalists' God-like life is not pacifism but it is clearly incompatible with any military undertaking. The whole of a person's emotional and spiritual energies are directed to God, and nothing must distract a man from this level of existence. This rules out military service, but to see it in a negative light, as avoidance, is to overlook the positive centrality of peace in Kabbalist teaching. God is revealed to man through ten emanations or aspects of Himself, the *Sephirot*. These emanations were arranged by the Kabbalists in a mysterious structure based on one they called the Foundation. The higher unknowable aspects of God rested on the Foundation and through the Foundation they flowed down to the level of Sovereignty by which God is revealed to the lower world. It was said that the symbolic name for the Foundation of God was peace.

The Holy life is not something that can be achieved in isolation. The unification of God's presence on earth imposes on the observant Jew a religious relationship with other human beings. "Who is a Saint?" The rabbis asked and the answer was, "He who does Lovingkindness to his Creator." One of the ways a man must train himself to acquire the quality of Lovingkindness is "to make peace between man and his neighbour..."[17]

The Palm Tree of Deborah, written by Rabbi Moses Cordovero, in Sfat, in the 1560s, has an evocative charm which speaks eloquently over the centuries. The Kabbalistic idiom may be disconcerting in terms of contemporary discourse but the spiritual message is perfectly conveyed within its own peculiar imagery:

> At times [the Sephirot] are separated from each other and it is necessary to perfect them and adjust them until they are alike and bound together in love and friendship. ... And when, God forfend, there is the flaw of sin in the world then there is an opposing hatred between them and there is no Unity nor bond among the Sephirot at all.

It is necessary to make peace between a man and his neighbour and between a man and his wife: "All similarly peaceful acts are acts of benevolence on behalf of the Upper Worlds."[18]

Cordovero and his friends formed a mystic brotherhood which strove to live a pure life so that they might be fit for their religious studies. Their hearts had to be the abode of the *Shekhinah*, the spirit of God; and they were to make their hearts fit for the *Shekhinah* by banishing all profane thoughts and concentrating on the words of the Torah and Holy things. "When a good man meets provokers, he should appease them and quiet them with goodwill –

drawing on great wisdom to weaken their anger that it does not overstep its boundaries to cause harm. .... The good man should not be angry with those that offend him, but he should constantly be willing to be appeased and desire to do kindness. The Crown, (that is the first and highest emanation of God) cannot spread its light on the man who bestirs external anger, even if it be for the sake of Heaven." One should note that proviso. Even if the motive is religious, whatever the moral justification, there is to be no conflict.

As expressed by Cordovero, Judaism comes close to the Christian principle of loving the enemy:

As God suffers our sins and shortcomings with unending patience and mercy till we repent, so we must suffer and bear insult. In particular we must not hate the wicked man but must look for his good points, remembering that God loves him also.

The Kabbalists were realistic about the Power of God. Power was one of the ten emanations. But it was related to evil. In Judaism, the one God who created all things created the evil impulse within us as well as the good. "Man is created with two inclinations, good and bad: the one belongs to Lovingkindness," says Cordovero, "the other to Power."

A century and a half later, Moses Hyam Luzzatto, one of the great spiritual exponents of Judaism, developed the concept that saintliness was opposed to power. Luzzatto was born in Padua in 1707 and died in Tiberias in 1747. His essay, *The Path of the Upright*, explores the nature of the religious Jewish life by drawing the reader towards the truth which is already within him, the potential of holiness. Luzzatto sees no connection between the law of the state and Torah law. Man's duty in the world is not to a state but to perform the commandments, the *mitzvot*, for the sake of the world to come. "For the soul has no love for this world. On the contrary it despises it. Man was created then for the sake of his station in the World to Come." Only Divine service can lead a man to perfection. This is a severe philosophy. Saintliness and separation involve effort. "A person must realise he is not in this world for repose but for labour and exertion." "A person should render himself rootless in the world and rooted in Divine service."[19]

Being Holy involves more than prayer and Torah study. It involves cleansing oneself of sin and transgression. "Do not take revenge and do not bear a grudge against the children of your nation." "Speaking falsehood is comparable to removing the foundation of the world." Holiness in the Jewish tradition does not involve depriving oneself of essentials but self-denial is certainly an element in the thought of Luzzatto. He has quite puritan attitudes towards sex and clothing. We are told that the Holy man takes the humble seat and wears modest clothes. The emphasis on humility and hatred of authority reminds one of Gandhi. The saintly man must not cause pain to any creature – even animals – and must show mercy and pity towards them. "Whose sins are forgiven?" Luzzatto asks. "The sins of those who overlook the wrong committed against them."[20]

Unlike Gandhi, these Saints do not act within a social sphere. The emphasis is not on the whole Jewish community but on the individual and his particular responsibility towards God. (Sanhedrin 37a) Man was created individually so that each man should say, "The world was created for my sake," that is to say that even though individual prayer or actions may seem insignificant, each plays its part in God's purpose.

In *The Way of God* Luzzatto moved even further from the political.

> God does not involve himself directly in the direction of nations in detail though it is possible that He should exercise His providence over them when it is required for the sake of Israel.[21]

The Jew is not to fight wars for God but to suffer for Him.

> When reciting the Shema [the most important Jewish prayer, affirming Jewish belief] each individual should resolve to be ready to give his life for the sake of God's Unity, and willingly undergo all types of torture and the cruellest of deaths for the sanctification of His Name. Such a resolve is counted as an actual deed. .... When a person actually gives his life for God it results in a very great illumination. This in turn has a tremendous effect in rectifying all creation and increasing its sanctity and enlightenment.

The willingness to suffer rather than to defend oneself or retaliate was partly a religious attempt to control the natural impulses in man, but it was also, emphatically, a reflection of the way God Himself behaves. God is merciful. Even when a man sins, God still moves and lives in him, There is still a Divine flow of Power, says Cordovero. "Thou art patient and bearest insult until man repents."

There has always been pressure on organised religion to reinforce and reflect civic virtues. However, the quietism of the Kabbalists greatly influenced the Hasidic Rabbis of the eighteenth century. Hasidism was not connected with society; it had no social or political programme. Such concerns were not appropriate to Judaism. This is why some orthodox Jews refuse to recognise the State of Israel. They argue that, even within Israel, they remain in exile from the Messianic kingdom. Outside the spiritual Jerusalem they may not fight. They refuse to recognise the state in any way. They do not pay taxes, use Israeli schools, take state benefits or do military service. They refuse identity cards, they do not vote in elections and they ignore Israeli courts. It is said that they are not pursued by Israeli police because the secular police are unable to distinguish between individuals who wear identical traditional dress. This seems unlikely. The Israeli authorities probably choose to turn a blind eye to Hasidic conscientious objection.

These dissenting Jews are members of *Neturei Karta*, which means in Aramaic the Guardians of the City. They are not guards in a military sense; the Jerusalem Talmud says that "religious scholars are the guardians and defenders of the City." A town had no teachers of Bible and Mishnah although it had trained police and sentries. No, said the Rabbis, sentries could not guard a town, on the contrary these men are the destroyers of the City. "Who then are the Guardians of the City?" "They are the teachers and scribes, for without them a city is fated to destruction."[22]

One must not regard the Hasidic refusal to recognise the State of Israel as a convenient way of producing a Torah-based argument for not serving in its army. The whole of life is Torah-based and the refusal to serve in the forces is a relatively minor consequence of an underlying concept of what is religious in Jewish terms and what is not.

Neturei Karta is not a structured organisation, nor does it have its own rabbis and synagogues. This is partly deliberate; it is only assimilated and Diaspora Jews who set store by material things. Funds and buildings are not regarded as significant. *Neturei Karta* represents "the pure ideal of the eternity of Israel". It has no plans and claims to have no politics. Its origins lie in a movement which broke away when the Hasidic communities in Palestine (the *Agudat Israel*) began to participate in the public administration of Jewish affairs in the Mandate. The anti-Zionists were followers of the 19th century Rabbi, Joseph Hayim Sonnenfeld, who adamantly opposed Zionism, not so much because it was Zionist but because it was secular. In the eyes of the Hasids, secularism was the real threat. Sonnenfeld in 1898 accused the Zionists of maintaining "that the whole difference and distinction between Israel and the nations lies in nationalism, blood and race, and that the faith and religion are superfluous".[23] The celebrated contemporary exponent of the philosophy of *Neturei Karta*, Rabbi I. Domb, is careful to point out that their anti-Zionism is not related to the success or failure of the State of Israel. Zionism is itself a negation of Judaism, the result of the intrusion of the Enlightenment or *Haskala* on the holiness and spiritual status of the Jews. For the Portion of the Eternal is His people.[24] The refusal to fight is based yet again on the concept that the Jewish people are unique. They are not in search of territory. They are not a people or state like any other. "Lo it is a people that shall dwell alone, and shall not be reckoned among the nations".[25] *Kadosh*, the Hebrew word for Holy also means separate. This separation from the peoples of the world is the basis of Jewish holiness. They are the People of the Torah whose values are not material values. Torah is eternal.

In December 1931 the *Agudath Israel* Central Organisation in Palestine sent a letter of greeting to the Moslem Conference in Jerusalem:

> The Jews have no intention of harming the rights of the Moslems to the places that are holy to them or to demand any right to those places, just as we wish that others should not harm our right to the places that are holy to us. ... We hope that a spirit of peace will be spread over this respected congress and will help remove all suspicions in the hearts of one segment of the population of the Holy Land about the other.[26]

The name *Neturei Karta* was first used in 1938 by students opposing the levying of a voluntary Jewish Defence Tax by the

Jewish Community in Palestine. Their opposition even to a voluntary tax suggests that they were not willing for a Jewish army to protect them. There was no feeling that Torah commanded a minority of Jews to pursue a religious life and leave the fighting to another section of the community.

Their refusal to participate on any level whatsoever is comparable with that of the most absolute of British and American wartime Objectors, the absolutists who refused alternative non-combatant service. In the 1930s *Neturei Karta* condemned some teachers in Palestine who had taken a week off to dig defensive trenches, the only purpose of which would presumably have been to shelter the civilian Jewish population. Self-defence entailed refusing to defend oneself in military terms.

The pacifism of *Neturei Karta* is not consciously formulated as pacifism. Their primary concern is with the character of Jews and Judaism. But a rabbi from Poland preached an inspired Hasidic pacifism which applied directly to life in the Diaspora. Aaron Samuel Tamaret was born in 1869, a poor innkeeper's son but also the grandson of the Maltsher Rabbi, Reb Arele. Tamaret was originally a brilliant young Polish Zionist but he became more and more critical of Jewish Nationalism and published pacifist sermons parts of which have continued to circulate in translations by Everett Gendler.

Unlike Christianity, Judaism does not attribute evil either to the devil or to original sin. God created all things and that includes the good and evil inclination within each of us. Tamaret explains that acts of violence come from the evil impulses in man. Sometimes these murders are a natural human response, unpremeditated like the murder of Abel. But there is also violence which is planned or justified by men's intellectual powers. Sometimes violence is exercised even in the name of religion. This kind of violence is far worse than the first because it is not natural to man; it is a perversion of his spirit, "This fraudulent evil," Tamaret calls it, "This evil justified by the mind – political evil – has become the greatest destroyer on the face of the earth." .... "This is the secret of all the wars, conscriptions and organised slaughters which have occurred in the world at large and against Jews in particular."[27] Tamaret makes a connection between the national aggression by which strong states attack weaker ones, and the persecution of the Jews by peoples stronger than they.

The whole purpose of Torah is to set this right, to counter the evil impulse in man. Israel was prepared to receive the Torah first by the experience of exile and slavery in Egypt and then by the redemption from Egypt. Jews are to be redeemed from their oppressors by remembering the lesson of that first Passover; they must remember that their God is the God of truth and justice. Non-violence purifies the atmosphere and prevents tyrants sending men to fight and be killed. For the great danger is that Israel will become complicit in their own oppression as they did in Egypt. "By what power was Germany able to send thousands of her sons to the slaughter? Because of the clod-like insensitivity of the rest of the nation, which coldly stood by and in fact even sang and cheered the plague of war with patriotic hymns and prayers." Tamaret is suggesting that a strong faith in God and non-violent resistance to war and oppression will redeem the Jews. He quotes the *Tosefot*, an ancient supplement of oral teaching which related to the Talmud but which was not included in it. " 'A man should concern himself more that he not injure others than that he be not injured.'[28] For when a man tries to keep watch that his fist not injure others, by that act he enthrones in the world the God of truth and righteousness and adds power to the kingdom of justice; and it is precisely this power which will defend him against injury by others."

Tamaret sweeps aside all Jewish arguments for the right of self-defence by claiming that self-defence for Jews depends on individual conscientious objection.

Neturei Karta certainly believe this and their opposition to the state was always complete. In the political sphere, *Neturei Karta* opposed the war of independence, made proposals for an internationalised Jerusalem and have maintained contacts with the PLO. Rabbi Domb points out that there is nothing particularly Jewish about military heroism. Plenty of other peoples have shown patriotic self-sacrifice which puts the Zionists in the shade. He cites the people of Britain during the Blitz, the Japanese suicide pilots and the Russians who threw themselves under German tanks with dynamite in their hands. "The mightiest armies are moved to fight and to win only by the will of the human beings who constitute them. The same human beings are on *both* sides of the front and are commanded by the same sort of human beings."

Peace or *Shalom* is not just a question of self-defence, it is actually translated as "the welfare of the people". Jeremiah XXX describes the traitor, the man who desires the destruction of the people. Peace involves the welfare of the people because it is only through peace that they can survive as Jews. War is contrary to the nature of Judaism. The founder and leader of *Neturei Karta*, Rabbi Amrom Blau, summed it up like this, "By the command of Torah, the Jew is bound to further the welfare of the state wherein he dwells. He entertains no thought of rebellion. The Torah forbids us to retake the Holy Land by force of arms. Jews abhor the murder of any human being for any reason whatsoever. In our entire long exile, there has never been an instance where the Torah justifies the use of murder, as the Sages point out in the Midrash."[29]

It is sometimes suggested by their opponents that, if *Neturei Karta* were to recognise the State, then they would also concede that wars of self-defence were an obligation for the Jewish people, that war is forbidden only so long as Israel is in exile. One must not over-simplify. The spiritual, mystical element in Judaism dominates the thinking of *Neturei Karta*, and to reduce their philosophy to a legal quibble makes nonsense of the Jewish values they claim to protect. There is real conflict between this group and their Zionist opponents. Many halakhic problems arise because the traditional law is inappropriate to modern situations. Religious, traditional and secular definitions of the terms involved may be subject to widely differing interpretations. What does one understand by Exile, or the State of Israel? The secular concept of a nation state bears no relation to that of an ideal state which for Jews signifies redemption, achieved only in a Messianic future. *Neturei Karta* define terms such as Exile within a spiritual perspective and even go a step further by claiming that it is impossible to understand on any rational level either God's will in History or the Jewish role in it.

This type of Hasidism works on a simple but not rational basis of reward and punishment from God. Good is rewarded and evil is punished. In this it has certain affinities with Christianity. There is the concept of guilt and punishment, and with it the idea that our sins may be wiped away and that in the future there will be redemption and a Messiah. Jews are in exile because of their sins. *Neturei Karta* agree that Jews are permitted to live in the land of Israel, seeking a way back to the roots of their existence. But that is all; before the Messiah comes we have no right to rule in the Holy

Land and the Zionist aspiration for governmental power is a rebellion against the people who live in it. The purpose of Jews coming to the Land at this stage "is not one of dominion and wars and victories but one of peace so that the *Shekhinah* may dwell in the midst of Jerusalem and to the Lord will be the dominion. Only then will our joy be complete and our security assured."[30]

The religious argument is based on a Talmudic interpretation of a passage from the *Song of Songs*.[31] The passage (see Appendix, page 225) is about the daughters of Jerusalem and is not explicitly about war. However, Rabbinic textual interpretation rests on more levels than the literal and this passage has become the authority for what are known as the three oaths. While in exile Israel is first forbidden to make war as an organised army, and secondly may not rebel against the nations of the world. In their turn (thirdly) the nations of the world are not to oppress Israel too much. This interpretation is not codified and does not have the same status as *halakha* or law but it is taken by many observant Jews as a commanding guide to relationships between Jews and non-Jews.

The *Golus*, or exile, is of a spiritual dimension and its end cannot be hastened even through prayer. Israel is scattered through the world so that its universal message shall also be spread through the world. At the end of time there will be an ingathering of all Jews to the Land of Israel; until that mystical moment Jews are forbidden to rebel against the nations of the world, that is the other nations who have a political and territorial identity as opposed to Israel's spiritual one. There can be no thought-out human solutions for Jewish problems because they are beyond the rational. Leading a Jewish life is not a reasonable existence. Observing the Sabbath and obeying the commandments does not lead to any obvious advantage or reward. It is a mystery. God's spirit rests on the People and the remedy of the world will come from the Jews.

Sereni and Magnes saw Israel as the only possible refuge for Jews. For *Neturei Karta* on the other hand, Israel "is the least secure place in the world for Jews."[32] It is a state that has been established with the help of anti-Semites, particularly the Germans, and has succeeded in secularising and assimilating the Jewish people so that they are just like any other, with political and social codes and procedures of their own. The holy language of Hebrew is used in a secular context. This is the "Transformation" of the Jews which Domb decries. *Neturei Karta* see Israel as a creator of problems rather than as a solution. Israel has created anti-Semitism, not solved it. It has disrupted Jewish life throughout the Arab world, destroying the stable communities in countries like Yemen and Morocco. As for the argument that the Holocaust made the State a necessity, the Jews had been freed from Auschwitz before the State was set up; they could and did settle elsewhere. Only harm can come from the State, and that harm is war itself. "If the Land is conquered before the coming of the King of Peace, grievous wars will follow and one people will gore another."

In the 18th century, when John Wesley was bringing a simpler and more direct form of Christianity to the working people of England, Hasidic masters brought Judaism to the ordinary Jews of Poland. People were made to feel they could be in touch with God in their everyday lives. Judaism had always depended on scholarship and meditation which were beyond the capabilities of ordinary people. But Hasidism took many of the ideas of Kabbala and used them to put simple mystical or ecstatic experience within the reach of every Jew. The founder of Hasidism, the Baal Shem Tov, taught that God was present in all things. Rather than withdraw from the world to discover holiness, one may search for the divine reality within all things and therefore within oneself. He and his disciples translated the Jewish spiritual tradition into a mass movement.

Like Kabbala, Hasidism originally put a great deal of emphasis on the important of individual acts and individual responsibility. Contemporary Hasidic movements have less feeling for the autonomy of the individual or for his conscience. Carrying out the Divine will is not a voluntary task; it is compulsory and there is in modern Hasidism an element of compulsive religious practice. "We are the blind slaves of *Shem Yisborach* (God who is to be Praised) and that slavery of our spirit is the greatest aspiration of a Jew."

Hasidic Jews followed charismatic Rabbis whose families tended to inherit the mantle of leadership. The elevation of the leader or *Zaddik*, the Righteous man, into a Prince of religion with his own Court ran contrary to many of the tenets of Judaism. Any orthodox Jew may associate himself with *Neturei Karta*, (it has been referred to as the conscience of Israel) but many of its adherents are followers of the Satmerer Rabbis who are descended from Moses Teitelbaum 1759-1841, the founder of Hasidism in Hungary.[33] One of his direct descendents, Rabbi Joel Teitelbaum (1887-1979), moved from Hungary in the 1930s and went to Rumania where he became rabbi in the town of Satmar. There he set the pattern of the conscientious orthodoxy which was to dominate his life and that of his followers. He combined scholarship with respect for the religious regulation of life. He persuaded his followers to respect the Sabbath and the laws of family purity, but he also attended to their needs with a social concern, running soup kitchens and caring for the disadvantaged in the community. He escaped the Holocaust first by hiding and later, after he was taken to Bergen Belsen in 1944, by being rescued when 1,684 people were allowed to leave for a neutral country. Eventually he settled in Williamsburg, New York where he became an extraordinary and successful leader. His community there grew to 30,000 Jews and he became Head of the Central Rabbinical Congress of Rabbis of the United States and Canada. He was a kind and generous man but on religion he was uncompromising. "If I am left with only one minyan of adherents [ten], I will not refrain from expressing my beliefs," he declared.

The religious authority of the Hasidic dynasties in a way contradicts their democratic appeal. But the tone is still populist, and the message uncompromisingly religious. In 1953 Rabbi Joel Teitelbaum became the spiritual head of the *Edah Haharedit* encompassing *Neturei Karta*, for which he became a formidable spokesman.

May Jews wage war or battles in our time? asks Teitelbaum. Using the texts described in this chapter, he argues that there is no longer any such thing as a Holy or obligatory war. The Gemora (component of the Talmud providing substantial commentary on the Mishna which is its core), Maimonides and the law all show that the concept is not relevant in our time. The State of Israel has neither a Sanhedrin nor a King so the concept of a Holy war is invalid.

Nor is a war of choice possible. It can only be ordered through a High Court of seventy-one members. Even Ezra said that laws valid only in time of war do not apply in our time. This shows clearly that war is forbidden. Israel is not permitted to do battle with its enemies. Torah does not command that Jews should go to war for Israel. On the contrary it commands that one should mediate for peace. Torah commands that not one drop of Jewish blood should be spilled for the Zionist state.

The politicians argue that they have no choice, but Teitelbaum insists that there is no such thing as an inevitable war. The United

Nations is there to mediate and the Arabs have not provoked the conflict. The violence in the Middle East was caused by the Zionist State provoking Arab opposition. War and rebellion against the nations endangers and wastes precious Jewish lives. "Their doctrine of political power at any cost can only bring Jewry to the abyss of destruction."[34] The underlying argument is not that war itself is bad but that it puts Jewish lives at risk. Rabbi Teitelbaum complains, "Even today when the war is over, they quarrel with the nations, angering them and thus jeopardising the lives of tens of thousands of Jews in many lands."

Jews in the Peace movements are apt to argue that Jewish wars of self-defence are justified and that Israel cannot survive without her Defence Force. Rabbi Teitelbaum challenges this view. He claims there is no justification even for a war of defence. The Jerusalem Talmud and the Babylonian Talmud disagree on the interpretation of the commandment "One should not stand idly by while one's fellow is being killed." But Maimonides says that it means one should intervene only if one is certain of being able to save the other person. A man is not obliged to give his own life. In any case it does not refer to a war situation. There was no justification for sending Israeli troops into Lebanon. "When was such a thing ever heard of amongst people who are the seed of Israel? Where will we have come to such a profanation of the name of G-d, so that all the countries look upon the Jews as murderers. (G-d forbid)."[35]

Gradually it emerges that the survival of the Jewish people is not the overriding aim. A Jew is an individual who keeps Torah and obeys its commandments, the *Mitzvot*. The Law is binding on an individual. It remains binding even if only one individual is left. Therefore the purpose of the Torah cannot be just to secure the Jewish people in the Diaspora or anywhere else. Torah is the personal obligation of every Jew. The individual following a religious life of Torah is far removed from the average Israeli citizen, who stands condemned because he is united to his fellow citizens not by religion, but by nationalism. This is a call for a return to the Holy life.

The notion of the Jewish people is as central to the pacifist thought of *Neturei Karta* as it is to that of Judah Magnes. Both regard the Jewish people as distinctive and unique. But there the similarity ends. For *Neturei Karta* the Jewish people are not in search of territory, and Zionism is a sin because it conceives of

Judaism in terms of the temporal and earthly. The Jews are not a nation like any other. This position comes close to that of assimilated anti-Zionists in the Diaspora who regarded their Judaism as a religion pure and simple, rather than as an ethnic or national identity which might impair their belonging to the state where they were citizens.

For *Neturei Karta* the Jewish identity is pure spirit. This means that, traditionalist and fundamentalist though the movement is, it is remarkably free of racism or exclusivity. Converts do not become Jews for material rewards but because life as a Jew is different. The exaltation of Torah depends on "the quality of the penetration of Torah into his very soul, to the extent of *ahava viraha*, purity of motive and conduct with which Torah has been studied and the greatness of soul with which an individual has been endowed at birth." One *Neturei Karta* advertisement reads, "In the soul of the Jew, in his tabernacle, there was only one kingdom, that of G-d. There was only one code of laws – the exercise of humanity." Since the specialness of the Jew is purely spiritual, *Neturei Karta* is in practical terms able to relate to and accommodate other religious groups, including the Arabs, to a degree which progressive secular Zionism with its competing territorial claims is unable to do.

The movement is not large: Rabbi Moshe Hirsch, secretary of *Neturei Karta* in Jerusalem estimated a membership of 60,000.[36] In Israel they may be found principally in the Mea Shearim district of Jerusalem and in Bnei Brak, where they form part of the strictly orthodox community, the Jews who probably seem most alien to non-Jews: the men in fur hats called *shtreimels*, the little boys with the regulation fringes escaping their shirts, and the wispy beginnings of sidelocks curling from under the ubiquitous skull caps. There are members too in Britain and the United States. Their tiny numbers, their lack of financial weight and their mystical fundamentalism, not to speak of their intolerance of other Jews, means that they are not taken seriously by those who do not share their beliefs and way of life.

Yet in terms of Jewish pacifism the philosophy of *Neturei Karta* is both profound and significant. It provides an intensely religious justification for Jewish dissent and non-violence. Although few people in the secular or progressive Israeli peace movements would be willing to recognise their shared roots, the common ground is there. *Neturei Karta* respects the same Hasidic sources as the most celebrated religious philosophers, Buber and Heschel, through whose writings the Jewish search for non violence has gained a wider public.

In a political and historical context *Neturei Karta* is the Jewish equivalent of the small Christian pacifist sects which have an influence beyond their numbers, and a contradictory bearing on the world of *real-politik* which they deny. It shares with these sects too a conviction that conscientious objection is a simple, immediate response open to any individual and does not require to be substantiated by scholarship or erudition. Other Jews both in the Diaspora and in Israel have to argue an individual case for taking up a minority pacifist position. In *Neturei Karta*, membership of the movement itself establishes the incontrovertible 'genuineness' of the religious objection to military service:

> We have no connection either with them [the Zionists] or with any of their affairs. We desire no benefit from them or through them, neither deliverance nor protection. Nor do we desire collaboration with them. .... We do not approve of any hatred or hostility and above all any fighting or war in any form against any people, nation or tongue, since our Holy Torah has not commanded this of us in our Exile, but the reverse.[37]

Neturei Karta is the institutionalisation of Jewish dissent and the relevance of this goes well beyond its own membership. It calls into question the ethical necessity of conforming to majority Jewish patterns of thought or institutions, just because they are Jewish. It challenges the right of any Judaism, however traditional, to claim a halakhic prerogative. Louis Jacobs points out that, "For all its emphasis on the mystical life and the purely religious aspects of Judaism, Hasidism is profoundly concerned with sound ethical conduct."[38] It is important to examine and understand the power this philosophy has for its believers and the rationale it provides for any Jewish pacifism. *Neturei Karta* has formulated a Jewish pacifism so convinced that it remains intact even when it involves dissent in a Jewish state, or refusing to retaliate with violence in the face of the Holocaust.

Chapter 5
The Land and the People
Magnes in Palestine

Magnes had a dream of Palestine, but it was a personal dream in which he, Magnes, reached a promised land.

> How cozy (sic) and comforting the thought of that Palestine to which many of us looked as a land of refuge from the impossibility of Western industrial civilization! Even now, as far as I personally am concerned, I should like nothing better than to till a piece of its sacred soil, to spend my idle days on horseback traversing the length and breadth of the Holy Land, awakening echoes of a wondrous past and piercing the mists that come from Mt. Hermon for a glimpse of the blessed future. I should love to have time each day for the study of Torah, and to teach my children the wisdom of our People in the sacred tongue of our tradition. And what joy it would be to help search out some of the archaeological treasures that might illumine many dark places in our history .... all this was possible under the Turk .... and I presume it will be possible for a long time under the British – for the politically circumspect.[1]

In 1923 Magnes agreed with his influential American friends that there was no future for him in the United States. His best course was to remain in Jerusalem and become the driving force behind the new Hebrew University. His work in the *Kehillah* had for some time centred on the importance of Jewish education and his move to the Hebrew University in Jerusalem seems on the surface to be a continuation of this concern. Jewish culture was always vital to Magnes and now appropriately he was transporting it to Jerusalem.

But Magnes was by choice and training a rabbi in the majority Jewish community in America, that is to say the Reform (non-orthodox) movement. In Palestine there was no such thing. Magnes in Palestine had lost his constituency and with it his profession. The only Judaism in Palestine was orthodox and the only rabbinate was also by definition orthodox.

To understand the religious setting in which Judah Magnes now found himself one must look at the Jewish situation in Palestine before the Mandate, when Palestine had been ruled by the Turks. The geographical and historical context provided precedents with which pacifist philosophy had to contend. The attitude of the religious community towards war and peace was partly determined (as in any Jewish discussion) by an examination of Jewish history. The past is used to give authority for the present.

In 70CE there were more Jews living outside Palestine than in it. In that year a Jewish military uprising, crushed by the Romans, ended with the destruction of the Temple. Although the Temple was destroyed by the Romans and not by the Jews, Jewish commentators later took its destruction to be the consequence of the Jewish revolt, and so Jews assumed responsibility. Jewish pacifism has not isolated war (right or wrong) from its unpredictable results. It is the evil consequences of war which persuaded Magnes to continue to reject war as a viable policy in any situation. Only when the extermination of Jews in Germany produced a situation which could deteriorate no further, did Magnes relax his position and admit that war might be the only recourse. In the Arab-Jewish confrontation, Magnes never saw war as an answer.

War had not been successful for the Jews. In 135CE the Bar Kochba revolt was crushed by the Emperor Hadrian and Jerusalem itself was destroyed. Harkabi has coined the phrase, the Bar Kokhba syndrome, synonymous with risk taking and suicidal heroism.[2] There was a further revolt and loss of Jewish life in 351CE. The revolts provided an important lesson in Jewish pacifism. Compromise and calm dealing with the political overlords seemed to produce dividends which could not be achieved by armed resistance.

The vulnerability of defenceless Jewish communities since 351 CE is an inescapable historic fact. Yet, being defenceless victims of anti-Semitism created in Jewish communities an attitude of mind and way of life that was conducive to pacifism. Recent attempts to prove that there has been an unbroken Jewish military tradition are not convincing. The number of Jews killed or expelled by hostile measures, whether physical or administrative, are a better indication of our vulnerability and our compliance. In the Middle East there was no exception. Inter-Arab conflicts of the late 8th century CE led to a further marked fall in the Jewish population of Palestine. In the 11th century there was once again an organised Jewish community but it was wiped out in the course of the Ist Crusade. The Latin Kingdom of Jerusalem collapsed and in 1211 three hundred rabbis from England and France set out to re-establish the community in Palestine. One must note that this was a religious endeavour, and unlike the Crusades was not backed by arms.

The expulsion of the Jews from Spain in 1492 increased the settlement of Sephardic Jews who came as refugees to Palestine and religious settlement continued after Turkish rule was established in 1517. By the mid 18th century, Sfat was the largest Jewish town in Palestine with a population of 3,000 Jews. It was there in the mountains above Galilee that Karo produced his full application of the law, *The Shulkhan Arukh*, that Luria (1534-1572) developed the ideas of Kabbala, and Cordovero wrote *The Palm Tree of Deborah*. From 1700 onwards religious Jews from Eastern Europe began to find their way to Palestine. Some of them came with Messianic hopes, followers of the false Messiah, Judah Ha Hasid, who created near hysteria by prophesying the imminent end of the world. Later, Hasidic followers of the Baal Shem Tov settled in Palestine and the size of the Jewish population steadily increased. By 1845 there were 12,000 Jews in Palestine. By 1880 Jews made up more than half the population of Jerusalem.[3]

Living in the Land was part of one's religious calling as a Jew and settlement was exclusively religious. The *Yishuv* (the settlement or community) adhered strictly to the law or *halakha* as practised in the traditional communities of Eastern Europe. There was *Heren* (excommunication) of those who criticised *halakha*. The lives led by the religious Jews in Palestine bore some resemblance to that of some Christian religious orders. Their life of study and devotion was supported by charitable contributions from the Diaspora. There was no need or compunction to earn a living or be self-supporting.

It was during the late 19th century that certain clear cut divisions were established in Jewish society in Palestine, a separation of communities within the community, which perpetuated themselves into the period of the British Mandate. When secular settlers of the first *Aliyah* arrived between 1882 and 1903, with aspirations to establish a productive and self-supporting Jewish community in Palestine, they were seen as rivals by the old Yishuv which was determined to retain its jurisdiction over religious questions: *Kashrut*, ritual slaughter, status and education. The religious community had no interest in the secular administration of Jewish villages or farms. Indeed, the socialist notion of egalitarian, self-governing communities, the kibbutzim, which were run on co-operative lines, was diametrically opposed to the formal application of *halakha* under the guidance of religious authorities. The Turkish administration allowed self-government to the different religious communities in Palestine. The Moslems had privileges, but the Jews also enjoyed autonomy and the old Yishuv had no aspirations to establish a state or extend the application of *halakha* to government in general, certainly not to the government of non-Jewish communities living in the area.

The secularisation of settlement left religious affairs entirely in the hands of the orthodox authorities. Though there was not necessarily agreement between the various orthodox and ultra-orthodox communities, the secular settlers and the Zionists left religious disputes entirely to the religious. Maybe this was an evasion of responsibility but it also made political sense. In 1897 the first Zionist Congress was condemned by the Rabbis who maintained that Zionism was contrary to the Jewish religion. Herzl, the Zionist leader, attempted to overcome the religious opposition by encouraging the growth of *Mizrahi*, an orthodox Zionist party. His followers were content to leave religious matters to the orthodox.

The First World War had a disastrous effect on Jewish religious life in Palestine. While the Turks ruled there, many Jews had retained their original nationality. Under the capitulation system, their affairs were looked after by the consuls of their 'home' countries. This came to an end with the entry of Turkey into the First World War in November 1914. Palestine was in the German field of interest; Jews who were subjects of the Allied powers were offered naturalisation and forced to do military service. The alternative was to leave Palestine. In order to try to protect the Jews in Palestine, the Central Council of the World Zionist Organisation met in Copenhagen in December 1914 and resolved to remain neutral.

The Turks did not remain neutral towards the Jews. Their commander-in-chief published a manifest opposing the creation of a Jewish State in Palestine; Zionist organisations were declared illegal and the use of Hebrew forbidden. The Jewish religious community found itself cut off from its economic support in the Diaspora. Aid from the United States became of vital importance and it was Magnes who helped channel both food and money to Palestine via Turkey. Once the United States entered the war the situation grew worse and the end of the war in 1918 left the Jewish population of Palestine down by one third with only 56,000 survivors.

The war left another doubtful legacy in the Balfour Declaration. This was no more than a letter expressing support for a Jewish homeland in Palestine and it was matched in December 1917 by a statement from the Grand Vizier of Turkey, Talaat Pasha, allowing free Jewish entry to Palestine. Both sides were vying for Jewish support. But by then Jerusalem and south Palestine were under British control and in September 1918 Turkish rule came to an end. Jews fought for the British, and supported the British application for a Mandate in Palestine. In the Arab world Jews were blamed for the peace settlement which incorporated the Balfour Declaration and prolonged a semi-colonial situation in Palestine.

Magnes was never seduced by the Balfour Declaration. It established important Jewish rights, but others had rights too. "The Joshua Method is not the way for us of entering the Promised Land, the retention of bayonets in the land against the will of the majority of the population. The Eternal People should continue its long wait rather than establish a Home ... except on terms of understanding and peace."[4]

Helen Bentwich, whose husband Norman was a legal officer in the Mandate Government from 1920-31, shared these doubts. Jewish herself, she had sharp things to say about the prospects of peace. "The Arabs and Jews don't love each other," she wrote in 1919. "And those people at home who talk so glibly of them lying down together like lions and lambs are ignorant of the real feeling here. The antagonism goes very deep, and the Jews are not as tactful as they might be in trying to make things easier."[5]

Peaceful coexistence did not get easier; Jewish religious quietism was eroded as both the British administration and the secular Zionists built up a relationship with the orthodox authorities in Palestine. The religious community were drawn into the political arena. There were elections in Palestine in 1920 and a Jewish National Committee was set up, the *Va'ad Leumi*, which was recognised by Sir Herbert Samuel as the representative of the Jewish People. The Turks had had a system of religious courts for the different communities. Each local *Beth Din* or rabbinic court had final authority. Now Norman Bentwich innovated by trying to set up a central rabbinic authority. Gradually *halakha* was adapted to participation in the modern political process. There were Orthodox disputes over women's rights to vote and over educational issues but, in the long run, most religious Jews registered to take part in Jewish elections and to pay Jewish taxes.

There was already a Sephardi Chief Rabbi in Jerusalem, the *Rishon b'Zion* or First in Zion. A new development was to have an Ashkenazi Chief Rabbi and the new post was lent stature by the distinction of its first incumbent, Rabbi Kook (1865-1935). *Mizrahi* and the Religious Zionists were now joined by a wider spectrum of the religious establishment and majority orthodox opinion was helping to shape the infrastructure of the future state.

The Chief Rabbi of Jerusalem, Rabbi Kook, a major figure in this development, was a notable mystic and humanitarian who has remained an inspiration to Jewish moderates. Like Judah Magnes, though in rather different idiom, he insisted that religion must concern itself with political and social issues. Moral principles of Judaism, faith in man and the universal love for all men must hold good in the public sphere. Religion is intended to bend life towards ethical and moral perfection. Secular political Zionism was not enough. It was spiritual yearning which would create a land in which Jews, Christian and Moslems would live as brothers. His optimism remains unsoured. The inner essence of the soul must have absolute inner freedom. "The uniqueness of the inner soul lies in its own authenticity." In the past Holy things had been detached from the things of the world, but in future a heroism of religious involvement will transform worldly things.[6]

Kook shared something of the Utopianism of the socialist settlers with whom he co-operated. His existentialism is as appealing as that of Martin Buber, and unlike Buber's it is an expression of orthodox Judaism. "We began to say something of immense importance among ourselves and to the entire world but we have not yet finished it. We are in the midst of our discourse." But Kook did not articulate pacifism and his co-operation with the civil authorities may have had effects different from those he would have desired. By integrating religious life into political life, he paved the way for religious support for a Jewish state, for the state to identify itself with exclusively orthodox religious interests, and for the military demands of the state eventually to become recognised as a religious imperative endorsed by the rabbinate.

Orthodoxy militated against conscience, just as Ahad Ha-Am had pointed out. Ahad Ha-Am (meaning One of the people) was the pen name chosen by Asher Zvi Ginsberg (1856-1927) who championed the place of conscience, not as modern self-indulgence, but as the authentic source of Jewish morality. In *The Law of the Heart*, 1894, he denounced the authoritarian written law of the Rabbis. Torah had codified the inner law, the law of moral sense and now he complained that "Conscience no longer had any authority in its own right; not conscience but the book became the arbiter in every human question."

In Zionism, (The Love of Zion he called it), he saw the spirit and culture of Judaism revitalised, but he also saw all the pitfalls of political Zionism.[7] He admitted that the ingathering of the Jews was not practical. "The truth is bitter," he wrote. "But with all its bitterness it is better than illusion." ... "Political Zionism cannot satisfy those Jews who care for Judaism; its growth seems to them to be fraught with danger to the object of their own aspiration." Under the Mandate the imperative of the Law began to align itself with political Zionism. Freedom of conscience, so vital to the early Zionists, would find no footing in Israeli law.

Magnes was neither orthodox nor secular. He was marginal to Jewish society in Palestine, and it is tempting to say that his

Judaism itself became less secure, now that he was deprived of his role as preacher and rabbi. His notebooks chronicle his agonising doubts about the existence of God. In the States Magnes had pleaded for an intense expression of Jewish ethnicity. In Jerusalem he found it hard to find a congregation which suited him and finally he joined in worship with a few personal friends. He was outflanked religiously by the traditional orthodox to whom he must have seemed hardly Jewish at all. Magnes had always had Christian Pacifist friends, and the Unitarian J. Haynes Holmes remained a correspondent. In Palestine, Magnes' contacts were primarily with other Americans, with the British, with an academic élite, with Palestinians.

In the States Magnes had been a maverick Rabbi. In Jerusalem he was Chancellor of the University with a public role to play in administration and fund-raising. His character was still American and for the rest of his life he admitted retaining a double identity as Jew and American.[8] His links with the States were important because the revolution of 1917 had destroyed the religious identity of Russian Jews; the USA was now the dominant centre of Jewish life. It was as an American Jewish leader that Magnes had assumed some responsibility for the welfare of Jews in Palestine during the First World War, and Jewish life in Palestine during the Mandate remained dependent on American support. Magnes retained his contacts with the American Jewish establishment, encouraging their financial generosity, and trying to guide their growing Zionism into what he believed were the right political channels. His pacifism remained undaunted but it was no longer inspired by the character of the Jewish people. Rather it was for the sake of the People. His role was to give the people the best protection that the situation could afford. This empirical pacifism, expedient to the moment, and intended to mitigate the permanent sense of conflict and crisis between two communities and the mandatory power, set the style of pacifism in Palestine, and later in Israel.

Magnes' confidence and energy were perhaps also changed. The task of talking to individuals and writing individual letters was altogether on a smaller scale than his previous existence. Magnes did not join *Brith Shalom*; it was not commensurate with his position as Chancellor of the University. But at the opening of the academic year 1929/30 shortly after vicious inter-communal clashes at the Western Wall, he had this to say: "One of the greatest cultural duties of the Jewish People is the attempt to enter the promised land, not by means of conquest of Joshua, but through peaceful and cultural means, through hard work, sacrifices, love and with a decision not to do anything which cannot be justified before the world conscience."[9] There had been violence on both sides. During August Zionist Youth groups had demonstrated against Arab construction work near the wall, and disputes over Jewish rights to pray at the wall ended in Yom Kippur services being disrupted and Jewish holy objects desecrated. Magnes' letters of 1929 show some despair. He wrote to Warburg from Paris saying how he had been torn. He had been happy, too happy, devoting himself to the University, had tried to keep the University out of politics. "But I see again what I knew before and tried to forget, that politics means lives, safety and the determination of moral and religious attitudes."[10]

Helen Bentwich wrote home in February 1932 describing the isolation of Jewish peace activists. Her husband had been dismissed from the Administration and now held a part-time post in the University.

> I can't think why such a calm, peace-loving person as Norman should be such a storm centre. He had taken a great deal of trouble over his first lecture at the Hebrew University, on 'Jerusalem, City of Peace' .... No sooner had he started than shouts came from the audience. 'Go and talk peace to the Mufti, not to us.' For a quarter hour they kept up the row .... throwing stink bombs, and showering pamphlets. ... [There was such a continuing disturbance that] In the end, the British police were called in, and Norman gave his lecture on peace with an armed guard standing on each side of him. It's bad enough to be persecuted by the British for being a Jew, but it's worse to be persecuted by your fellow-Jews for being the kind of Jew you are.[11]

Magnes in America had formulated a Jewish pacifism based on a notion of the land and the people, a Zionist Jewish homeland and the morally elect Jewish people. In Palestine he was confronted with a real land and the reality of the Jewish people very much at variance with the ideal. Magnes had already admitted that his dream was not reality. "Unfortunately I know that if Palestine is to be peopled by Jews from the rest of the world, not even the strictest

British–Zionist immigration laws can keep proscribed ideas and dangerous Jewish persons from entering."[12]

In America Magnes had known two types of Jew: the influential American Reform establishment and the radical Eastern European immigrants in New York. For him Jews had never been ordinary people; they embodied particular virtues of brotherly love, of co-operation and non-violence characteristic of the *Bund*. In Palestine the Jewish population was less marked out and less different from populations elsewhere and he could no longer rely on the natural virtue of the people to justify his pacifism. Magnes assumed the responsibility of speaking, not with the voice of the people, but on behalf of the people, who were themselves too ignorant to appreciate the moral implications of their Jewish heritage.

He advised Weizman not to press for increased immigration. In another letter, to Felix Warburg, he expressed the view that Jews had no superior right to Palestine and the situation seemed very similar to the Great War. Each side talked of its own isolation and war to gain total victory. "Whereas they should be talking also of their own sins and of ways of stopping the war and living at peace. And if the Arabs are not capable of this, we Jews must be, else we are false to our spiritual heritage."[13]

The following winter he defended himself when Stephen Wise attacked *Brith Shalom*. Magnes denied that his own views had disturbed opinion. Events disturbed opinion. His own views helped Jews keep faith with Zionism. "As it is, we are hated and feared, perhaps also despised, not just in Palestine but throughout the East." The Arab question *is* the Jewish question. "What is the nature and essence of Jewish nationalism?" he asked. "Is it like the nationalism of all the nations?"[14] On 30 July, 1932, he wrote in his journal that there should be change without violence. The Jews were not cruel. They were the merciful, the children of the Merciful. Persecuted people were either brutalised or filled with pity, and for Jews it must be the latter.

Majority opinion was moving in other directions. Historians debate whether the non-violence of the Jews was *faute de mieux* forced on them by circumstances, or whether it was a matter of religious and ethical conviction, but it seems indisputable that non-violence was for so long the Jewish response that the early settlers in Palestine, whether secular or religious, believed it contrary to Jewish tradition to take up arms. Those who first in Russia and later in

Palestine took up arms in self-defence did so consciously as a last resort. It was only when they and their opponents became used to the concept of the fighting Jew that military reactions began to seem both normal and prudent.

> Out of blood and fire and tears and ashes a new specimen of human being was born, a specimen completely unknown to the world for over 1800 years, 'the fighting Jew'. That Jew, whom the world considered dead and buried never to rise again, has arisen. For he has learned the simple truth of life and death and he will never again go down to the sides of the pit and vanish from the earth. ....
>
> The world did not pity – or else it got used to – the tens of thousands of human beings taken like sheep to the slaughter in Treblinki (sic). The world does not pity the slaughtered. It only respects those who fight. For better or worse, that is the truth.
>
> All the peoples of the world knew this grim truth except the Jews. That is why our enemies were able to trap us and shed our blood at will.[15]

Leo Pinsker (1821-91), an assimilated Russian Zionist, suggested that Jews must have a state of their own before they would get equal respect. "No people, generally speaking, has any predilection for foreigners. This fact has its ethnological basis and cannot be brought as a reproach against any people. .... Since the Jew is nowhere at home, nowhere regarded as native, he remains an alien everywhere."[16]

Persecution is not all pogroms. Helen Bentwich recorded the genteel anti-Semitism of the British; during one period of political tension the British onlookers at the Club clapped when she lost points at tennis.[17] Her wounded feelings help one understand what Pinsker meant when he described the Jew as the adopted child of his fatherland, never the legitimate child. Zionism, the determination to find a land for the landless Jews, was an expression of Jewish feelings of marginality in Western society and of alienation from the cultures that rejected them. Jews were special because the persecution of the Jews had made them special. The terrifying persecution of Jews under Nazism seemed to justify more than ever the Jewish special claim to a homeland in Palestine. It was the Land of Israel covenanted to Abraham and Jacob in the Book of Genesis. It had unique religious and political significance.

It is this duality of need, of necessity coupled with religious desire, that has torn the Jewish peace movement apart over Israel and seemed to face it with unanswerable problems.

Yet Magnes reasserted his vision of Zion. It was to be a living centre for the Jewish People and for Judaism. It should help to maturity the slumbering spiritual and intellectual forces of the whole Semitic world and Jerusalem should be the sanctuary of the three great religions. His pacifism now became particular to the land of Israel. It depended on the identity of Palestine as the Holy land, a land Holy to three different world religions. Magnes did not regard the Mandate as a simple colonial situation. Considering the Arab question, he felt that the land belonged to all, that there should be some sort of trusteeship to establish an international state whose inhabitants would never be conscripted "in behalf of any war whatsoever, offensive or defensive." Questions of a Jewish state or serving in a Jewish army did not arise.[18]

But instead of heading a mass movement and addressing crowded meetings as he had in the States, Magnes now set the pattern for Jewish pacifism in the Middle East. Palestine was a patriarchal and élitist society. Pacifism was a matter of high level meetings and contacts between Jewish leaders like himself and leaders of the Palestinians. The new style reflected the social fabric of the Middle East but it has proved a long-standing handicap to Palestinian/Jewish dialogue.

The shift from public to private speaker was forced on Magnes partly by his lack of Hebrew. In the States he had been a great orator, exploiting his command of his mother tongue, English. In Palestine he spoke in Hebrew from notes which he had painfully translated. He could use English as a spokesman but not to shift public opinion. Pacifists were a tiny minority; he spoke for almost no one but himself.

In February 1937 he was sixty years old and confessed himself "racked by religious doubt, by pessimism as to the world and Palestine, by scepticism as to the efficacy of the pacifist point of view. The pain deep down is sometimes unbearable." Five months later he expressed these thoughts in public. "The failure of my own people is the hardest to become reconciled to." They had returned to a small, already populated land. Rights were meaningless. Jews had to get on with the Arabs. The Jewish ethical tradition, their ideals of justice and the way they had suffered themselves from other nations meant that they had a duty in Palestine to make peace.[19] It was both a practical and ethical duty. Yet he saw that Jews resettled in Arab lands would be no more secure than in the Diaspora.

When he met Nuri Pasha in Beirut in 1938 there was misunderstanding. The Arabs believed he had accepted a permanent Jewish minority in Palestine. Magnes' only solution to the problem was a prolonged mandate. Meanwhile, the Jewish community at large had become respectably Zionist. It was a response to Hitler, and it was as a response to war against Hitler that in October 1939 giving the address as usual at the opening of the academic year, Magnes gave his students permission to go to war against the Satanic persecution.[20] He likened his "belief that the taking up of arms, though never righteous, is inevitable at this juncture," to changing his religion, and not a change to a higher belief but to a lower one. "This is apostasy from the pacifist faith. One may still hold this faith, but without having the strength at this moment to carry it through in practice."

What followed was a cry from the heart, his incessant pacifist credo. He declared that no war was righteous, not even that one. No one had tried to avert it "through contrition for the last war, through renunciation of conquered possessions, through justice at home and abroad, through real sacrifice." It was not possible to divorce religion from politics. The Prophets had been concerned with the political situation of their day. Wars of religion were not righteous, he said. 'Thou shalt not Kill' was a literal command and war infringed it. He was "transgressing His word knowingly".

Hitler's success was creating a growing Zionist consensus. The Biltmore Programme of the Zionist Congress of 1942 won widespread Jewish support for its declaration of the right and the need for an independent Jewish state in Palestine and pressed for this to be made an Allied war aim. Against the majority, Magnes disagreed. To divide up the land between the Jews and Arabs would lead to endless problems. It would leave no room for further Jewish immigration, and both sides would resort to terrorism, the Jews to expand their land holding, the Arabs to assert their claim within any Jewish state.

Magnes persisted with the bi-national idea. In August 1942, with Martin Buber and Henrietta Szold, he instigated a new group, *Ihud* or Unity Association. It was not a political party; it was an association of friends, some of whom had been members of *Brith Shalom* and later of the League for Arab Jewish Friendship. It included members of the Labor Federation but its secretary was a German rabbi, Dr. Kurt Wilhelm, so that in *Ihud* religion and politics were integrated as Magnes had always desired. "Politics is one of the most profound of mankind's spiritual concerns. How men are to live together and be governed is a spiritual question with far-reaching implications." Buber and Magnes campaigned for a bi-national state; the Arab population had to be a working and active partner in development. A settlement which gave either side dominance was bound to lead to catastrophe.[21] Richard Crossman, the British Labour MP, took a practical view: parity between the two communities would ensure there was deadlock on any vital issue. The bi-national idea may have been innovative political thinking but it could not gain popular support from either side since it satisfied the aspirations of neither. Yet for Magnes and Buber it spelled peace. Magnes was not interested in democracy that rested on numbers of people. He had never pressed for a Jewish majority.

There are moments when Magnes' attitude to the Arabs (like that of Buber) seems colonial and disparaging. After the Holocaust Magnes urged peace on the grounds that the Jews, with one third of their population gone, could not afford to lose a single life more. They were vastly outnumbered by the millions of Moslems who would be prepared to die in a Jihad (a holy war). The Holy War is a concept unknown in Judaism. Magnes said poetically that the Arabs had time on their side and the space of the desert.[22] Magnes was not saying that Arab life was less precious than Jewish life; he was recognising the existence of ideologies which regarded human life as expendable.

Magnes and other Jewish intellectuals shared many of the Western attitudes towards the Arabs which are analysed and castigated by Edward Said as *Orientalism*.[23] The racist theories of the anti-Semites (which were without scientific basis) provoked a Semitic Jewish response which was equally illusionary: Arabs and

Jews were brothers, the heirs to a common Semitic heritage. Hebrew poets in Palestine gave literary expression to their curiosity, their fascination, their acceptance of the Arab aspects of the land where they were living Jewish lives.

Avot Yeshurin incorporates Arabic into his Hebrew; he writes, "Fragrant is father's prayer shawl" but the *tallit* (prayer shawl) wraps a curious Arabic phrase which seems simultaneously to be a common form of address, and to translate the Shema, (the essential Jewish prayer). The two people or the two languages may become one, and his seeing them as one may constitute a betrayal of his own Jewish inheritance. The father's prayer shawl may demand retribution.[24] Yehuda Amichai's poem *An Arab Shepherd is Searching for His Goat on Mount Zion*[25] connects the fears of the Arab shepherd with the Jewish father. Both search for reassurance, and there is a hint that this can only be provided by the beginning of a new religion, that existing concepts do not allow for what is needed. Edward Said would probably condemn this literary work as idealising, stereotyping or disparaging 'The Arab'. Some of it is – to lose a goat is not the same as losing a son. Abraham Shlonsky in *The End of Adar* beautifully romanticises the images of the land, the golden bracelets of the Bedouin women. With their wells and pitchers, the women somehow seem closer both to the landscape and to biblical symbolism than modern Jews.[26]

But Hebrew literature at least admits a common human destiny, and is offered by Israelis to demonstrate that there are Jewish ways of seeing which do not cast the Arab as national enemy. Before dismissing this sort of fellow feeling between Jew and Palestinian as wishful thinking in the light of the conflict, one should recognise that it is an idea to which Palestinians themselves have contributed. Edward Said himself has written eloquently of a shared exile, the common diaspora experience, of juggling multiple identities; when he writes about being a Palestinian in the States he comes close to describing what it is like to be a Jew of similar class and education.

Jewish Arab relations in the Mandate were a matter of class as much as of race. Magnes and his academic friends were not always complimentary when speaking of their own people, the Jews, and the attitudes on both sides, Jew and Arab, reflect the period. English religious intellectuals like T.S. Eliot did not hide their disdain for the urban mob or the small man. Watching newsreels of Nazi rallies one can understand why Jews too mistrusted the crowd.

Popular opinion was suspect. This is why Buber attached no importance to majority rule.[27] He pinned his hopes of co-existence on the Arab intelligentsia rather than the population in general.

Their diaries and letters show that the Bentwiches and Magnes and others of their circle enjoyed social contact with an Arab élite. In their early days in Palestine the Bentwiches crossed the Jordan to lunch with Emir Abdullah (Feisal's brother) in his winter camp and play chess.[28] This is one of the weaknesses of the pacifists during the mandate period and since. In 1932 Arthur Ruppin spoke sadly of the constitutional plan for an Arab-Jewish state, "But what good does it do that a small circle has reached agreement when there is no prospect of making the draft acceptable either to the Jews or to the Arabs?"[29] Magnes and his university friends wrote articles, corresponded with their contacts in the USA and Europe and held high level meetings with like-minded Arab spokesmen and community leaders. But neither they nor their Arab colleagues reflected the attitudes nor antagonism of the people at large.

Jews in contemporary peace movements, and some Christians too, like to claim Buber as their mentor and inspiration. They admire his writings on Jewish Arab relations collected by Mendes-Flohr in *A Land of Two Peoples*.[30] If some of his writings convey a pacifist view, it is not one that represents the full measure of Buber's thought. His espousal with Magnes of the bi-national idea did not amount to pacifism and Buber never claimed (as Magnes did) to be a pacifist. Indeed he denied it, and it is instructive to compare his thinking with that of his student and fellow Zionist, the pacifist, Hans Köhn.

On the other hand, if one starts with Buber's philosophy of personal interaction based on the mutuality of the I/Thou relationship, it is difficult to arrive at anything other than a pacifist conclusion.[31] The personal relationship insisted on in Buber's philosophy hardly seems to allow for the use of force between two individuals. Never to regard the other as an object, but always unconditionally as another self, would seem to be the most pacifist of philosophies, and one is pulled up short by what appears to be a break in continuity between Buber's writings on the personal and the social scale. He attempted to bridge the gap by putting the

Jewish individual before the nation, and making the nation dependent on the individuals within it. The Jewish relationship to other nations can only be seen in these terms.

> Nations can be led to peace only by a people which has made peace a reality within itself. The realisation of the spirit has a magnetic effect on mankind which despairs of the spirit. This is the real meaning of Isaiah 2.2. (And it shall come to pass in the end of days, That the mountain of the Lord's house shall be established as the top of the mountains, and shall be exalted above the hills; And all nations shall flow unto it.)[32]

Buber's current popularity and the uncritical advocacy of a version of his philosophy which appeals to modern religious taste, help disguise the fact that his thought underwent considerable change over his long lifetime. His attitudes to Zionism and the Jewish state were affected first by his move to Palestine and later by the establishment of the state of Israel.

In 1921, in an essay on nationalism he sees the ideal community as a natural one. The uniqueness of Israel is a difference which sets it apart from other peoples but it is not a superiority. Jewish nationalism must not assert that Israel is 'like unto the nations'. Israel's destiny is an idea. It must not deteriorate into false nationalism, nor a specific political program. The land is the 'healing of Israel'.[33] A state in Palestine is 'a station in this healing process.' One finds Buber often uses organic language and metaphor which imply that the desired religious outcome is also the natural process.

Like Ahad Ha-Am, for whom love of Zion (says Buber in an essay, *On Zion*) was love of Judaism, Buber interprets the specialness of Israel in mystical, spiritual terms.[34] His theology is bitterly opposed to a false messianism linked to the acquisition of territory.[35] None the less, by 1939, when he wrote to Gandhi, Buber's ideas had shifted from the ideal of 1921 to the real. "The land is not an idea, it is holy. Only the real land can be holy. An idea cannot be holy and a land cannot just be a symbol." Buber did not give up the claim to the land. He sees the Jews not as a colonial power employing native labour as the British did in India but as working the land themselves.

Köhn dared to suggest that Buber, who had edited *Kalevala*, the national epic of the Finns, had adapted this nationalism to the Jews.

Buber would have denied that,[36] and pointed out that whereas
Goebbels said that Right was what benefitted the German people,
he, Köhn, emphasised that in the case of the Jewish people the
means must fit the end. However, for Buber, the claim to the land
entailed acceptance of the right to defend the claim by military
means.

> We do not want force. We have not proclaimed, as did Jesus,
> the son of our people, and as you do, the teaching of non-
> violence, because we believe that a man must sometimes use
> force to save himself, or even more his children. But from time
> immemorial we have proclaimed the teaching of justice and
> peace; we have taught and we have learned that peace is the aim
> of all the world and that justice is the way to obtain it. Thus we
> cannot *desire* to use force. No one who counts himself in the
> ranks of Israel can desire to use force.

The *havlaga* or self-restraint practised in Palestine was precious to
Buber. He believed that force provoked a violent response and he
was utterly opposed to Jewish terrorism which constituted a
breaking of the faith.[37] Buber saw Palestine as a refuge and place of
healing. It was not essential to have a Jewish majority or a Jewish
state and he was at odds with Ben Gurion over this.

When Gandhi insisted that Hitler must be confronted with non-
violence, Buber responded in a famous exchange of views that
Satyagraha *had* been practised in Palestine but he would not follow
Jesus. He would resist evil by force. Buber abandoned any idea of
confronting Hitler with non-violence. "If there is no other way of
preventing the evil destroying the good, I trust I shall use force and
give myself up into God's hands."

Buber was sensitive to Arab aspirations only up to a point. The
situation in Germany called for desperate solutions. There was a
pressing need for a refuge in Palestine for Jews from Nazi Europe.
Buber saw this as a just claim and one that might be defended by
force.

For all his insistence that one must not withdraw from the
practical reality of politics, Buber's philosophy leaves unanswered
questions. There is a seeming break in sequence between his
idealisation of the unconditional mutual relationship on which

natural communities are to be gradually built up, and the real social tensions which existed increasingly in Palestine.

In this predicament Buber supported the formation of *Brith Shalom* in 1925 and participated in *Ichud* in 1942. Both movements encouraged the building of relationships between Jewish and Arab communities but neither movement was pacifist. Both movements were a means to Jewish survival, and Buber made no distinction between survival in Palestine and in Hitler's Germany. British armed intervention in Palestine was an intervention as necessary to Jewish survival as the armed opposition to Hitler ten years later. Buber accepted the necessity of arms.

The irony is that the pacifist Köhn went to America and became an eminent writer on nationalism. The rise of Fascism and Nazism convinced him of the need for armed resistance against extreme forms of nationalism. He became anti-isolationist, a strong believer in American intervention, and ceased to regard America as a colonial or imperial power. By 1939 Köhn was no longer pacifist. Nor was he dismayed at abandoning pacifist principles. Köhn now saw peace as something that had to be fought for.

Buber on the other hand, a non-pacifist by now residing in Israel and remaining fiercely attached to the land, seems to have begun to have doubts about the use of force. The establishment of the State of Israel in 1948 confronted him as never before with the problems of politics and he did not like them. His views began to echo those of Köhn, the pacifist Zionist, twenty years before. In July 1946 Buber had condemned the bombing of the King David Hotel, British Military Headquarters, by Jewish terrorists (freedom fighters?). "The redemption of Zion cannot be achieved but by the rule of the sacred law ... whose essence is respect for the life, property and honour of one's fellow human beings". His disgust was even more marked after the escalation of the war and the murder of Count Bernadotte, United Nations envoy in September 1948. "In the commandment 'Thou shalt not kill' can also be heard the commandment 'Thou shalt not kill the soul of your people'."

In October 1948 Buber wrote in *Be'ayot Hazman*, "It is characteristic of modern warfare that each of the two fighting sides is convinced his is a war of defence." The Jews had begun the attack through peaceful means. Israeli political policy was equal to Arab armed aggression. Natan Hofshi, the pacifist, wrote the same thing in the same month. As a pacifist he widened the concept of aggression to include political aggression as firmly as military, and he condemned both.

It is possible that Buber had previously (like Magnes) countenanced the use of force only in stopping the Holocaust. Until the War of Independence he had expected peace and co-operation between Jew and Arab, based on the beneficial Jewish influence on agriculture and on society. Later, with a Jewish government, he saw the reality of a military government based on Arab inequality. He began to look critically at the Jewish record in Palestine. Every situation resulted from another. Things were left undone. Inactivity influenced the future. "Always in every situation it is possible to do *something*, some correct undertaking which determines to some extent the character of the next situation."[38]

Buber began to question Jewish policy and insisted on his right to do so. One must bear in mind that he had always been a dissenter from Orthodoxy. He gave up religious observance after his Bar Mitzvah and, we are told, developed a deep aversion to the Law, to *halakha* in all its forms. He was never acceptable to the Orthodox as a teacher of religion. Buber was someone "who with complete radicalism stood aloof from Judaism as a cult, and whom nobody ever saw in a synagogue during the almost thirty years he lived in Israel."[39] He had no patience with those who claimed that it was disloyal to the Jewish People to admit Jewish errors or criticise Jewish policy. He refuted the idea that Jewish censorship or self-censorship was necessary in the interest of the Jewish People.. "Labelling people who hold different opinions as people who do not have the national interest at heart... creates a noxious atmosphere. ... How can the knowledge that there are individuals who do not subscribe to the accepted definition of the interests of the Jewish people harm the view of those who are trying to limit expression?"[40]

Yet we have to ask what is going on in Buber's philosophy and whether it is really a help to have religious language and concepts applied to an actual situation. Buber said there could be no generalisation. One had to deal with each individual situation. "We must be quite unromantic and living wholly in the present, out of the recalcitrant material of our own day in history fashion a true community."[41] The material was recalcitrant because his language avoided analysing it. He spoke a vernacular of the spiritual, and there was a religious call on him to embrace the real land and supply the real need of Jews under Hitler, their desperate search for safety and survival. His Judaism and his love of peace were in conflict and, given the choice, he chose Judaism.

For Magnes on the other hand there was no conflict between his pacifism and his being a Jew. Each entailed the other; they were synonymous. He could not choose between them; he had to live in the real land as both pacifist and Jew.

It comes as a shock to Jews to realise that Jewish religious attachment to the Land is not unique but is a known phenomenon of political geography. Our situation as Jews may be singular but we react to it in normal human ways, and the relationships between populations and territory may be discussed dispassionately within modern academic disciplines. An essay by Yosef Shilhave relates Jewish territorialism to this wider intellectual world. He describes the emotional, cultural and religious ties that develop between a population and a territory. Group consciousness of this kind is known to be connected with a people's concept of its own identity.[42]

At the time Magnes lacked this intellectual formulation but he saw land as a real location, one's country in which one lived one's life. He recalled that he had been born and raised in a land without fear but that the land of Israel was a land of fear. In 1937 he put it quite clearly that an individual Jewish state had not the capacity to solve the Polish/German Jewish problem. It was a false messianism. Zangwill had said "Give the land without a people to the people without a Land" but there were people there and it could therefore be settled by Jews only in a way compatible with the rights of the Arabs. He pointed out again and again that Jewish land had been legally purchased and that the rights of the Arab farmers, the fellah, must be protected. But he also saw clearly that the resettlement of millions of Jews from Europe could not be solved by resettling Arabs from Palestine.

Magnes saw that real people, the Jewish People, could not possibly be redeemed by the geographical land. It was not large enough to hold them. The solution and safety it offered were not real.

As a Zionist Magnes was constantly frustrated by the view of his fellow Jews, both Zionists who were fiercely anti-Arab and

Americans who were anti-Zionist. Magnes by his example
established that it was possible to oppose Zionist policies without
being anti Zionist. While recognising on some subconscious level
that the existence of a Jewish political entity depended on force of
arms, at that time wielded by the British, Magnes remained
doggedly in Jerusalem, arguing that the future of the Jewish
homeland depended on peace. He had very few supporters. Self
Defence was the order of the day.

Resentment against the British had fostered the self-identity of
the Jews who formed their own armed resistance movements. There
were real grounds for their suspicion. The British had always had
an emotional partiality to the Arabs whose support they needed in
the Middle East. The White Paper of 1939 was yet one more
restriction on the admission of refugees from Hitler who might have
survived if allowed to enter either Britain or the Mandate. The
Anglo-American Committee of enquiry which was set up in May
1946 recommended policies very similar to those advocated by
Magnes: a continuation of the Mandate, (probably under United
Nations supervision) and increased Jewish immigration, but it was
accepted neither by the Zionists nor by the British with whom they
were already virtually at war. On 29 June, 1946, the British arrested
Jewish political and religious leaders in Palestine. Two thousand
Jews were interned and on 26 July the Irgun responded by blowing
up the Mandate Administrative Office in the King David Hotel.
There was escalating violence between the Jewish and Arab
communities and from November 1947 this amounted to a state of
war until the Jews gained military superiority in April 1948.

As a pacifist Magnes realised that it was not enough to disarm the
enemy. Peace was not just a matter of Jewish principle. It had to be
coaxed out of the Arabs. His peace initiatives now involved a
concern for the welfare of the Palestinian population which has
persisted in the Israeli peace movement till today. At a high level he
met on equal terms with Arab leaders. He argued that Jewish funds
should benefit the Arab population as well as the Jews. He argued
against partition and he constantly upheld the rights of the Arabs to
land holdings. For Magnes, Jewish rights were inseparable from
Palestinian rights. There was no ethic which made Jews more
valuable. All were the same. The land should be shared by equal
partners. For either side to achieve its real aim and to gain
dominance would deprive the other. This was why Magnes opposed

the creation of a partitioned state. He wanted a bi-national solution which would create and preserve an atmosphere of co-operation between the two peoples.

To see Jewish historical and geographical attachments in a sociological context is not to deny them or decry them. By remaining a Zionist Magnes recognised that there are real needs and real feelings among populations. It is natural for individuals to look for security, for a place to live, for stable relationships and a community to which to belong. Religious needs and identification are an additional psychological and social reality. Magnes did not deny the difficulties of pacifism. Pacifism presents very real problems of response.

One may even look at Magnes' career in Palestine and ask what his discussions, his deputations, his meetings, his letters had to do with the pacifism he had preached in the States. The answer lies in the setting. Pacifism in America raised issues of conscientious objection and civil liberties. In the Middle East pacifism had to concern itself with problems of territory and populations. Then as now, the territory was in dispute and the populations denied and discriminated against each other.

After the establishment of the State in 1948 where the state itself became synonymous with Jewish religious identity both in Israel and in the Diaspora the problems Magnes warned about and the solutions he proposed were quickly forgotten. But in the long term they can probably not be evaded and his legacy is not just to the small pacifist groups in contemporary Israel but to the community as a whole, as we have to come to terms half a century later with the realities of Zionism he felt unable to avoid.

In the context of his career, Magnes' removal to Palestine, his exile from his own milieu, was a disaster. If he had stayed in the States and been able to pursue a career like that of Wise, there would be no feeling of a lost potential, of a man uprooted and wasted. Yet from the point of view of Jewish pacifism, Magnes' relocation in Palestine is something for which one must be profoundly grateful. After the United States had made peace, first in 1919 and then in 1921, conscientious objection was no longer on the agenda. The Arab Jewish conflict in Palestine ensured that Magnes spent the rest of his life in a situation where he was forced to explore further and further the dilemmas of pacifism in a 'war' situation. For pacifist as rabbi this new setting presented a different

category of challenge. It is not easy for a Jew to be a pacifist in any
context but it is more problematic where one protagonist is actually
'The Jews' (to be accurate, the Zionists). Until Magnes arrived in
Jerusalem and found himself continuing to act as a pacifist in this
new Jewish setting it would not be possible even to be sure that his
pacifism would survive the transition. As it is, his career in Palestine
puts his whole philosophy in a new perspective. His great
achievement as a pacifist was to demonstrate that Jewish pacifism
remained a valid principle even in a Jewish conflict. "When I talk of
peace with the Arabs, it is not just a tactical ... move in *real politik*; it
is a result of a *Lebensanschauung*, a given view of life."[43]

His example has not been an easy one to follow, but his note
books show that it was not easy for him either. He never gave up
trying: he wrote, he talked, he negotiated, he persuaded. In spite of
ill health he insisted on leaving Jerusalem in April 1948 and
travelling to the United States to speak to members of the
Administration, to try and arrange a ceasefire in Jerusalem, to
negotiate an armistice, to encourage American support for a
Trusteeship rather than partition. On June 10, still in America, he
had a stroke and he died in harness the following Autumn. He was
too ill to return home to Jerusalem but he was still writing, still
trying to negotiate some sort of confederation with the Arabs.

Louis Fischer had paid tribute to Magnes[44] and Magnes confided
in Louis Marshall's son, James:

> He says that my 'constant companions' are God and the
> 'common people'. That indeed would be my great aspiration;
> but I must say that I have had very little companionship, if any,
> with God. When I see people, who believe they are on some
> intimate terms with Him, I envy them and wonder if it is true. I
> find that He turned His face away from me many years ago.
> That has been for me probably the most fundamental problem
> of my life. As to the common people, well, I have little more
> knowledge of them, and I do feel rather intimate with some of
> the hard-working people, whom I stop on the street sometimes
> for a little questioning or a little chat. Gandhi's strength is that
> he knows all about God and the way to him is always open.
> How happy Gandhi must be![45]

Written late in life, this passage may stand as Magnes' testament to
Jewish pacifists. Self-deprecation and religious doubt are part and

parcel of what he left. So is the awkward admission that it had not been easy for him to be a Jewish pacifist, that for some Christians or for Gandhi religious pacifism might be somehow simpler, or carry more conviction. Magnes had demonstrated that, problematic though it is, Judaism through pacifism provides practical ways of responding on a human, individual basis to the divisive and threatening situations which confront us. Pacifism, like ourselves, if it is to operate at all, has to operate in a complex and uncertain world.

Chapter 6
The Loss of Innocence
Abraham Cronbach and Jewish
Pacifism in the Second World War

Sooner or later any discussion of Jews and pacifism comes up against the question of the Holocaust. Is it conceivable that Jews could stand by and not use force to try and prevent the extermination of the Jews? The Second World War agonised both Harris and Magnes; neither saw any alternative to fighting Hitler although both men continued to insist that it was against their religion. Jews today lead their lives very much aware that, if Allied soldiers (including Allied Jewish soldiers) had not been prepared to fight, Jews and Judaism might not have survived. But the dilemma for a Jew is not necessarily different from that of a Christian pacifist. It must be made clear that a refusal to take part in war is not an alliance with one side or the other.

But it happened that Hitler's growing persecution of the Jews coincided with manifestations of Jewish pacifism stronger than ever before. All pacifism flourished in the inter war years. The reaction against the slaughter of the First World War provided a broader social base for peace movements both secular and religious. The War had been "the war to end wars", and in Britain the Jewish Peace Society flourished without offending against the general mood. In the United States Rabbis Stephen Wise and Emil Hirsch preached non-selective pacifism reminiscent of the Quakers. "War is the violation of every one of the ten commandments. Thou shalt not kill. War says thou must kill .... and the only excuse you have for killing is that if you don't kill, you will be killed yourself, and where there is a question between you and the other, of course you take the benefit of the doubt for yourself."[1]

From 1924 onwards the Central Conference of American Rabbis urged "an uncompromising opposition to war. We believe that war is morally indefensible." The Conference welcomed every government proposal for outlawing war and for international law and adjudication; it set up a Committee on International Peace.

None the less, the rabbis were careful. "We do not champion extreme attitudes. We do not adhere to the doctrine of non-resistance."[2]

By 1926 the resolution before the CCAR was more specific. "Peace is not only a religious ideal but a fundamental necessity...The great atrocity of human history is War itself." Throughout the whole inter-war period the Conference opposed military training in schools and colleges. In 1927 it affiliated with the National Council for the Prevention of War but the Rabbis remained wary of absolute pacifism and did not join the American Peace Society.[3]

In the United States, Reform and Conservative rabbis found that pacifism was no longer an obstacle in their careers. In 1922 a chair of Jewish Social studies was established at the Hebrew Union College in Cincinnati and its first incumbent, Abraham Cronbach, was a lifelong pacifist. He was threatened with dismissal in the early days when he tried to set up a Jewish pacifist organisation but over the next decade pacifism became respectable. In 1932, at the request of the women's synagogue organisation, the National Federation of Temple Sisterhoods, he published *The Jewish Peace Book for Home and School*. Stories, from both Jewish and non-Jewish sources, demonstrate ways in which children can follow the great figures of history in working for peaceful solutions to conflict. Cronbach pursues a serious educational purpose. He explains the cost of war both in human lives and in taxation. He outlines in simple terms the workings of the World Court and the Kellogg Pact. In particular he explains that heroism is not synonymous with bravery in war; there are other peaceable models for courage and self-sacrifice. This is one of Cronbach's recurring themes. In May 1923 he initiated a Decoration Day at Spring Grove Cemetery, Cincinnati; Jews, Catholics and Protestants met to honour the heroic dead of civilian life and the ceremony continued every year until 1941.

Cronbach describes with some affection how in post-Biblical literature even Joshua and David, the warrior heroes of Israel, are divested of their military character; they fast, they study Torah, they are portrayed as scholars themselves. He reminds us that in the Passover *Haggadah*, the wicked son in the story is often drawn wearing armour as if he were a soldier. In a final anthology of readings and prayers he quotes the beautiful and universal passage from Midrash Rabba Deuteronomy V 14.

> If a man have a foe, he seeks and ponders how to do him harm. God is not thus. Though all peoples grieve Him, none the less, when they sleep, their souls ascend into His presence; as it is said in Job 12:10: 'In His hand, is the soul of every living thing.'

What is remarkable about this book is its backing. It was financed by American Reform Judaism and published by the UAHC Department of Synagogue and School Extension. Pacifism was now majority opinion and even Wise regretted his change of mind in 1917. "The war came and to my everlasting shame I took side. .... Without reservation or equivocation, I herewith affirm that the pulpit of the Free Synagogue, while I stand in it, will never give support to war, to any war whatsoever. .... I would as little support a war to crush Hitlerism as a war for the strengthening of Jewish claims in Palestine."[4]

Cronbach's book faithfully reproduces at classroom level what was debated within the Central Conference of American Rabbis. It represents the feelings of both Rabbis and congregants at that time. There could not be a greater contrast with the isolated protest of Judah Magnes only fifteen years earlier.

The rabbis did not confront the issue of Jewish pacifism direct. It was still important to emphasise that Judaism and Americanism were identical.[5] Jews must never risk being associated with the Red scare of Bolshevism. Yet, like other Americans during the inter-war years, many Jews abandoned their religious identity and dedicated themselves to the American-style social ethic which found expression in Roosevelt's New Deal. Citizenship and radicalism were again concomitant.

Or so it seemed. In 1929 citizenship was denied to two applicants (Mrs Rosika Schwimmer and Professor D. MacIntosh, the Dwight Professor of Theology at Yale Divinity School,) because neither would give an undertaking to defend the United States in time of war. The following year the Conference protested with a resolution. "No person mentally, morally or otherwise qualified shall be debarred from citizenship by reason of his or her religious views or philosophical opinions with respect to the lawfulness of war as a means of settling international disputes." They also opposed all proposals for universal conscription. "Conscription bills tend to war not peace."

Albert Einstein is often mistakenly cited as a Jewish pacifist. He opposed the First World War and in March 1929 he agreed to serve on the Board of the newly formed Jewish Peace League.[6] However, Einstein objected to war only because, like many others in the inter-war years, he regarded German Culture and militarism as one and the same, and the persecution of racial minorities as a form of civil war. Because of this, he naturally believed that the Second World War was unavoidable and, though he urged Israel to remain neutral in the Cold War, he made his position clear. "I am not what you might call a religious pacifist. Besides I consider it preferable for men to fight rather than to be butchered without lifting a finger. That was just about the alternative in the case of Hitler's Germany. Nor do I favour unilateral disarmament. What I advocate is an armed peace under supranational control."[7]

However, in 1932 Einstein arrived in the United States, a very eminent Jew on a much publicised personal peace crusade. Jewish pacifism was newsworthy. The Rabbinical Assembly of America (Conservative) made a strong statement, "We believe all war to be wrong, whether as an instrument of national policy or a means of settling disputes." The resolution discussed by the CCAR in 1931 was even-handed. "While adherents of the Jewish faith have at different times so interpreted their religion so as to justify their personal participation in warfare, so it is in accord with the highest interpretation of Judaism, conscientiously to object to any such personal participation."[8]

Rabbi Bernstein urged the conference to come down more firmly on the side of Jewish pacifism. His colleagues preferred to allow a variety of interpretations within Judaism. It was one of the fine characteristics of Jewish religion as shown in the Talmud that it allowed such differences of opinion, insisted Rabbi Enelow.

Rabbi Feldman was very conscious that in Judaism no innovation was possible unless it carried the authority of tradition. "Judaism never took the Quaker position in the matter of war, non-resistance and non-participation." "For those of us .... who feel as keenly as we do and are very sympathetic to the non-resistant attitude of Quakerism, and should like to line up on that side," what was needed was for them to be able to "still feel that we are within the historical and ethical position of Judaism". The eminent Samuel

Cohon looked to the ethic: whatever the fact of Jewish participation in warfare in the past, it was in accord with the highest principle of humanity as professed by Judaism for the individual to object to taking part in war.[9]

The Reform American rabbis were evolving a new pacifism authorised by their own non-halakhic, universal, ethical Judaism. Jewish law no longer proved an obstacle; but there remained a problem with American law. Religious objectors were exempted from service only if they were affiliated with some organisation or religious body that expressed such objection as part of its platform. Unless the Conference made an official pronouncement it would not be possible for individual Jews to be conscientious objectors.

Christians did not necessarily face this problem. The Quakers and Christian peace sects had pacifism as part of their platform. There are no equivalent Jewish peace sects and this is sometimes put forward as proof that Jewish pacifism cannot exist. The fact is that, although some contemporary Hasidic movements come close to it, Jews do not have sects at all; the sect itself is a Christian concept involving dissent from a Church. It is a mistake to expect Jewish pacifism to conform to a Christian pattern.

Jewish structures are different. Jews pray in congregations. The laws which limit travel on the Sabbath day mean that congregations have traditionally lived within short walking distance of their synagogues and make up a local community. In the contemporary situation individual Jews may decide to travel some distance to the synagogue of their choice, but on the whole each congregation is centred in a locality, employs its own rabbi and appoints its officers by a democratic process. Within each congregation there may be consensus but there is not necessarily unity. A congregation is a social as well as a religious unit and its members may embrace a wide variety of individual beliefs and observance. The rabbi will reflect the opinions of his congregation because he has been chosen by them. In as much as pacifism is a minority position, pacifist Jews whether rabbis or congregants are likely to remain isolated figures in their local congregations.

There was no easy answer to this quandary. The following year, 1935, there was another attempt to establish pacifism as the mainline Jewish platform. "We believe that the time has come to change the traditional attitude of our faith towards war." "Be it therefore resolved that this conference declare that henceforth it stand opposed to all war, and that it recommend to all Jews that, for the sake of conscience, and in the name of God, they refuse to participate in the bearing of arms." That all Jews should oppose all wars was strong stuff; the motion was not defeated but it was decisively deferred to the next conference.[10]

Both during this period and later in the Vietnam war American pacifists tended to differentiate between wars of American intervention or aggression, which they opposed, and wars of self-defence in which they would be prepared to participate. This is a traditional Jewish differentiation between the just and unjust war and one might expect to find it used to justify a war against Hitler. Yet the pacifist Rabbis were beginning to look at the inconsistencies of selective pacifism. Rabbi Joseph L. Baron pointed out that if force was justifiable to defend the United States then surely it could also be used to achieve justice elsewhere or to forestall invasion. He underlined the fallacy of claiming to be pacifist and then making an exception where United States security was involved. "We cannot justify morally an exception of a selfish nature."[11]

It seems important that this point was made before the Holocaust because it goes some way to explain why even during the Second World War there remained Jews and Rabbis who were not willing to support the war against Hitler. There were Jewish pacifists for whom no self-interest, whether American or Jewish, could invalidate their pacifist ethic.

Initially, Germany's repudiation of the military clauses of the Treaty of Versailles and the rearmament of the United States stimulated the peace movements. Commitment to peace constituted opposition to German militarism. But the growing pessimism of the Conference is evident throughout the thirties. Germany was a risk to peace but it was a greater risk to the Jews. Though the Conference persistently pressed for a peaceful solution to the problems of minorities in Germany, most of the rabbis, including Wise, were shaken. The invasion of Ethiopia, the Spanish Civil War and the unchecked expansion of Nazi Germany made pacifism look like appeasement.

Cronbach wrote, "Like the man in the jest who so feared death that he committed suicide, nations wage war because they dread war. One nation's military preparedness inspires other nations with the terror of what might befall them should war occur; and with their fear arises the inclination to hasten war before the menace grows. ... In brief, preparation for war takes the lead among the causes of war. It is a deadly link in a vicious circle." [12]

Cronbach's struggle to keep Reform Judaism on pacifist lines resulted in two major statements, his address to the CCAR Conference at Cape May in 1936, *War and Peace in the Jewish Tradition*, and his book *The Quest for Peace*, published the following year.[13] His style is predictably academic, even pedantic. There is regrettably little of Cronbach's own voice and what there is is often painstakingly objective and scientific. He must persuade with facts. But his work and the rabbinic debates on Jewish pacifism which accompanied it broke new ground.

For Magnes the tradition and the people were everything. The mission of the Jews dictated their pacifism. For Cronbach, history, the people and its mission had become suspect. He somewhat inconsistently anthologised from the Jewish tradition while insisting that to Liberals the tradition offered no binding precedents.

Speaking in 1936 with refreshing honesty, Jonah B. Wise recognised the lack of a Jewish pacifist tradition. "The Quakers have behind them not the resolution of a conference but a history of actual devotion to peace. We have no such history behind us officially or as a religious group. ... If we are actually interested .... in a peace program, we should begin to make peace part of our teaching." He was echoed by Rabbi Eppstein who said that if Jews did not have a tradition for peace, it was high time they started developing and creating such a tradition.

So it was with an awareness of doing something new that the Rabbis reaffirmed their 1931 Wawasee resolution:

> The Conference of American Rabbis reaffirms its conviction that conscientious objection to military service is in accordance with the highest interpretations of Judaism, and therefore petitions the government of the United States to grant to Jewish religious conscientious objectors to war the same exemption from military service as has long been granted to members of the Society of Friends and similar religious organisations.[14]

Pacifism was not the only Jewish position, but it was a possible one. The pacifists compromised, but they achieved something realistic and significant. 'Interpretations' is in the plural.

Abraham Cronbach was born in 1882 only five years after Magnes but he seems a different generation. He grew up in a poor and predominantly Christian area of Indianapolis. This isolating experience threw him back on the sustaining comfort of Judaism. Yet his religious devotion seems to have been illumined by the Christian spirituality which he tasted at school and in his neighbourhood church. To the little boy, God was not chastiser, but a blessing, support and helper. "In choosing the ministry," he wrote, "I pictured the minister not as a public speaker but as a counsellor and a consoler." [15]

Cronbach's inner spiritual life afforded no escape from the material world. All around him he saw painful evidence of social deprivation. Even when Cronbach became a Rabbi, his Judaism found expression in the exploration of social issues, and it was a natural progression in 1915 for the pacifist Rabbi with his social conscience to move to New York to serve as associate to Stephen Wise at the Free Synagogue. The difference between the two men became clear in 1917. Unlike Wise, the modest Cronbach had no aspirations to power or influence. The war revealed to him, he later said, how propaganda based on untruth could change people's ethical outlook so that the kindest of people could act with real savagery. Cronbach remained pacifist and was asked to leave the Free Synagogue. But he was not equipped like Magnes to become an orator or public figure. Though Cronbach was briefly Rabbi at Akron, Ohio, he persuaded himself that his views on public questions made it impossible for him to hold a position within the regular Jewish ministry.

Cronbach lacked both confidence and magnetism. His congregations inevitably absented themselves, his classes dwindled. When confronted with any group of people he seems to have failed beyond reasonable understanding as both preacher and teacher. Yet he could leave no social assumption unquestioned, no ingrained prejudice unchallenged; it was as if he wanted all Jews to share his modern uncertainties.

Out of this open-mindedness he dared to remain a pacifist regardless of the political context. He took no refuge in a polite pretence that all men are loving brothers. Instead he began to look at the way people perceive their opponents. He questioned the role in which Americans and Jews cast their national enemies. In 1919, like Magnes, he pleaded for suspended judgement on the Russian Revolution. That sermon led to his resignation. When the Nuremberg laws caused very real doubts among his colleagues,

Cronbach again remained the lone pacifist. In 1935 he did the unthinkable and discussed with "leaders of the American Friends Service Committee the feasibility of bringing together under their auspices some representative Jews and some representative Nazis or Nazi sympathisers that the two groups might discuss their points of conflict and explore the possibilities of reconciliation." [16]

He wrote without official backing, a solitary voice that received no response. A preliminary meeting of Jews failed to materialise. On one level one can say that he was naive to hope for dialogue with Nazis. But what sense is there in suggesting that without dialogue there can be no understanding, unless one is prepared to talk to the enemy? When dealing with the psychology of the Holocaust, we deal in retrospect. Cronbach was a man who seems to have applied contemporary psychological understanding of the Holocaust before the event.

In the Second War as in the First, Cronbach was to take an obstinate and isolated stand. This inconspicuous and diffident man, by many standards a failed rabbi and a laughable preacher, becomes an isolated figure, feeling his way towards ideas that were ahead of his time and often very much in tune with our present preoccupations.

At the end of the war Cronbach, who had worn a yellow star out sympathy with his fellow Jews in Germany, begged for Jewish magnanimity and forgiveness at the war crimes trials. "All that we Jews crave is surcease of our sufferings. We have no wish to inflict sufferings upon others." He recognised that the war and even the final solution had arisen as part of a grim recurring pattern, "retaliation for grievances , real or imaginary. That vicious circle of retaliation and counter retaliation must be broken. We Jews hereby offer to break that vicious circle."

Cronbach is sometimes labelled a religious humanist, as if he had ceased to be a Jew at all. Taking his life as a whole one can now see that he was expanding the current notions of what constituted Jewish mission; he was helping to modernise both the role of the rabbi, and religious understanding. As a student in Cincinnati he had come under the influence of the Professor of Philosophy at the University, Professor Wyland Richardson Benedict, a friend of William James. William James' *Varieties of Religious Experience*, published in 1902, was not the first psychological interpretation of religion but even today it remains an essential work. It insists on the need for psychological understanding of the religious experience and challenges religious particularism (whether Jewish or Christian) by dwelling on the characteristics of religious experience in general, rather than on the merits of any single religion. Cronbach took this new learning to heart.

The Reform background in which he went to work was in need of fresh input. Hebrew was despised. American Jews worshipped in English and on a Sunday. Yet synagogue attendances were falling. The old fixed ways of Reform Judaism had become conventional in themselves. Respectability had taken over. Instead of responding with a return to tradition, as Magnes had done, Cronbach looked to revitalise Judaism with the latest developments in social and religious understanding. Fixed services and formal sermons failed to satisfy the spiritual needs of the people. He abandoned the Bible as a basis for preaching. "Slowly the thought developed in my mind that my goals lay ... in the realm of the spiritual. Whenever I have adhered to that ideal, results have been gratifying; when I have forsaken that ideal, results have been disappointing."[17]

Cronbach always asked "not how can people serve Judaism but how can Judaism serve the people?" As he saw it, religious education should be to help individuals, not to perpetuate Judaism. The young Rabbi innovated. He introduced consolation services and abandoned the Reform prayer book. "The spiritual values of religion depend on no ritual conformity." To those who denounced Judaism as superficial, Cronbach replied that it was not necessarily so. "There may be within us a longing for God. As the Psalmist says, 'My soul thirsteth for God, for the living God'."[18]

Cronbach asked about the symbolic and emotive use of words; what do we mean when we use words like 'soul' and 'God'?[19] In New York before the First World War, he had talked to a Freudian analyst and then, when Cronbach was working in the hospitals and prisons of Chicago, Emil Hirsch lent him books on psychoanalysis. In Chicago where he served more as counsellor than rabbi, he wrote his first article on Psychoanalysis and Religion.[20] Later, at the Hebrew Union College, he urged that the psychology of religion should be included in the rabbinic course and in 1932 he offered his colleagues a survey of *The Psychoanalytic Study of Judaism* in which the anthropological and psychological hypotheses of Freud, Reich and Fromm are set out with asperity.[21]

Cronbach was sceptical about much of this psychological material, particularly where the emphasis was exclusively sexual or where it was unsupported by real evidence. But he welcomed whatever offered insight into human behaviour or religious practice. The universal human need for religion, (high in the hierarchy of needs, the anthropologist would put it) validated Cronbach's own need for Judaism. He began to identify God as a religious concept signifying a reverence for human personality, but it was still to the Talmud he turned for moving passages with which to make his point. "Alas for him who said "I have been humiliated, be my fellow humiliated; I have been cursed, be he also cursed." Let him remember that when one humiliates and curses a human being, it is God's image that one humiliates and curses."[22]

In Cronbach's thought, respect for the other man is inseparable from his awareness of ethical relativity: that what is to one man Good will be to another man Bad. Cronbach is always sensitive to another man's fears, to the social pressures which create the criminal, to the deprivations, both in society and in relationships, which damage an individual and make him vulnerable. But one wonders whether Cronbach's idealism evades the real problems of dialogue with those who may not share his respect for the lives and rights of others. Ethics may be relative, but an ethical framework which deprives others of the right to exist is not something with which one can coexist. For the Jews in the Holocaust this became only too evident.

But Cronbach pointed out that war had not saved them. "Within a few years six million Jews perished through violence. The method of hatred and revenge, whatever it achieved, did not deliver the Jews from those unprecedented horrors. The men who overthrew my proposals (for talking to Nazis) did not intend that cataclysm. Yet the rescue of our people was hardly among their accomplishments."[23] What Cronbach termed ethical relativity is not properly speaking relative at all. Cronbach emphasises that the other man believes as fiercely as we do in his own conviction as to right and wrong. But is Cronbach really maintaining that we cannot make value judgements which distinguish between one ethic and another? His understanding of the psychological causes of Nazism and aggression do not amount to an endorsement.

Yet when the writer Vorspan asked him to sum up his message, Cronbach insisted that freedom depended on the principle of Live and let live. "Learn to respect differences. Let Catholics be Catholic. Let Protestants be Protestant. Let Orthodox Jews be Orthodox Jews. ... Curb your harshness and antagonisms. Let mutualism and co-operation flourish. Let religion forsake bankruptcy by practising the love and justice it professes. As individuals and nations let us differ amiably. Freedom means more than an end to persecution; it means also an end to animosity. Freedom means love and respect for every creature of God, even for our enemy."[24]

Cronbach's preaching love of our enemy sounds Christian, but there is a tolerance here which goes beyond Christianity. He does not turn the other cheek, he does not wish to transform the enemy, or redeem, or alter. He seeks to respect the other and understand. Understanding the other involves understanding ourselves. In this context Judaism becomes not the only or right way; he abdicates the position of superiority. By embracing a religious absolute he also abandons it.

Cronbach is suggesting that our ingrained religious prejudices and attitudes contribute to conflict and provoke antagonism. It is the Ego, our self-importance, which once affronted leads to animosity and prejudice against those who are not like us. Religion is the domain of ideals and values. These values are present in Jewish writings but this is irrelevant. The values would remain true even if the books opposed them. "It is not the writings that give worth to the ideals. It is the ideals that give worth to the writings".[25]

A relentless anthologiser of other people's views, Cronbach had no opinion of himself. But some of his colleagues called him a Saint. He was a man for whom the spiritual was not the opposite of the material, but the opposite of inferior, who confessed that his most precious experience in life had been the moment he took his adopted baby daughter in his arms on the train journey home and for the first time fed the baby a bottle. The tenderness which he rarely expressed is demonstrated for him in the texts he so carefully quoted.

In a paper delivered after the war, *The Logic of Pacifism*,[26] Cronbach concludes with the undisguised maturity of psychological insight. This is not naïvety: "If the real cause of the frustration be inaccessible or unknown or forgotten or if it be someone too powerful to tackle, the retaliation is deflected to some scapegoat", he explains. Aggression and retaliation are displacement of our immature irrational fears. "Those unconscious or barely conscious workings of our minds underlie most if not all of our illusions and mistakes." He was suggesting that these were the causes of Nazi anti-Semitism. But he does not leave the argument there; his analytical eye is also turned on his own side, the Jews, the West, on the Cold War as sternly as on the Holocaust:

> These are the forces which mislead people into the belief that armament and that war contribute to national defence....
>
> How it would advance the cause of international peace, if people at large understood the psychological phenomenon of rationalisation, so that 'national defence', the rationalisation for war, ceased to be regarded as the reason for war!
>
> Of all the outrages against the Jews committed by Hitler, none is more calamitous than this: he has banished from the hearts of many of us the will to peace.[27]

Conscientious objection in Britain during the Second World War is often presented as the happier sequel to suffering endured in the First World War, of lessons learned by the Government. During the second reading of the Conscription Bill in 1939, Neville Chamberlain conceded, "We all recognise that there are people who have perfectly genuine and very deep-seated scruples on the subject of military service and even if we do not agree with those scruples, at any rate we can respect them if they are honestly held. .... We learned something about this in the Great War, and I think we found that it was both a useless and an exasperating waste of time and effort to force such people to act in a manner which was contrary to their principles."[28]

In real terms the number of objectors probably went up during the Second War. In the First World War there were 16,000 objectors, perhaps 0.125 per cent of 6 million enlisted. In the Second War there were 59,000 objectors, about 1.2 per cent of the 5 million conscripted.[29]

From a Jewish perspective, however, this was a more difficult war. In 1914 the Jewish community, because of its foreign origins, was at the very worst suspected of sympathising with the enemy. This was a false charge which could be contradicted by all-out Anglo-Jewish commitment to the war effort. After the Munich agreement the insecurities were immeasurably greater and of a different nature. Jews had been successfully excluded from the Reich and from the German People. Was it possible that the same could happen in Britain? In the autumn of 1939 the Jewish Community was accused of engineering the war itself in the interests of world Jewry. No display of British patriotism could ward off this double-edged accusation. The existence of Jewish pacifists might in itself prove an asset, normalising the Community reaction by bringing it into line with the rest of the population.

It is legitimate to ask why it was that not even the rise of Hitler could alter the convictions of the few Jewish pacifists. But this is a question asked in retrospect: we know that the Holocaust happened and for this reason we perceive the war itself as a Jewish issue.

Hitler and the Germans under his command systematically slaughtered certain populations selected by physical, racial, ethnic, religious or political criteria. Among them were six million Jewish civilians and civilians of Jewish descent. Their extermination coincided with the Second World War during which, coincident to acts of war, to bombing, sieges and military campaigns, there were other civilian deaths outnumbering the Jews who died. So, in saying there is a special problem for Jewish pacifism, one is already making a distinction between the systematic political murder of a population (for which the term genocide may perhaps be employed) and the civilian casualties of war, say the millions who died in the siege of Leningrad. Pacifists would not make a distinction between civilian deaths and those of the military. One million German soldiers lost their lives in the first year of the Eastern offensive. None the less, a Jewish belief in non-violence has to take into account the peculiar Jewish devastation of the Second World War.

From the Jewish perspective there was another major difference between 1914 and 1939. One might assume that once the British government was at war with Hitler, the Jewish and British interest might be seen as identical. This was not always so. The safety of the Jews was a Jewish priority not a British one. 'Jew' had always had a negative connotation; Nazism had now made that distaste explicit and even respectable. British political anti-Semitism was polite but by no means negligible.[30]

Discussing the absence of non-violent civilian resistance to the German occupation of the Channel islands, including the passing of measures against the Jews, the Belgian historian, Jean Jacqumain reminds us that before the war Guernsey excluded Catholics from certain offices and in Jersey Jews and Freethinkers were similarly excluded.[31] Viscount Rothermere, owner of *The Daily Mail* and *Sunday Dispatch*, was a dedicated supporter of Mussolini, Hitler and their policies, including the treatment of Germany's Jews. "The German nation", he wrote (10 July 1933) was "rapidly falling under the control of its alien elements. .... It is from such abuses that Hitler has freed Germany."[32] Perhaps the Jewish cabinet minister was now regarded as an alien element? Hore-Belisha was forced to resign from the War Office in January 1940 and prevented from becoming Minister of Information because he was a Jew, whereas in the First War Lord Samuel and other eminent Jews remained in government without question.

German and Jewish opposition to Hitler was barely comprehended by the patriotic and partisan English. By November, 27,000 refugees had registered for National Service[33] but each individually had to appeal to the Tribunal against certificate B which restricted the right to travel. Jewish refugees from Hitler remained interned as enemy aliens while British-born Nazi sympathisers were for the most part returned to liberty.

In Cincinnati Abraham Cronbach was only too aware of the situation. "The status of Jews in every part of the world has deteriorated. We Jews in supporting the World War only helped prepare the way for the Nazi horror which has engulfed us. Even in America Jews are complaining of new discriminations." [34]

In Britain, already at war, not only attitudes but practical politics underlined the worsening Jewish position. In the First War the Jewish Community had been courted by both belligerents, in the Second, Jewish interests and even Jewish lives were of no account. The prosecution of the war even militated against the Jews. British courtship of the Arabs entailed the limitation of land sales in Palestine. The furthering of imperial policy worked at direct odds with the resettling of Jews from Europe. This dichotomy explains but does not excuse the apparent alliance with Hitler of certain Zionist resistance groups who were unwilling to give armed support to the British authorities in Palestine. In America Stephen Wise and the Zionist leaders were by no means convinced that American intervention would save the lives of Europe's Jews. Rather they hoped that the United States might put pressure on Britain to allow emigration to safety in Palestine.

It would be comfortable to pretend that the extent and nature of the Holocaust was not fully realised. Reading the *Jewish Chronicle* for the years 1939 and 1940, one is uneasily aware that this was not so. On 22 December, 1939, there was a full description of the Nazi onslaught on Polish Jews. A week later there is a report of mass executions in Buchenwald.[35] The brutal slaughter of the Jews in Poland was being fully reported at the very time when Hore-Belisha's resignation from the war office and political future were in question. Relief workers knew what was going on. In January 1940 Clarence Pickett, Director of Quaker Relief, suspended operations in Poland until such time as the Jews should receive their share of assistance.[36] On 9 February, 1940, *The Jewish Chronicle* was banned in Switzerland because its reports of Nazi atrocities in Poland were "not neutral".

There is a knowing and a not knowing. When the special benches for Jews were removed from German parks in September 1939, it was taken by *The Jewish Chronicle* as a good sign, an end to apartheid. The population figures for German Jews told another story: a population of 522,000 Jews before the Nazis came to power had fallen to 185,000 by 1 October, 1939. The benches were no longer needed; there were to be no Jews left to sit on them. Jews were nowhere safe. A pact with Germany might involve their expulsion from Britain. A German invasion of Britain might recreate a Poland in the reception areas, a Warsaw Ghetto in London. The Century Insurance Company refused life insurance on a Jewish woman in August 1940 and this was interpreted as anti-Semitism. It could just as easily have been actuarial realism.

In this despairing and disastrous setting it is easy to believe those who say there was no Jewish pacifism in Britain during World War Two. Any Jew who for political or religious reasons decided to register as an objector, had another issue to face in 1940. The debate as to whether or not a Jew could be a pacifist no longer hinged on the question of Jewish loyalty but on whether the peace movement itself was anti-Semitic. The Jewish Peace Society which had been revitalised by John Harris and his son Hugh was particularly strong during the twenties and early thirties. Its success coincided with that of other peace movements of which the most significant was probably the Peace Pledge Union. It was initiated by Canon Dick Shepherd who had been an active peace campaigner since 1924. In the thirties Jewish pacifists did not regard the Peace Pledge Union as anti-Semitic. When Dick Shepherd died in 1937, Rev. John Harris spoke at a memorial meeting in Golders Green.[37] The PPU became formalised in July 1935 which was after Hitler's rise to power; 80,000 people signed the Pledge and at its peak in the late thirties the PPU had 113,000 supporters.

The peace movement lost mass support when appeasement failed to curb German expansion. The Munich agreement did not prevent Hitler from taking over the whole of Czechoslovakia. The British were now resigned to fighting Hitler. In religious terms the peace movement was still Christian dominated but in the context of 1939 the word Christian can also be read as meaning 'not Jewish'. In addition there was secular opposition to conscription both from left and right, from socialists both national and international. In the peace movement which survived, a proportion of members were not pacifists but had a political objection to fighting Hitler.

Contemporary Jews were justified in asking how far the peace movement was a Raven in Dove's clothing. For a time it seemed to be dominated by members or ex-members of movements like the British Union of Fascists. During the first year of the war, the government outlawed various groups that were in sympathy with the Nazis. These included the Link and the British Union of Fascists. Some of their leaders and members re-emerged as the British People's Party but they also found an outlet in peace organisations. In October 1939 the pacifist British Council for Christian Settlement in Europe, which had as its Secretary the fascist sympathiser, John Beckett, of the British People's Party previously of the British Union of Fascists (BUF), also involved leaders of the Peace Pledge Union.[38] Members of the extremist Nordic League were instructed by their leaders to join the Peace Pledge Union.[39] A pacifist arrested at a BUF meeting was in possession of anti-Semitic literature.[40] *The Jewish Chronicle* open-mindedly published a letter from Beckett who had repudiated his former alliance with Mosley but the Peace Pledge Union were disowning their Fascist sympathisers. Another prominent pacifist, Lord Tavistock, was engaged in peace talks with the Germans in

Dublin and shared a peace platform with the Independent Labour Party. His Peace Meeting in April 1940 was still led by Beckett.[41] Lord Tavistock, a Christian Socialist, issued a disclaimer, but, as in a considerable part of the peace propaganda of that time, there is an anti-Semitic flavour that may not have been obvious to the contemporary eye.

However, the peace movement can also be viewed politically as an anti-capitalist movement rather than as purely pacifist or uniformly anti-Semitic. Its attacks on Jews were largely on Jewish capital and it was obviously acceptable to some Jewish socialists. In 1941 the People's Convention, a left wing group pressing for peace terms, included Jewish band leaders such as Ben Frankel who argued that the movement gave no support to Hitler but, on the contrary, was intended to encourage the German workers to remove Hitler from power. The Peace Pledge Union distanced itself from peace movements such as The Link which were nationalist rather than pacifist in character but it remains difficult to disentangle the two faces of the anti-war lobby. John Middleton Murray, editor of *Peace News,* made no effort to do so and *Peace News* carried anti-Jewish views from both left and right. The circulation of *Peace News,* 22,000 in September 1939, rose to a peak of 38,000 in November. Only after the end of the phoney war was there a change of mood and then there were problems in publishing *Peace News* at all.

In April 1939 conscription was announced for men aged 20-21 years. The Bill became law in May and was followed by full-scale conscription on 1 September. Conscientious objection was allowed if there was a genuine religious or ethical background to the objection. The Ministry of Labour and National Service thought that the objection should be to all war, a true pacifist position, but Tribunals allowed political objection, i.e. an objection to this particular war. Objectors in the Second World War included non-pacifists whose sympathies lay with Germany. One also knows from the fall in figures after the end of the German Soviet pact, that during the period of the pact objectors also included socialists whose sympathies lay with the German people. But there were also true pacifists who still believed that non-violence could defeat

Nazism. In Denmark the Nazis appeared to have been defeated by non-violent resistance.[42]

Both pacifists and tribunals were better organised than in the First World War. Seventeen pacifist groups joined to set up the Central Board of Conscientious Objectors to speak for the rights of C.O.s, to provide information on their rights under the act and prepare them for tribunal appearances. Tribunals were more fairly composed than in 1916; the military were no longer represented and, though biblical texts were again sometimes used to argue against religious pacifists, unfavourable tribunal decisions were not so frequent, and disobeying them no longer led to direct imprisonment. The government deliberately avoided the cat and mouse situation when objectors who were court-martialled for disobeying orders were imprisoned, released and re-imprisoned for the same offence.

In this altogether easier atmosphere one finds that, contrary to general belief, Jews objected along with the rest of the population. "The Jewish Conscientious Objector is a rare bird," conceded an editorial note in *The Jewish Chronicle* of 26 January, 1940, but one such (no doubt sincere) individual had appeared before the Glasgow Tribunal basing his case on the commandment Thou shalt not kill. "Any Jew who fights is not a strict Jew and has turned away from his faith," he had argued. God had fought for Moses. Jews were not to fight on their own behalf. The contrast with 1916 is marked. *The Jewish Chronicle* reports the case without derision or consternation. It is accepted that Jews like any other community will include those who refuse to fight on religious grounds. The editorial comments mildly only that the individual seemed muddled and to be uncertain even whether Moses was a Jew. A letter the following week supported the Jewish religious objection, reminding readers that the Torah urged that peaceful settlements should always be sought before resorting to force.

Lionel Cowan of Manchester[43] recalled that in December 1937[44] an article under the by-line "Watchman" had opposed war in these words. "Jews, the immemorial sponsors of the peace message, cannot shirk the supreme task. A warlike or even despairing Jewry is a Jewry recreant to its trust and lost to hope."

It is an important response to the Holocaust. The survival of an authentic Jewish identity depends on a refusal to resist force with force, even if in physical terms that renders survival less likely. A sermon of the week suggests that suffering in silence, "Israel's heroic silence", may hasten the redeemer.[45] The redeemer is the Messiah. The Jewish concept of the Messiah (unlike the Christian) does not imply divinity. But the Messiah will come as the agent of God to fight for the Jewish people, and his kingdom will bring perfection to the world; it is the Utopia which Isaiah describes as the peaceable kingdom when the lion will lie down with the lamb, the swords shall be beaten into plough shares and they shall not teach or wage war any more. The argument that God fights for the Jews is one that is taken up by other pacifists, most notably the Mennonites. It rests on the words of Moses in Exodus, "The Lord will fight for you and you shall hold your peace."[46] The Messianic theme is recurrent in Jewish pacifism but it is here voiced less in the hope of an actual redemption than to insist that heroism is not necessarily synonymous with bearing arms.

Jews certainly were dying in large numbers, and how they were dying and for what reason had already become a political question. When the Germans invaded Poland they justified gunning down the Jews by describing the implacable armed resistance they had encountered from armed Jews sniping from their houses. There is no evidence that the Jewish population resisted more or less than the non-Jewish Poles. Jews in the Polish army fought with the army. Nationalist and socialist Jews fought in the resistance. Religious Judaism has no military tradition. Hasidic Jews appear to have offered no resistance at all and yet it was often they who were singled out for extermination because they were made conspicuous by their distinctive dress and behaviour.

Judge Wethered of the South Western Tribunal kept an analysis of applicants who appeared before him between March 1940 and March 1942. He records 18 Jews. This was in an area which apart from Bristol had no sizeable Jewish community and one might suppose that the numbers were higher elsewhere.[47]

Because Judaism was not officially a pacifist religion, these Jews objected on personal moral grounds and not officially as Jews. Wethered's figures show that the distinction is hardly significant. The majority of pacifists in his area were not members of the peace sects: In a total of 3,353 objectors there were 662 Methodists and 531 members of the Church of England, but only 439 Brethren and

302 Friends. So the majority of objectors came from religions that were not officially pacifist. That included the Jews.

The British Jewish pacifists of the Second World war achieved a normalisation of Jewish pacifism. The system allowed them to object as individuals and to take alternative service without becoming part of a specifically Jewish group.

The American system made it difficult for pacifists there to survive without group identity and support. It was because the American Jewish pacifists became visible that the Rabbis were obliged to make a response. Throughout the thirties the CCAR was painfully aware of the dehumanising of German Jews under the Nuremberg laws, and pressed the American government to use its influence on their behalf. Even after 1939 when Britain and France entered the war (but the States did not), American Jews did not assume that German Jews could be helped by an American declaration of war. American Jews hoped for American mediation. Hitler himself had threatened that if war was declared on Germany, the Jews would pay the price. The Holocaust was presented by the Nazis as a German response to foreign 'Jewish inspired' aggression.

The normal arguments of American pacifist movements continued to apply during the Second World War. America was not itself being attacked and selective objectors argued that the war was not in the interest either of Americans or of European Jewry. One cannot repeat often enough that the War Resisters' League, the Quakers and Jewish pacifists themselves never regarded their pacifism as support for Hitler. The peace movements did everything in their power to rescue the Jews, to press for the relaxation of immigration quotas both for the States and for Palestine and to provide for refugees.

There were evidently specifically Jewish arguments against entering the war. Anti-Semitism was not absent from the American political scene. Father Coughlin and the American neo-Nazi movement made an impact and some Jews opposed the war lest American entry might be seen solely as Jewish-inspired involvement in a Jewish war. On the other hand, American isolationist groups were regarded as anti-patriotic and anti-Semitic.[48]

The continuing Americanisation of American Jewry between the wars blurred the dividing line between pacifism that was Jewish and that which was Christian. One hears anecdotes of Jewish conscientious objectors in Britain in the Second World War who 'became' Quakers because Jewish pacifism was unacceptable to the Community. The Friends themselves deny that they accept pacifist recruits simply as pacifists. Pacifism is a consequence of membership of their Christian religious society, not its cause. However, in the States it definitely appears that some Jewish objectors became Quakers. Bernard Gross of Philadelphia claimed to have become a Quaker while retaining a Jewish identity. These Jews denied that there was anything specifically Jewish about their pacifism. They had been exposed to the moral and cultural climate of a multi-ethnic society in which it was no longer appropriate to claim membership of any exclusive denomination.[49] Jews joined the War Resisters' League and the Fellowship of Reconciliation.

The 1940 Selective Service Act recognised conscientious objection only on religious grounds and although the concept of religion was widened by a judgement in 1943, (U.S. *v* Kauten), to include individual conscience, the Jewish objector found, as in Britain in the First World War, that draft boards and appeal courts assumed that the Old Testament furnished clear proof that a Jew could not be a pacifist.

The problem was not easy for the rabbis. All the arguments for Jewish patriotic conformity and participation were as valid as they had been in the First World War; and in 1942 the additional Jewish issues involved militated more than ever against Jewish pacifism. The Rabbinate were aware that political capital might be made by the Fascists if American Jews refused to participate fully in a war which many felt was being fought on their behalf.[50]

In 1940 the CCAR passed a resolution accepting that pacifism could be based on the Jewish tradition. The Rabbinical Assembly (Conservative) repeated its judgement, "We recognise the right of the conscientious objector to claim exemption from military service in any war to which he cannot give his moral assent, and we pledge ourselves to support him in his determination to refrain from participation in it."[51]

Although in general terms one can optimistically quote these resolutions as evidence of rabbinic support for Jewish conscientious objectors, in practice communal support was not forthcoming even though the terms of the legislation meant that there was a recognised need for "a responsible Jewish agency to which conscientious objectors could turn for advice and for practical assistance."

The National Service Board for Religious Objectors invited Jewish representation. The Reform rabbis resolved to set up a Committee to deal with the Board, and to ask for the co-operation of the Conservative Rabbinical Assembly. There was a good deal of confusion. Reform rabbis had already met with Isidor B. Hoffman, Chairman of the Social Justice Committee of the Rabbinical Assembly, and had refused to join the Conservative movement in a plan for the public registration of Jewish objectors. Rabbi Israel explained that they had been incapable of doing anything at all because the Orthodox group completely repudiated the idea that there could be such a thing as a Jew who would be a conscientious objector on religious grounds.[52] In June 1942 the Jewish Reconstruction Foundation, the third non-orthodox movement in the United States, recognised the right of Jews to interpret Judaism in terms of a pacifist philosophy of life.[53] With the Community divided it is not surprising that nothing was done that went beyond consultation.

But, as so often, real life stole a march on theory. Jewish law has always been realistic; woven into the tradition is the complicit acknowledgement that the law must reflect the *minhag*, the local custom of the people.[54] American objectors were obliged to perform alternative service. The noncombatant work was not paid and objectors had to live away from home in civilian public service camps. The Peace Churches which administered the camps supported their own members within them; of course, the Jewish pacifists had no such support. "Six Jewish conscientious objectors have been in need of financial help, and are being aided by the American Friends Service Committee and the Brethren Service Committee. Of these, only two are unable to repay these committees."[55] The rabbis were worried at the idea of Jews being supported by Christian charity. Yet, unlike the Peace Churches, the Central Conference of American Rabbis was fully supportive of the war effort. There was no way in which either the CCAR or the congregations would ratify official financial support of Jewish objectors. Individual charity was the only possibility.

Bernard Gross, one of the Jewish objectors, had been unsuccessfully pressing the pacifist Rabbi Isidor Hoffman to set up just such an independent Jewish peace movement. Isidor Hoffman had studied in Jerusalem as a young man, both at the American School of Oriental Research in 1924-5 and at the new Hebrew University. There he had encountered the pacifism of Judah Magnes and met Ernst Simon and Arthur Ruppin, the pioneers of *Brith Shalom* and the bi-national idea. He had moved in Jewish intellectual circles where peace and coexistence were major talking points. He spent the rest of his life working with Jewish students in America, first at Cornel and then after 1934 at Columbia University. But he remained constant to his early experience. He became an American member of *Ichud* and continued to be concerned with Jewish Arab relations. More important, he was one of the few from that earnest early group of peace lovers in Jerusalem who remained a pacifist during the Second World War. It was Hoffman who had the experience and the competence to establish and then to run the first Jewish pacifist organisation in the world.

At first Hoffman had not been enthusiastic about a segregated Jewish peace organisation. He had been active in various peace movements during the thirties and he was now vulnerable.[56] John Haynes Holmes writing in *Opinion*, September 1940, describes some of the pressures faced by an un-named pacifist rabbi friend: the rising war fever, the jittery opposition of his congregation and its officers. Hoffman was personally attacked in *The American Jewish Congress Weekly* of 3 March, 1942.[57] Abraham Cronbach too had failed in another attempt to set up a Jewish peace organisation at Cincinnati. Jewish pacifists still had no religious representation of their own but belonged to non-denominational organisations like the War Resisters' League.

But it was not as simple as all that to divest Jewish objectors of their Jewish religious identity. Howard Schoenfeld's prison memoir describes the impression made on himself and other Jews by Christian absolutists from the Union Theological Seminary who had no need to be in jail at all. They had refused to register for the draft even though as students preparing for the ministry they would have been exempt from service. The depth of their religious conviction was contagious; when the Christians prayed, the Jews followed. "Al Herling, Stan Rappaport and myself, joined together and recited an ancient Hebrew prayer."[58]

Michael Young, writing on Jewish conscientious objection in America in the Second World War, says that approximately two hundred and fifty Jewish men refused to serve in the American forces.[59] Many Jewish objectors had no wish ·to challenge the American government; they wished to offer a religious representation within the existing provisions, and to "engage in constructive social action on behalf of peace and justice". Now as never before there was a need for a specifically Jewish peace organisation to provide economic and moral support for Jewish objectors and represent their interests on the Consultative Council.

It was over this period of late 1941, and throughout 1942, that Hoffman and his graduate students at Columbia joined with Cronbach to amalgamate three existing groups of Jewish anti-war activists. The Jewish Peace Fellowship began modestly enough with groups in Columbia and New York as well as Cronbach's group in Cincinnati. New chapters were set up in Philadelphia and Los Angeles and its small membership grew to over one hundred. Its first Newsletter appeared in August 1942.[60] The membership was tiny but there was now a Jewish pacifist organisation with a committee and officers.

Hoffman, the Vice-President, took on most of the administration and was later to represent Jewish objectors, liaising with the Friends' Service Committee. The Jewish Peace Fellowship, under its first chairman, Reform Rabbi Arthur Lelyveld, took over responsibility from the Friends' Service Committee for the upkeep of Jewish objectors, and funds for this purpose came from Jewish organisations including the Jewish Welfare Board.

In March 1943 the War Resisters' League began to object to the conditions under which objectors worked. Objectors were still offered no choice of alternative service and worked without payment. The League became more absolute in its pacifism, more militant on behalf of objectors, and more secular. Finally it broke off relations with the Consultative Council of the National Service Board for Religious Objectors. (From June 1943 – April 1944 the Jewish Peace Fellowship also protested that pacifists' work was unpaid; during that period it made no contributions to the National Service Board and Jewish objectors seem to have been supported instead by the Joint Rabbinical Committee set up by the members of the CCAR and the Conservative Rabbinical Assembly.)

Secular Jews like Abraham Kaufman, who was executive secretary of the War Resisters' League from 1928-47, were happy to remain within the non-denominational protest movement. But Hoffman's pacifism was not tactical or political. He resigned as a Vice-Chairman of the League. Jewish pacifism implied religious conduct, a personal way of peace as well as a public one. "A continual calling towards peace, justice and compassion," he called it.[61] The similarity to the Quaker model is inescapable. But, in the Jewish Peace Fellowship, Jews were declaredly drawing on their own tradition, only part of which was shared or could be shared by Quakers.

For the first time there was a pacifist organisation which was specifically Jewish and, though its absolutism has at times been shaken, it has remained a unique organisation. It began to issue a succession of papers on Jewish peace issues and to publicise the religious foundations of Jewish pacifism. It also began to campaign actively not simply within the pacifist camp but representing peace causes in the Jewish community at large. Its continued existence bears witness that for Jews as for Christians there is a minority pacifist position which may legitimately be founded on their religious principles. Its pacifism holds good regardless of cause.

Chapter 7
Conscience or Compliance?
Non-Violence and the Holocaust

Between 1096 and 1204 the Crusaders passed through Europe on their way to defeat the infidel. The journey to the Holy Land was long and there were substitute unbelievers nearer to home. Jews were sitting targets; in the towns and cities of Europe entire communities were wiped out in thousands. But by 1932, wholesale, deliberate slaughter of Jews in democratic Europe was no longer a feature of living memory. The question why didn't the Jews resist the Holocaust presupposes both that they knew the Holocaust was going to happen, and that there was a correct preventative response.

November 1939. Vienna railway station. The Berlin correspondent of a Danish newspaper reported panic among the Viennese Jews being herded onto the trains. There were several suicides and escapes occurred. To refuse to get on the transports East, to escape, to kill oneself: all were ways of resisting. So was doing everything possible to remain alive. Yet we ignore the appalling scenes at so many railway stations and, equating resistance with guns, ask always, Why didn't the Jews resist?

When individual Jews refused to leave Vienna, did they know they were all destined to be killed? The reaction of individual Jews and of the community structures depended very much on how they perceived their situation and the appropriate response.

The Germans took care to disguise the nature of the final solution. Euphemism concealed actual policy and allowed even party members the comfort of self-deception. At the time Jew and non-Jew alike were led to believe that Jews were being moved East to live and work in specially designated Jewish areas. "But we imagined we'd only be sent off somewhere as labourers and would stay there till the war ended. Besides, we were sure they'd only send us among Jews. In either case people were resigned to make the best of it."[1] So successfully was the Holocaust denied that revisionist historians can still maintain that the slaughter of the Jews never took place. If they do accept that there was killing of some Jews, it is rationalised in terms of realpolitik, anti-Communist measures which were amply justified by the comparable savagery of Stalin's concentration camps. In other words, every Jew is identified as a Bolshevik and a danger to the Western European/American democratic ethic. This is an attempt to appropriate to the non-Jewish side of some perceived dividing line, the whole system of values which are shared by Jew and non-Jew alike within the common and pervasive European culture.

When we accuse Germans or Jews of not recognising the enormity of what was taking place, we should remember that the Holocaust ran counter to these values. The failure to believe in it was in some ways an insistence that the values still held good in Germany. Those values did indeed to some extent continue to establish a norm of what was and what was not acceptable. This was why it was vital to the Nazis that they should deny the Holocaust was policy. When the synagogues were burned down by the Germans in Wloclawek in Poland, it was the Jews who were forced to sign a document accepting responsibility for the damage and who were made to pay for the arson.[2] Exposure of the truth was in itself a form of non-violent resistance. There is evidence that a direct and public challenge (for instance by a German "Aryan" on behalf of a "non-Aryan" spouse) disturbed the Nazis. In order to prevent embarrassing publicity, public appeals were sometimes successful, whereas complaints made in private within the bureaucracy had no effect.

In Munich in 1943 when the young German students in the protest movement The White Rose were brought to trial, the indictment accused them not just of treason or opposing government policy but of spreading propaganda about the *alleged* slaughter of the Jews. "These seditious pamphlets....contain statements concerning the alleged atrocities of National Socialism, namely the alleged murder of the Jews and the alleged forced deportation of the Poles." The leaflet had said only that "300,000 Jews had been murdered in the most bestial way, a crime that is unparalleled in the whole of history." Even to report that Jews were being killed merited a death penalty, and met with a denial.[3]

The identity and values of a people change, responding to changing circumstances and reacting to historical experience. From a modern

Israeli viewpoint, the correct response to Hitler would have been efficient armed resistance, and the Jews are to blame for not providing it. "Hitler alone is not responsible for the death of six million – but all of us and above all the six million. If they had known that the Jew has power, they would not all have been butchered .... the lack of faith, the ghettoish-exilic self-denigration .... contributed its share to this great butchery."[4] It is reassuring to believe that a military solution would have been effective. It suggests that the Holocaust was preventable and therefore need never happen again. Yet this "might have been" is unreal; could an untrained Jewish force have succeeded when the regular armies of France and Britain, and later of the United States and the Soviet Union, took several years to put a stop to the German Reich?

This allegiance to a military code of values is very much the current response to the stark facts of Jewish history. Jews no longer see their long tradition of non-violence as something to be proud of, but as one of powerlessness, in which they, an oppressed people, were and still are in need of liberation. Jews' powerlessness in the Holocaust particularly distresses them. There is an idea that it would have been more honourable for the Jews to die fighting, taking enemy lives with them. The point is made by the historian, M. R. D. Foot, describing the Warsaw ghetto uprising in the Spring of 1943. "Those twenty-eight days of absolutely hopeless, absolutely heroic revolt provide a passionate denial of that other popular stereotype, of Jews who shambled off unprotesting to the slaughterhouse. That was what Jews had often (not always) done before, over twenty centuries of persecution: this time they fought back."[5] Foot, who was himself decorated for wartime service with the French Resistance, uses language that is loaded with value judgements. "Shambled" implies that the wretched state of the Jews was something they had chosen rather than a humiliation forced on them by physical and psychological victimisation. "Unprotesting" ignores the futility of the many protests made about the treatment of Jews both by the community leaders, foreign governments and by individuals. Jews are not answerable for the way they have been stereotyped by an inhospitable non-Jewish society. Nor are they obliged to regard as superior the stereotyped non-Jewish definition of what constitutes absolute heroism.

Viktor Frankl sees things very differently from Professor Foot and his vocabulary reflects this difference. "Our generation is realistic for we have come to know man as he really is. After all, man is that being who has invented the gas chambers of Auschwitz; however he is also that being who has entered those gas chambers upright, with the Lord's Prayer or the Shema Yisrael on his lips." Frankl, a Jew, a psychologist and an Auschwitz survivor does not differentiate between Jew and Christian. Psychology proposes a general human truth which overrides religious and racial characteristics. "The uniqueness and singleness of each individual gives a meaning to his existence."[6.]

But it remains true that there are characteristics of Judaism and the cohesive Jewish community which are particular to them. Killing the enemy in Jewish law is never an event in isolation; killing is only justified as a means to an end. If Jewish defeat is a foregone conclusion, whether or not it is heroic to kill one's enemy is in Jewish terms religiously debatable. Maimonides was of the opinion that one might break a commandment to save one's life but, if one was going to die anyway, then one was bound to observe all the commandments.[7] One hasidic historian says the question, " Why didn't they fight back?" is asked either by non-Jews or Jews who have taken over the values of the gentile world.[8.] For better or worse the mainstream of Jewish history has been entirely non-violent.

Reacting against this, one member of a synagogue said to me. "You won't find any Jewish pacifists here. You had six million of them. How many more do you want?" At least he was recognising that in the Holocaust there had been a confrontation between violence and non-violence, a mass of people whose only resource was to maintain the normal religious, social and cultural values of their lives. The general tendency today is to deny their moral stature. They are even blamed for their compliance. Jewish historians and memorial ceremonies now emphasise resistance and the ghetto uprisings. Armed resistance there was but it was not in the mainstream.

Since Jewish reaction to the Holocaust was largely non-violent, one must consider the paradox that pacifists too have been critical of the response. Gandhi ignored Buber's request that he should support the desperate Jewish plea for free settlement in Palestine.[9] He maintained that wide scale, militant pacifism could defeat the

Nazis and save the Jews. Gandhi preached *Satyagraha*, a soul force, a positive heroic mentality which he found lacking in the Jews. Replying to Gandhi, Buber commented sadly that it was lacking not only in the German Jews, but in the Germans, the Italians and all other peoples submitting to fascist tyranny. Gandhi was not alone in demanding more of the Jews than of other peoples, some special reaction, some extra heroic example. But the Jews of Europe were not in a colonial situation. Europe was not India, nor South Africa. Unlike the Indians, Jews were a landless minority whose German rulers were prepared to wipe them out; Buber had lived too long in Germany to believe that Hitler could be removed by non-violence.

None the less, the White Rose group did suggest that passive resistance could stop Hitler: they urged people to refuse to contribute to collections of money and materials, to boycott Nazi cultural and academic programmes, to sabotage industry, ignore Party newspapers, distribute protest propaganda and oppose the war. Professor Huber wrote,

> What I intended was .... to rouse the student body, not by means of any organisation, but solely by my simple words; to urge them, not to violence but to moral insight into the existing severe deficiencies of our political system.[10] ....
>
> Perhaps most of the readers of these leaflets do not see clearly how they can practise an effective opposition. They do not see any avenues open to them. We want to try to show them that everyone is in a position to contribute to the overthrow of this system....the only means available is *passive resistance*. The meaning and goal of passive resistance is to topple National socialism, and in this struggle we must not recoil from any course, any action, whatever its nature. At *all* points we must oppose National Socialism wherever it is open to attack.[11]

Jews too had faith in the power of the printed word. At least fifty underground publications in Yiddish, Polish or Hebrew were published in Warsaw between 1940 and April 1943.[12]

The White Rose epitomises non-violent resistance to Hitler and it resulted typically in the execution of its members. Was it futile to protest when the end result was death? Or did the initiative of a few apparently insignificant Christian students matter in the sense that it was an affirmation of their own belief in the real identity and values of the German people? There are Jews who aspire to share the cultural norms of well-armed European nation states; it is salutary to remember that to the students in the White Rose group, militarism and totalitarianism were un-German. Their concept of German identity was Christian; they insisted it entailed a combination of freedom and moral responsibility, both of which they continued to exercise under the Nazi regime. To them the Reich did not look heroic at all. "Goethe speaks of the Germans as a tragic people, like the Jews and the Greeks, but today it would appear rather that they are a spineless, will-less herd of hangers-on, who now, the marrow sucked out of their bones, robbed of their centre of stability – are waiting to be hounded to their destruction...."[13] These are Germans talking of Germans under Hitler. Jews have used similar language to describe their disappointment in Jews.

Passive resistance meant refusing to co-operate at every level and at every opportunity. There were Jews in positions of authority who did defy the Germans in this way. In the ghetto of Vilna, German regulations stipulated that typhus patients were to be selected for the gas chambers. The doctors in the hospital falsified thousands of medical records, fictionalising case histories, and keeping them updated to pass German scrutiny, in order to save the lives of their typhus patients.[14] In Venice, Giuseppe Jona, the Professor of Medicine and community leader, destroyed the records of Venetian Jewry and then killed himself to prevent the Nazis getting hold of the names.

However futile it may seem in retrospect, individual families also defied the Nazis. There are Jews who claim that their family's survival depended on non-co-operation with the Nazis. A French Jew in Jerusalem told me that his family simply did not register when all Jews were ordered to do so. Another survivor, Valentine Senger was a boy in Berlin when his mother put the word "none" on the religious register at his school and withdrew from the Jewish community.[15] Even half- or quarter-Jews were on the Police list but the local Sergeant Kaspar did not put the family on his list. He altered the religion given on their card and in 1935 he changed the card for a new one. It was he who pointed out that this meant the family had to stop going to the Jewish relief kitchen for food; they did not act nor look like Jews. Another eyewitness recalls how she pretended to be the illegitimate child of a mixed couple. This reduced her classification to only one quarter Jewish. In fact she was completely Jewish by descent and was 'passing'.[16]

Passing as non-Jewish, then as now, raised all sorts of questions. It can be interpreted as a denial of one's people and one's religious identity. Many Jews would rather die than do that, but it is not the only view. According to Maimonides, the paramount commandment to save life made conversion to Christianity or to Islam permissible if one's life was at stake. This was not the attitude of Jews in the Middle Ages who suffered death or committed suicide rather than deny their faith. To die for the sake of one's faith was victory over the Christian oppressor, martyrdom for the Sanctification of the Name, *Kiddush Hashem*. But then the objective of the Christian anti-Semites in the middle ages was to save Jewish souls through conversion. By killing themselves Jewish families thwarted that purpose. The objective of the Nazis was to exterminate Jews. It could be thwarted by remaining alive. "Only by living can you honour your family," Samuel Oliner was told by Malvina, the Polish peasant who saved him.[17] One Pole estimated that for every Jew saved (and he put the figure at 40,000 Polish Jews) there were ten non-Jews involved in that survival. Many Poles, like Malvina, saved Jewish children by teaching them the catechism and passing them off as Catholics, a fresh identity which was so deeply implanted that some of the children never abandoned it. It raises the impossible question whether the survival of the life of a human being constitutes Jewish survival. In Nazi eyes it did. They regarded it as resistance and the penalty for Poles and Jews alike was death.

There is a distinction to be made between Gandhian non-violence which is partisan, used to achieve political ends, and pacifism which is an individual's decision that he is not prepared to use force against another man. The Nazi regime took the German pacifist movement very seriously indeed. One of the most celebrated of German pacifists, Kurt Hiller, was incidentally a Jew but his pacifism derives from international socialist rather than from Jewish inspiration. In 1926 he founded the Group of Revolutionary Pacifists and urged the League of Nations to abolish conscription in all countries. Compulsory military service, he said, was the worst form of slavery.[18] He was imprisoned in a concentration camp in

1933 and 1934 before leaving the country, not to return until well after the Second World War.

Another leading Jew in the German peace movement was the publicist Berthold Jacob, which was the pen name of Berthold Saloman. Like Köhn, Jacob had volunteered to serve with the German army in the First World War and had returned from that war an ardent pacifist. He became a journalist and campaigned against secret German rearmament under the Weimar republic. An article of his in the pacifist weekly *Weltbuehne* contributed to the exposure and dismissal of Hans von Seeckt, Commander in Chief of the German Army. In 1932 Jacob emigrated to the supposed safety of Strasbourg and from there led the exiled German League for Human Rights. He was considered such a danger that he was abducted by the Germans in 1935 while on a visit to Switzerland. Swiss government intervention led to his release six months later. 1940 found Jacob in Paris where he had been interned by the French. He escaped again, this time to Lisbon. Yet again he was considered important enough to be kidnapped by the Gestapo and taken to imprisonment in Berlin where he died from the effects, in the Jewish hospital in February 1944.[19]

Pacifist complaints about Jewish reaction to the Holocaust assume that pacifist non-cooperation and propaganda, if properly undertaken, could have prevented the extermination of the Jews. But pacifism is not necessarily a solution. It is a course of action which justifies itself from its own inherent morality rather than in the end result.

A third major criticism of Jewish non-violent reaction to the Holocaust comes from psychologists who complain about the Jewish determination to carry on as usual in circumstances that were quite out of the ordinary and demanded a non-habitual response. Those children taken into non-Jewish homes who co-operated in the deception adapted admirably to all that was demanded of them by abnormal circumstances. Bettelheim accuses the father of Anne Frank of being unrealistic in his plans to hide so many people over an unforeseeable period. At the very least the family members should have scattered rather than remaining as one family unit.[20] Inge Scholl, surviving sister of Hans and Sophie, who wrote the White Rose leaflets, puts it differently: "Perhaps genuine heroism lies in deciding stubbornly to defend everyday things, the trivial and immediate, after having been bombarded with so much oratory about great deeds." A Dutchman who saved Jews in hiding expressed amazement at the willingness of the Jewish authorities to co-operate with the Germans rather than engage in subversion.[21] With hindsight their co-operation looks like collaboration. The phrase 'like sheep to the slaughter' is quoted out of context to suggest a mindless obedience.

Psalm 44 where the phrase is found is a protest poem with a strongly pacifist tone. It reasserts that it is God and God alone who fights for his people, and renounces the use of weapons. "For I trust not in my bow, neither can my sword save me." Then comes the reproach that, though the children of Israel have gloried in God and given thanks unto His name, even so "Thou hast given us like sheep to be eaten; And has scattered us among the nations." It is not the Jews who have behaved like sheep. Their God, having taken them metaphorically as His sheep, is now accused of treating them literally like sheep for the table. The psalmist insists that the people are not to blame. This is unjust punishment. "For Thy sake we are killed all the day/ We are accounted as sheep for the slaughter." The Hebrew (*Chashav*) does not mean to be counted. It means to be thought of or considered. The role of sheep is not one that the Jews take for themselves; it is the way they are perceived by others, not as human beings but as animals whose proper destiny is to be slaughtered. The role is one which the writer of the psalm decisively rejects. The misuse of this quotation reveals the way in which language has been misappropriated to make the Jews party to their own destruction. Yet the idealism of the original psalm contains the real dilemma of pacifism, an unrealistic expectation that ideal behaviour will necessarily achieve a particular desired result.

Clearly there exists a feeling that the Jews did not react in ways that now seem appropriate. It prompts one to ask what is it that they or we perceive as resistance? Perhaps Jewish response is seen in a negative light because the Holocaust was successful. We ourselves are unable to accept the reality of what happened and we search for ways of evading the outcome. It could be suggested that, unlike ourselves, the Jews of Europe were unable to evade the inconceivable reality that confronted them and that their non-violent responses constituted an unparalleled testimony to the ideal of peace and non-violence which is the Jewish inheritance. Jewish non-violence was remarkably consistent over a wide variety of Jewish belief and commitment and may reflect a quality in Judaism which should not be under-estimated.

Nitza Spiro has made a comparative study of the Jewish response to persecution from the Biblical period of Lamentations, through the Rabbinic period and during the Crusades. In the Biblical period the Jews fought wars, not always with happy results. Fighting was not a preferred course of action and was not regarded as holy. Iron which was used for making weapons was not to be used in the building of the altar. Because he was a soldier, the great King David was not permitted to build the temple; that task was left to his son Solomon, the wise. Lamentations responded to the defeat and destitution of war with that most celebrated of pacifist verses

Let him turn his cheek to him who smiteth him, and endure full measure of abuse;
     For the Lord will not cast off His servants for ever.[22]

The Hebrew is ambiguous. It could be a statement, as it is in the Authorised Version, or it could be a command. But the New Testament pacifist image of turning the other cheek, is already anticipated in this most despairing of Jewish biblical texts.

Spiro points out that following the Roman period, there was a profound reaction against armed rebellion which had always seemed to lead to disaster. The Jewish death toll following the Bar Kochba rebellion against Rome is given by Josephus as 600,000 out of a total population in Palestine of 2-2$\frac{1}{2}$ million.[23] After the Trajan revolt 112-115 AD, 1.2 million Jews were killed in Egypt alone.[24] The deaths were regarded as the result of resistance, that is self-inflicted, rather than as the result of enemy action. It became imperative to save lives, and compliance seemed to offer the best chance of survival.

In theological terms the Jews were paradoxically always putting themselves centre stage, shouldering the blame for each and every disaster. Jewish history like all other events was in the hands of God. Exile and persecution were seen as a just punishment for Jewish shortcomings. Persecution by non-Jews was very often regarded as an internal Jewish affair, a punishment from God. This narrow, inward looking view of events served as a psychological defence mechanism. If the cause of anti-Semitism could be identified within Jewish society, then at least there was some hope of the Jews being able to bring it under control. In the meantime Jewish religious survival depended on physical endurance; and survival of the people on religious observance. Holiness was what mattered and what must not be compromised. But Holiness itself excludes violence.

Hilberg, the impressive chronicler of the Holocaust, comments on the lack of armed resistance and sabotage among the Jewish arms workers.[25]

> The entire Jewish tradition hampers the development of a general hostility pattern. In the Jewish religion revenge is a task relegated to God. The Jewish community tends to frustrate every impetus to strike out in anguish. Anger is regarded as provocative in the sense that it may invite further hurt.[26]

The attitude is described in terms of the Jewish tradition but it is one that is familiar to any pacifist. If aggression provokes aggression then non-aggression should result in the avoidance of conflict. It is argued that the animal who submits to a stronger rival is not usually annihilated.

Jewish history suggested that to rebel costs lives; Nazi policy and ruthless reprisals reinforced this lesson. Wherever they went, the Germans gave defeated populations a chance to retain their own individuality in exchange for co-operative involvement in German policy. Italian and Danish authorities seem to have held on to their own integrity rather more successfully than groups who were less clearly differentiated from the German. German Jews still saw themselves as Germans. Isaiah Trunk, historian of the Judenrat, describes how the National Union of Jews in Germany (the *Reichsvertretung* and later the *Reichsvereinigung der Juden in Deutschland*) "hoped to come to terms with Hitler and make life for the Jews somehow bearable".[27] He implies that the leaders of the Jewish community did not take the threat of extermination seriously.

The survival of community structures was probably to the Jews themselves important evidence of Jewish survival. Jewish organisations took charge of the registration of Jews and the organisation of contingents to go East. Jewish bodies regulated Jewish education, food distribution and relations with the German authorities. There were German and Austrian Jews who after they were transported to Polish ghettos went on wearing their original Stars of David with *Jude* in German.[28] It was put down to snobbery but at the same time it was an honest insistence on their different identity because, once they were accommodated in Polish ghettos, the German Jews lost their own social and family structures[29] and were under the authority of the Eastern Jewish Ghetto organisations, in other words the German Jews became dependent.

Maintaining control over one's own communal affairs can be seen as an important element in retaining self-determination, taking decisions, acting within the dictates of one's own ethical or religious tradition. The resettlement actions and the gradual liquidation of the ghettoes always left open the possibility that, by co-operating with the Germans, lives would be saved.

This was the rationale which lay behind so many of the Jewish ghetto councils. Gens, ruler of Vilna Ghetto, faced dilemmas which forty years later still aroused great anger both in Israel and in the Jewish community in London when they were faithfully reproduced in the play *Ghetto* by Joshua Sobol. Gens's armed Jewish police enforced law and order in the ghetto and enforced selections in neighbouring towns. Whether this assisted the Nazis or merely avoided more ferocious Nazi intervention is still a controversial question. In the Channel Islands the worst excesses took place in Alderney, where the Germans took direct sole control, there remaining no alternative local structure after the Bailiwick of Guernsey evacuated the island.[30] What is clear is that when Jews deny the facts of their own involvement, or blame Jews for facilitating the Holocaust, it diverts attention from those who were truly responsible for the appalling events that were taking place. Co-operation is not collaboration.

The Jewish community endured the Nazi measures up to the point where life itself was threatened. In the thirties, Sereni found Jews were unwilling to leave Europe for Palestine. One should not assume that Jews were being wilfully blind to their situation. About fifteen Jews refused the opportunity to be evacuated from the Channel Islands before the German take-over, and one may jump to the conclusion that this was foolhardy. It is salutary to be told that some of these Jews were nurses who deliberately remained in their posts. German Jews, who believed their lives were in danger, exploited all possibilities of escape. But entry visas to settle elsewhere were hard to come by. There is no evidence that emigration could or should have been arranged for the total Jewish population of continental Europe. In other words the Jewish leaders had to continue to operate as Leaders within a no choice situation.

Powerless in their dealings with the Germans, Jewish leaders saw themselves in a protective relationship with their own people, keeping selections to a minimum, themselves retaining some vestige of control over who was or was not selected in the hope perhaps of maintaining essential services.

Compliance at gun-point is not pacifism. Everywhere the Germans were skilled at exacting compliance from defeated populations. In occupied France, for instance, reprisals were carried out after feats of resistance. Innocent civilians were shot. Resistance was seen as opposition. The Jews were manipulated in the same way. Klok, a baptised Jew and member of the Polish Socialist Party, was said to have assaulted a Polish constable while defending a clandestine radio station, in Warsaw, December 1939. The Jewish community was ordered to hand him over, otherwise five hundred of the Jewish intelligentsia would be arrested. Dr. Weiss protested "His name was entirely unknown to Jewish circles. .... These unfortunate Jews were, of course, completely innocent of the whole affair but this did not prevent their arrest." Klok was a young man about twenty years old, and according to the Nazis he was the head of a secret organisation directed against them. He was obviously disowned by the Jews not simply because he had a Christian identity but because of his resistance work, in which they were unfortunately and unjustly implicated. The Jews protested their own innocence, but they were seeking refuge in being innocent by German standards. In Jewish law the assumption had always been that to obey the law of the land in the diaspora would ensure survival. The Polish Jews seem to be betraying their own cause, but only because they were as yet unaware that Nazi law made no distinction between the Jew who assaulted a policeman and one who did not. Observing Nazi law could not save a Jew; the law itself condemned all Jews. Jewish confusion noticeably reflects the same confusion among the Nazis. The Jews were accused of a particular act of subversion and punished for failing to hand over its perpetrator. The inference is that a Jew might indeed survive provided he did not engage in clandestine resistance, and that the non-violent tradition of the Jews was still appropriate to their situation.[31]

The Polish Jews in Chelmno felt that the German Jews were too willing to comply with orders. They arrived in Lódz provisionless because they had obediently left their luggage "to be sent on afterwards" when ordered to do so. But Hildgard Henshel, wife of Morris Henshel, last head of the Berlin Community, described the round up and evacuation from Berlin. "The evacuation had indeed become a reality and many took Veronal to put an end to all doubts. ..... The behaviour of the victims was admirable. It was clear to everyone that resistance was impossible; the only form of resistance was suicide."[32] For others however, the only resistance was to stay alive. An orderly evacuation held the possibility of survival.

Some rabbis, as Leo Baeck did in Theresienstadt, wished to spare their people the mental torture of knowing the truth and so withheld their own discovery of the Holocaust. Similarly the remarkable Janusz Korczak refused the Nazi offer of freedom and remained with the children of his orphanage as they were transported to the gas chambers, deliberately reassuring them in order to avert panic and allow them to die with dignity. Evidence to the Eichmann trial[33] shows the havoc that could be wrought in the Nazi routines when children were left to their own resources. Boys refused to take off their clothes or use the numbered pegs before going to the so-called 'shower rooms'. Some of them even managed to respond when a boy from the Sonderkommando, a Jew himself, told them not to let the Germans see how frightened they were but to sing. They sang the prayers and songs they knew from their Jewish homes.

The story illustrates how it is possible to see the same actions in a both positive and negative light. Keeping people calm and sane could be seen as a humane step designed to prevent panic and confusion. But loss of order might have hampered Nazi plans for evacuation. Were Jews given a false sense of security because they were following instructions from their own leaders? Rudolf Hoess, Kommandant of Auschwitz, described women caring for others, calmly. Women who became hysterical were shot.

Maintaining normality became a matter of principle. The intellectual, artistic and religious dimensions of normal life in some of the Polish ghettos or in the transit camp Theresienstadt were a defence of human values against a less than human enemy. Jews continued to paint, to draw, to compose, to write diaries. In Theresienstadt Raphael Schächter directed Verdi's Requiem with an orchestra and 150 singers, even though few of those who were there at the first rehearsal also survived to perform.

The camp and the ghetto appeared to have a permanent Jewish existence of their own. A miniature society existed that could survive the loss of part of its population even when that loss was inevitable and arbitrary. Survivors barely conceived the demise of the unit itself. Once again one is forced to ask what constitutes non-violent resistance. Community leaders often saw their role as one of damage limitation; their aim became one of ensuring daily life continued to meet with German approval. The community character survived though individuals within it were unsaveable.

Non-violent and spiritual resistance was not the monopoly of the religious. Psychologists and doctors continued to make observations and plan research even in the camps. The Dutch physician Elie Cohen who survived to publish his observations on Human Behaviour in the Concentration Camp spoke of a medical thesis written from inner necessity.[34] Victor Frankl was another who persisted in his work. He emphasises man's need to find meaning and he quotes Nietzsche on man's "need for an aim, a goal, a Why. He who has a why to live for can bear with almost any *how*."[35] But there is a moral emptiness at the heart of this psychology. The Nazi had an over-riding aim: it was to serve the Führer, to execute the final solution as smoothly and as efficiently as possible. Jewish non-violence was attached not to any aim but to living in accordance with one's own values, whether secular or religious.

Primo Levi was perhaps mistaken in making a distinction between himself, an unbeliever, and the religious or political idealists. "They had a key and a point of leverage, a millennial tomorrow so that there might be some sense in sacrificing themselves, a place in heaven or on earth where justice and compassion had won." One of the most evocative acts of spiritual resistance must be Levi's own. In Auschwitz, exhausted and starving, he tried to convey to a young Frenchman walking to work at his side the significance of the Canto of Ulysses in Dante's Inferno. Levi, who was himself to become a poet and notable writer, communicated Dante's inspiration and craftsmanship, the vagaries of translation, the levels of meaning lost and found in Dante's poetry, and his own Italian classical education. Doing justice to Dante, and showing compassion towards his companion, Levi gave all he had to give. Later in *The Drowned and the Saved,* Levi admits his debt to his culture, to those lines of Dante "which made it possible for me to re-establish a link with the past, saving it from oblivion and reinforcing my identity". Levi saw this identity of his as secular and Italian rather than as Jewish but that is to narrow the concept of a Jewish identity, to remove it from the way in which Jews really live their lives. Levi's identity was that of a Jew, a highly educated Jewish Italian intellectual. Because the Jews of Europe were exterminated as Jews, we tend to define the loss as the destruction of Jewishness. Jews are part of society. Levi represents that significant part of the intelligentsia of Europe which was being wiped out.

Levi admits his own aversion to violence, not as a virtue but as a fact of life. He describes camp inmates who found dignity in returning blow for blow. "Here I must admit to my absolute inferiority: I have never known how to 'return the blow', not out of evangelical saintliness or intellectual aristocracy, but due to intrinsic incapacity...Trading punches is an experience I do not have, as far back as I can go in memory; nor can I say I regret not having it. It is indeed because of this that my career as a Partisan was so brief, painful, stupid and tragic: I had taken on a role that was not mine."[36] Levi knew his own role: it was to teach a Frenchman about Dante in the death camp; physical violence was not in his character. Given the proverbial midrashic choice between the book and the sword, Levi chose the book.

When the Talmud forbids Jews to raise arms in exile it is not pacifism for its own sake. It is a practical policy induced by fear of repercussions on the Jewish community. The law of the state is law; it is a matter of life or death that Jews should always comply. Hasidic stories from Poland show how ingrained was the non-violence of the Jews and how this was seen as a specifically Jewish quality which distinguished them from the host communities. On one level Poles and Jews did fight together amicably against the Tsar ('For your freedom and for ours') but oral history reveals how far this went against the Jewish grain. In 1905 when Jews became strikers and revolutionaries against the Tsar there was amazement. "Jews what is it you demand? Is shooting correct Jewish behaviour?"[37] A parable by Shtaynberg makes the same moral point. One day the needle met the bayonet, the needle was terrified but managed to ask what it was that the bayonet pierced. "People, people," came the reply. The needle laughed at the ridiculous reply. I make shirts and dresses and suits out of cloth. But what can you make out of people?" One Jew thought this story worth telling to an SS officer[38] but in the camps two cultures had met, the military and the non-violent, each of which was incomprehensible to the other. For Nitza Spiro points out that the non-violent tradition was not altogether negative in its effects. "By freeing the mind from aggression and the need to retaliate, the Jew was able to concentrate on the positive aspects of Jewish values which supplied his life with meaning and distinguished him from outside society."[39]

The survival of this spirit means that even today it is still possible to find orthodox criticism of the Warsaw Ghetto uprising. The resistance of two hundred people, split into twenty-two groups and holed up in bunkers cannot be compared with the revolt in Warsaw in 1944. "A revolt under circumstances that offer no chance for victory can be undertaken only by people who have despaired of life. .... This is clearly suicide. .... To die a hero's death just for the sake of dying a hero's death is not compatible with the Jewish faith even if no one else is endangered by it." The uprising which is so widely acclaimed coincided with the liquidation of the ghetto and probably lost more lives than it saved. It could not have been carried out by Torah Jews.

> Heroism under such circumstances is not to die a false hero's death, something any foolhardy youth can do in a hopeless situation. Heroism in these times is to live like a hero in the ocean of suffering, and by doing so to fulfil the Divinely imposed role of heroism.
>
> The supreme inner heroism is not to give up a single moment of life because of outer pressure. Only Jews who believe in Gd★ are capable of such heroism. Only Jews who know how to value a minute of life for what it is, especially a moment of life clouded by suffering and trials, a moment of elevated life like our brethren in the ghettos.[40]

Jewish behaviour in the Holocaust was a product of this tradition and Rabbi Albert Axelrad, a Reform champion of Jewish conscientious objection, has no hesitation in calling it heroism.[41] The Hasidic writer quoted above shares his view. "Let the orthodox Jewish writers establish a memorial to those heroes of the spirit in

★Orthodox Jews do not employ the full name of God; Gd and Hashem are used as substitutes. Where quoting such sources, I have respected this practice, and also the abbreviated Common Era dating of their journals which they provide alongside the full Jewish date.

the ghettos and camps, who have sanctified and are sanctifying Hashem in their lives and who have sanctified and are sanctifying Hashem in their deaths. Let them not skip over the inner heroism which even secular Jews attained, in whom a ray of love was ignited during those great moments. Let them not long for false heroism, which has no basis in Judaism."[42] The non-violence was not accidental nor that of a splinter movement. It was the product of a pervading ethic, common to every Jew.

Asked whether traditional Jewish non-violence was moral choice or simply expedience, one must answer both. Jewish tradition is simultaneously ethical and pragmatic. In Judaism there is no separation of the real and the ideal. At every painful step Jewish institutional response to the Holocaust was an attempt to mitigate its effects. Non-violence often seemed to hold out the hope of survival. But the affirmation of a Jewish identity went beyond this, into an area where rationality no longer holds sway.

> When one views events from a Torah perspective, the perception is diametrically different from the experience of seeing the same thing through secular eyes. The Torah Jew is inculcated from early childhood with a special sense of *areivus* (responsibility) of one Jew for the other and for all mankind. When one's heart is overflowing with love for Gd, then that love naturally flows over to man who was created in the image of Gd. The tighter one clings to his roots as a Jew, the more profoundly one thinks and acts as a Jew.[43]

Jewish secular non-violent resistance was matched by those who recklessly continued to carry on with religious practice even at moments of great peril. For the Germans unleashed tremendous fury on Judaism itself. As they invaded Poland, they burned synagogues and prayer houses. Jews were marched through the streets wearing their prayer shawls, the orthodox were deprived of their side locks or shorn of half their beards to make them look ridiculous, Bible scrolls were burned. In the Warsaw Ghetto the Germans closed all synagogues, *yeshivas* (religion schools) and *mikvehs* (baths), supposedly to prevent epidemics. Public prayer was forbidden even in small *minyans*, the groups of ten men, which in orthodox Judaism is the minimum number needed for public prayer.[44] In Wloclawek which had a Jewish population of 20,000 the Germans raided Jewish prayer meetings on the Eve of the Day of

Atonement 1939, "dragged them to the barracks in ritual garb. They forced the Jews to sweep the floor of the barracks with their praying shawls, while they took photographs of them and jeered at the Jewish religion".[45] A decree in Warsaw introduced penalties ranging from ten years in prison to the death penalty for visiting the *mikveh*, the ritual bath to which observant orthodox women went every month after menstruation before resuming marital relations. Women risked their lives to continue with the ritual. Some went to small towns where the baths were still open, some bribed officials.[46] Other women pleaded for the right to go to the *mikveh* before being executed.[47] Orthodox Judaism demands meticulous observance of commandments which give religious regulation of every day life. Some Jews persisted in the rigid observance of this Law even in the appalling circumstances of the Holocaust. Women were desperate to circumcise their own children before they too died.[48]

Jewish obstinacy in the face of religious persecution is not unique. The persecution of French Protestants in the eighteenth century and the forced conversion of their children bore similarities to the persecution of the Jews.[49] This suffering is said to have established some sort of solidarity between the Jews and French in Protestant areas during the occupation.[50] Pasteur Aimé Bonifas who was himself deported to Buchenwald has described the undercover Christian observance in the camps, including even an ordination service.[51]

Jewish religious obduracy must not be regarded as primitive or unthinking. Victor Frankl describes the comfort he found in praying, giving one man a proper burial in the last days of Auschwitz. Jews belong to a questioning tradition and compliance was by no means a foregone conclusion. There were instances of pious Jews violating the Sabbath or eating food forbidden by Jewish law, deliberately retaliating against God for deserting His people. The prisoners in Ghetto Heidemühle in the Kalisz echoed the outrage of Psalm 44 and arranged a trial with God as the accused.[52] But the concept of God was still there; Jews still saw the Holocaust only as a Jewish religious issue.

The survival of the religion sometimes seems to take precedence over the survival of men. A Hasidic Jew who had escaped a massacre wilfully returned to his ruined home to bury the dead. Assimilated German Jews were just as obdurate. The child of a Jewish father recalled that after the Grosse Aktion in 1943 there were only eight adults left in their Berlin community, all of them married to non-Jewish women. There were three part-Jewish children who used to help Rabbi Martin Riesenburger arrange secret services on Rosh Hashanah and Yom Kippur.[53] Many Jews risked their lives to attend these services. At the Eichmann trial one witness, Kleinman, described how a fourteen year old boy was beaten because he brought some prayer books to the hut. The boy did not complain. "It was worth it. I brought my friends a few prayer books so they could pray."[54] Jews remained faithful to their God. Hostages prayed at the point of death. "I remember Oh God and I tremble when I see every city built on its hill top, and the City of God degraded down to the lowest depth. And despite all this, we belong to the Merciful God and our eyes look to the merciful God."[55]

Religion retained an integrity all its own. Jews put on prayer shawls and *tefillin*, binding the law to their arms and foreheads, as they went to their deaths. One SS Colonel Paul Blobel failed to understand the serenity of Jews in the face of death. "They apparently do not value human life. Therefore they were able to march so calmly."[56]

Life is the highest value in the Jewish tradition. There is a Jewish tradition of martyrdom. In Jewish traditions that envisaged an afterlife, martyrdom ensured an instant entry to Heaven but Rabbis ruled that during the Holocaust it was more important to preserve the body against the enemy wishing to destroy it. But one cannot generalise. Some individuals did choose to die; there were values which were worth dying for. Rabbi David Shapiro refused Catholic offers of shelter in Warsaw and stayed with his people.[57] For many individuals, staying alive as long as possible was not an end in itself. When the Kozhenitser Rebbe died a natural death even that was seen as religious victory. "At that time (1941) it was considered a great honour and divine reward to pass into eternity in a natural manner and thus avoid the sadistic Nazi torturers."[58] But Jews facing the inevitable death at mass shootings or in the camps yet again appropriated to themselves ways of the explaining their manner of dying. Religion endowed the deaths with meaning.

"'We should not be mournful,' said Shlomo Zelichowski to the Jews of Zdunsk Wola, 'but rather be proud of our sacrifice. Maybe this will be accepted as an expiation for other Jews.'"[59] The word Holocaust means burnt offering. Many Jews find it an unacceptable word for the Nazi destruction of the Jews because it implies a God who would find such a sacrifice meaningful. None the less there were orthodox Jews who regarded their own deaths as atonement either for their own sins or for the sins of other Jews. By 'other' Jews they implied those Jews who had assimilated, Jews whose lapse from strict fundamentalism was seen by some as contributing to the Holocaust. Another interpretation lent meaning to Jewish deaths by suggesting they would in some way further God's purpose for His people. Interpreted in this light, the killing of the Jews might be seen as a necessary condition for the establishment of the state of Israel in 1948. It is often said that without the Holocaust there would be no state. One survivor suggested that Jews had been 'chosen' to die in order to ultimately defeat Hitler. If Hitler had not wasted his resources on killing the Jews he might have won the war.[60] Others explained that Jewish suffering in the Holocaust was to prove the failure of Christianity. One Holocaust survivor who retained his faith speaks for many: "Our religion is proven true because it works. Our religion never permitted us to commit the crimes that their religion permitted them to commit against us."[61]

The Nazi aim was to dehumanise, and the Jews defeated this by remaining Jews. Their often foolhardy behaviour was a form of spiritual resistance best explained perhaps by these words:

> The only thing that remains is the I in me. I find suddenly some strange pleasure in knowing that when I die, I will die the same, unchanged, as when I was me. It matters very much. Yes, as I was. Keep that last thing. Hang onto it as to the last wall.[62]

The integrity of one's own identity became paramount and for most Jews that excluded violence. Violence was identified with the Nazis. To behave like a Nazi was to become un-Jewish.

"Are you still the Chosen people, Herr Rabbiner?" demanded a Nazi officer in Bergen Belsen after knocking down the Klausenberger Rebbe. "Zicher, to be sure. As long as we are not the oppressors, we are the Chosen people."[63]

There is a difficulty in concluding with this Jewish witness. The special Jewish dimension of so much Holocaust material might suggest that Jews reacted differently from other victims of the death camps. All victims of the Nazis who died without retaliation made a statement that must be respected. But in the end how people are seen by others and how they see themselves are interrelated. Jews died in the Holocaust because they were Jews. They reacted as human beings and Jews. Jewish reaction on the whole was a demonstration of dignified non-violence and non-retaliation. One may recognise how these non-violent attitudes were based on and are explained by Jewish identity and Jewish religious belief. They were worthy of the tradition and in keeping with it.

Chapter 8
A Crisis of Conscience
Abraham Heschel and the War in Vietnam

The thought that I live a life of peace and non-violence turns out to be an illusion. I have been decent in tiny matters on a tiny scale, but have become vicious on a large scale. In my own eyes my existence appears to be upright, but in the eyes of my victims my very being has become a nightmare.

***

Vietnam is a personal problem. To speak about God and remain silent on Vietnam is blasphemous.[1]

Abraham Joshua Heschel has been called "a jeweller of words", and "a son of the prophets".[2] He wrote in a religious language of his own creating. Like the generations of Hasidic rabbis from whom he was descended, Heschel offered people immediate access to God. As he put it in his famous book on the Sabbath, "The higher goal of spiritual living is not to amass a wealth of information but to face sacred moments."[3] Heschel presented Jews with a cycle of Sabbaths and seasons, of *mitzvot* and rituals, Jewish tradition so revitalised and personalised by his imagery that the heavenly became accessible. This makes Heschel's work both immediately inviting, and deeply mysterious. We are to be religious Jews, to find spiritual opportunities within our lives. Heschel immersed himself in a Judaism which explores the Hasidic relationship between God and man, and in which "no part of life does not share the divine".[4] Our wonder at God's creation and our own existence within it relates us to God who has created us and has His purpose for us.

One may entertain a niggling doubt that Heschel's mood of wonder is sometimes too optimistic. Those who are incapacitated, unable to see, who are suffering or clinically depressed may not share Heschel's "radical amazement".[5] Atmosphere is not everything. But Heschel himself survived the Holocaust still able to affirm the psalmists' experience of a human existence conducive to faith in God. "Life is His and ours. He has not thrown us out into the world and abandoned us. He shares in our toil; He is partner to our anxieties. A man in need is not the exclusive and ultimate subject of need: God is in need with him." For Heschel the intimate significance of a candle, a prayer, a religious dimension communicates itself as a universal intimation of what man ought to be. "Jewish existence is living shared with God. The quest for right living, the question of what is to be done right now, right here, is the authentic core of Jewish religion. It has been the main theme of Jewish literature, from the prophets till the times of the Hasidim, and it has been explored with a sense of urgency, as if life were a continuous state of emergency."[6]

Heschel's writings appealed to Christians as much as to Jews. Unlike Harris or even Magnes, Heschel was, in theological terms, centre stage, an individual and respected voice in contemporary theological debate. At a time when the Neo-Orthodox were reiterating religion based on traditional authority, Heschel and the Christians who admired him claimed a direct awareness of God and a personal relationship to Him. Steeped as Heschel was in the normative texts of Judaism, he wrote, "I am not just a dwelling place for other people, an echo of the past... I disagree with those who think of the present in the past tense. I have one talent and that is the capacity to be tremendously surprised, surprised at life, at ideas. This to me is the supreme Hasidic imperative."[7]

Heschel was born in 1907 into a Hasidic Rabbinic family and he himself became a rabbi in Poland very young. But he continued from his classical Jewish studies to a Yiddish grammar school and then to Western style philosophical and religious studies in Berlin. The rise of Nazism drove Heschel from Germany to teach in Poland from where he was again rescued in 1939 by his professorial appointment at the Hebrew Union College in Cincinnati. Reform Judaism was not where Heschel belonged and after the war he became Professor of Jewish ethics and mysticism at the more traditional Conservative Jewish Theological Seminary of America where he remained until his death in 1972.

Heschel's books are still in print and still affectionately used. His theology of "radical amazement" remains a source of inspiration. His words on Vietnam are all but forgotten. Yet at the time Heschel was regarded as "the supreme Jewish voice and leader on

Vietnam"[8]. He asked how it was possible to believe in God and not to speak about Vietnam.

Heschel was not just a scholar and mystic. True to his own theology, he involved himself on behalf of the poor and the oppressed in civil rights and in black issues. Opposition to the war in Vietnam was for Heschel part of his obligation as a Jew. With Daniel Berrigan and Richard Neuhaus (Catholic and Protestant), he became a founder and national co-chairman of Clergy and Laity Concerned about Vietnam, and addressed the conference of 2,500 clergy which met in Washington DC at the end of January 1967. He personally pledged himself to risk fine or imprisonment to help conscientious objectors. After American withdrawal he pressed for amnesty and at the inter-religious Conference on Amnesty in Washington, March 1972, shortly before his death, he delivered a talk on The Theological, Biblical and Ethical Considerations of Amnesty.[9] The Jewish Peace Fellowship continue to put his name with that of Leo Baeck, Abraham Cronbach and Isidor Hoffman beneath the list of their current executive committee.[10]

Heschel's objection to war is not an afterthought; it arises inevitably from the main body of his philosophy. Consciousness of man reveals God and man's relationship with God imposes a moral duty. This transcendent meaning demonstrates that what we do must also be meaningful. The presence of God is experienced primarily in other human beings, so it is they who have an absolute claim on our conscience. "The fear you must feel of offending or hurting a human being must be as ultimate as your fear of God. An act of violence is an act of desecration."[11] Heschel reasserts the Jewish foundation of something postulated more directly in Christianity: God is seen in man and the Holy is expressed in human existence. Heschel reminds us that Jews when praying speak of the eternal life which God has planted within us. "The law of the Sabbath tries to direct the body and mind to the dimension of the Holy. It tries to teach us that man stands not only in a relation to nature but in a relation also to the Creator of nature."[12]

Because we are created by God we do not own ourselves or our own existence. Both we owe to God. We are commanded into being and with that command go other requirements. We have a moral responsibility. We are answerable to God. This is our conscience, a seemingly non-Jewish concept given orthodox credentials. Heschel does not rest his argument on the legal details of *halakha*. Behind the *halakha*, inspiring and informing it, is the *agada*, the non-legal writing of the Torah which discloses the relationship between man and God; all we do must be compatible "with our certainty of the compassion of God". God's concern is for justice, compassion and love.

Heschel called his essay *The Moral Outrage of Vietnam* and he made his religious position clear.

> Prayer then is radical commitment, a dangerous involvement in the life of God......
>
> The most basic way in which all men may be divided is between those who believe that war is unnecessary and those who believe that war is inevitable; between those to whom the sword is a symbol of honour and those ... seeking to convert swords into ploughshares.

Heschel denied that war was inevitable,

> Worse than war is the belief in the inevitability of war. There is no such thing as inevitable war.[13]

Heightening his argument with his own unique idiom, Heschel has striking things to say about issues that are problematic for modern pacifists. Modern warfare is waged by modern democracies. Heschel admits that most of us prefer to disregard what governments do on our behalf. "The atrocities committed in our name are too horrible to be credible... So we bear graciously other people's suffering." The distancing of political decision-making means that "Our presence in Vietnam has become a national nightmare, our actions are forced, we dislike what we do."

"We must continue to remind ourselves that in a free society, all are involved in what some are doing. *Some are guilty, all are responsible.*" The italics are Heschel's. Heschel reasserts the need for the individual to find his own unique voice. The depersonalisation of war should not be an alibi for individual helplessness. "Modern war is a mechanical operation. But peace is a personal effort, requiring deep commitment, hard, honest vision, wisdom and patience, facing one another as human beings, elasticity rather than dogmatism."

Heschel speaks as a Jew for peace but far from suggesting that this sets him apart from other human beings, he identifies himself as a human being and specifically as Vietnamese. "This is the demand of the hour: not to rest until – by excluding fallacies, stereotypes, prejudices, exaggerations which perpetual contention and the consequent hostilities breed – we succeed in reaching the people of Vietnam as brothers." Adamantly he rejects the generalisation, the stereotype which classifies 'the other' and creates the enemy.

"Though not a native of Vietnam, ignorant of its language and traditions, I am involved in the plight of the Vietnamese." To the Christian pacifist a universalist response comes naturally. For a thinker as distinctively Jewish as Heschel, this is a significant statement. Heschel rejects that tendency in Judaism to concern itself only or primarily with the Jewish interest. He refuses to separate himself from humanity,

> At this moment praying for peace in Vietnam we are spiritually Vietnamese. Their agony is our affliction, their hope is our commitment.
> God is present wherever men are afflicted.
> Where is God present now?
> We do not know how to cry, we do not know how to pray!
> Our conscience is so timid, our words so faint, our mercy so feeble.
> O Father have mercy upon us.[14]

Robert McAfee Brown, Protestant and Professor of Religion at Stanford, has described how he and his Stanford colleague, the Catholic Michael Novak, invited Heschel to join them and contribute to *Vietnam: Crisis of Conscience*. They wanted to address the American religious communities with a book written by a Catholic, Protestant and a Jew. Heschel was a much revered spokesman in inter-faith relations, and inter-faith dialogue inspired the religious peace movement.

In 1955 Will Herberg suggested that the three monotheistic religions co-existed in America, each subscribing to the national religious identity, a moral consensus. His book, *Protestant, Catholic, Jew*[15] has become a classic text in the sociology of American Judaism. Theologians and sociologists were taking a fresh look at the relationship between religion and the state. While the Vietnam War was in progress the sociologist, Robert Bellah, began to publish his piercing observation of Civil Religion in America, those rituals, symbols and ethical norms which represented the values of the nation.[16] The Vietnam war could be regarded as the assertion of

American values against the quite different values of the communist world.

When Vietnam was partitioned under the Geneva Accord of 1954 the United States refused to subscribe because the North was to be governed by a Communist regime. In the South, a Catholic, Diem, became Prime Minister, but with so little popular support that two years later he suspended the local democratic system in the villages. By 1961 when Kennedy became President of the United States, communist guerilla warfare in South Vietnam had assumed global significance. If Vietnam fell to the communists, Laos would follow and Cambodia, then Thailand, Indonesia, Japan and the Philippines. It was believed that the outcome of the conflict in Vietnam would finally decide the future of the free world and that the security of the United States itself was at risk. The orthodox Jewish community in America accepted this domino theory. Although there were small demonstrations in Israel against the war, Israel supported American action in Vietnam. It was generally felt that in Vietnam, as in the Middle East, Herberg's nation of religion and democracy stood against the Godless forces of Communism.

In 1961 President Diem was re-elected but he remained in power only with the help of American military advisers, the helicopter pilots, who ferried his troops. By late 1962 there were 12,000 American advisers in Vietnam.

Vietnam, like America, was a multi-cultural, multi-ethnic society. There were both Vietnamese and Chinese communities. There were Buddhists and a Catholic minority as well as Communists. There were professional people assimilated to western culture, very often French educated. The American GI was not fighting the faceless oriental Gook he imagined. Like the United States, Vietnam was populated by individuals with complex religious, political, social and cultural ties.

Religious protest against the war began in Vietnam itself. Mahayanna Buddhism had a historic relationship to the tenth century Vietnamese struggle for independence.[17] Buddhist opposition was provoked when Diem refused to allow the flying of flags on Buddhas's birthday in 1963. Between June and August that year six Buddhist monks set fire to themselves in protest. Diem promised to make concessions but instead, in August his men raided Buddhist centres. Thirty monks were injured and 1,400 people arrested in Saigon in disturbances and protests.

In November 1963 the Americans sought to provide stable government in Saigon by assisting an army coup in which Diem was assassinated. In the same month President Kennedy was killed and his successor, President Johnson, felt that he could not afford to lose control in Vietnam. American combat troops were secretly deployed. The following Spring, 1964, an *ad hoc* committee of young people in New Haven Connecticut, the May 2nd Committee, organised the first protest march.

At that early date of 1964 the Central Conference of American Rabbis (CCAR) also called for a negotiated settlement but the secret U.S. peace package with Hanoi did not materialise. North Vietnam was bombed and less than a year later, in March 1965, 3,500 Marines landed at Da Nang. In June 1965 American military involvement was no longer secret; the State Department announced that troops were to be sent into direct combat.

Two American Christians, a Quaker and a Catholic, burned themselves to death in protest. It is interesting that no Jews seem to have killed themselves in sympathy. This form of Buddhist protest would be out of keeping with Jewish pacifism. Not all protest was so horrifying. Students for a Democratic Society sponsored draft resistance; 35,000 people marched on Washington to press for a negotiated settlement.

At this point the anti-war movement reflected neither majority American nor majority Jewish opinion. The CCAR was consciously moving ahead of popular opinion, when it declared in 1965 that there could be no military solution to the fundamental social and economic problems of Vietnam. Polls between January and August 1966 "showed that a majority of Jews supported the war (56 per cent) although, in comparison with other groups, a relatively large percentage (34 per cent) did feel the war was wrong."[18] The Committee on Justice, Peace and Church-State Relations declared itself "proud of the vigor with which the Reform movement has expressed its moral distress concerning the war in Vietnam and its will for a cessation of the conflict .... placing us squarely at the side of those Protestant and Catholic groups which have expressed their religious concern at this issue." The rabbis felt that U.S.

government policy was forcing its citizens "again and again to violate our own American ideals of liberty and self-determination." Their objection was to war itself:

> We recoil in moral horror from the use of obliteration bombing, of napalm floods of fire, of defoliation and the destruction of crops with the consequent threat of famine engulfing the innocent, [all prohibited by Biblical law on warfare] even when they are used against a known opponent. How much more do we reject these abominable techniques when they fall indiscriminately on the supposed foe and on the non-combatant inhabitants of a land that has not known peace for twenty years. The cheapening of human life in this process is inevitably linked with the brutalisation of American youth sent to use the tools of violence under the banner of our country's ideals.[19]

Rabbi Eisendrath (1902-73), for many years the energetic and controversial Executive Director of the Union of American Hebrew Congregations, had been a pacifist for most of his life.[20] In January 1966, with Rabbi Weinstein (President of the CCAR) and Rabbi Balfour Brickner, he joined the National Committee of Clergy and Laity Concerned about Vietnam [21] and his Conference lecture of 1966 explored the ecumenical aspects of pacifism. "We must root out of our preaching and our teaching all our once vaunted superiority, as supposedly evinced by our alleged non-pacifist tradition, over the so-called exclusively Christian gospel of turning the other cheek. In the first place, I am not so certain that this distinction is altogether true – even historically." He went on to quote what he called the explicit admonition in the Book of Proverbs. " 'If thine enemy be hungry give him bread to eat, and if he be thirsty give him water to drink,' and its still more exacting rabbinic commentary: 'If thine enemy rise up early in the morning and come to thine house to slay thee, even then, if he be hungry give him bread to eat, and if he be thirsty give him water to drink'."[22]

Definitions of conscientious objection had expanded since 1945. The Encyclical *Pacem in Terris* issued by Pope John XXIII in March 1963 provided new authority for Catholics to be conscientious objectors. The Just War concept existed in Christianity as well as in Judaism. In 1966 the Committee on Selective Service recognised "that there is a growing body of opinion that the term 'conscientious objection' should now apply also to those who do not reject all war but who refuse to participate in a particular war." (This is known as selective objection, not to be confused with Selective Service, the U.S. draft system which compelled some men to serve while exempting others.) The Peace Committee were split on the issue of selective objection when they reported back the following year, and the principle was not clearly recognised by American law.

The definition of conscience was also being extended to include those without a formal religious belief.[23] The American Civil Liberties Union were pressing for conscientious objection based on moral, social, philosophical or religious grounds, and it was suggested that the time had come for the Conference to broaden their own statement of 1936. Quakers were dubious about non-religious objection and the Schecter case in Baltimore later established that American objection still had to have a religious basis.[24] But there was recognition that conscientious objection to war was not a Christian monopoly. Membership of the Jewish Peace Fellowship rose. In 1965 Rabbi Michael Robinson became President of the JPF and it is said that it was he who insisted on affiliation with the Fellowship of Reconciliation which took place in December.

FOR originated in the friendship of a Lutheran German and a Quaker Englishman before the First World War. Its basis was explicitly Christian but it had acquired individual Jewish members who found its overall aims acceptable.[25] The American and later the International Fellowship of Reconciliation took the view that, if peace was to be meaningful on a world scale, it involved finding common ground between pacifists of many different beliefs. Thirty-six rabbis were among the signatories of an FOR advertisement appealing for an end to the war which appeared in the New York Times, January 23, 1966.[26] IFOR became multi-denominational and has ever since provided much needed support to the minority Jewish Peace movement affiliated to it.[27]

Multi-faith opposition in IFOR was reflecting the protest movement in Vietnam. There Buddhists believed that all men were brothers on a level that was above divisions of race or culture.[28] Rabbi Jacob Weinstein described how he and other members of the Emergency Clergymen's Committee for Vietnam, had met the Buddhist leader, the venerable Tic Nat Hanh, in a school house on the outskirts of Saigon. Tic Nat Hanh had written to Martin Luther King, appealing to him and all religious leaders in America to protest against the war. "The monks who burned themselves did not aim at the death of the oppressors but only at a change in their policy. Their enemies are not man. They are intolerance, fanaticism, dictatorship, cupidity, hatred and discrimination which lie at the heart of man. .... Intolerance, hatred and discrimination .... these are the real enemies of man – not man himself. In our unfortunate fatherland we are trying to say desperately: do not kill man, even in man's name. Please kill the real enemies of man which are present everywhere, in our very hearts and minds."[29]

Eisendrath and his colleagues went too far for some of their congregants in opposing Vietnam. The celebrated establishment Emanu-El congregation of New York withdrew from the Union and it was estimated that 25 Reform Congregations supported them, four per cent of the total.[30]

Reform Rabbis were themselves making a conscientious objection by refusing to serve as military chaplains. During the civil war the great Reform Rabbi, Isaac Meyer Wise, founder of the Conference and of the Hebrew Union College had "attacked the military chaplaincy as a violation of (the American constitutional separation of) church and state. But he argued that if there were to be chaplains at all, rabbis should be included."[31] Military chaplains were part of the uniformed army service paid by the government. Army regulations meant that chaplains were not free to comment on political issues. The rabbi in uniform was subordinate to his commanding officer. Since 1950, in order to meet the needs of Jews in the forces, the chaplaincy draft had been mandatory in the Reform movement. The result was that over the years about 40 per cent of newly ordained rabbis had been drafted to serve for two years without alternative.

Pacifists were granted exemption provided they gave notice of their objection on first entering the rabbinic colleges. Nine of the current students had been granted conscientious objector status. There was deferment for postgraduate study, and rejection of those physically unfit to serve. Through 1966 and 1967 the Committee on Chaplaincy and the President of the Conference emphasised that the need for Reform rabbis in the forces must over-rule any objection they had to the war. Yet of the 1968 class of 20 men, only four were under orders or awaiting orders; five were exempt because beyond the government quota. Rabbi Eugene Lipman admitted that very little attention had been paid to the actual working of the system. It had become almost a condition of ordination and the selection of chaplains had been made by a final-year lottery. In his judgement "the CCAR should have questioned the morality of this system a long time ago."

"You know how it is. You want to look and you don't want to look," wrote Michael Herr, graphic reporter of the Vietnam war.[32] It was some of the chaplains who brought the war home to the Conference. The chaplains as part of the army had seen the war for themselves. They had worked in the battle zone where "pacification was another word for war," where they saw the terror, the corpses, the going crazy.

The churches did not have a mandatory chaplaincy and recent decisions by the Yeshiva and Rabbinical Assembly (Conservative) prompted the Reform rabbinate to reconsider. The students asked for Selective Service to be replaced by Universal Service, either in areas of social need or in the forces. But the committee urged that opposition to Vietnam should not stampede them into a change which might destroy the chaplaincy system. Instead, those who objected to the war should be allowed a selective objection.[33]

Rabbi Michael Robinson, of the Jewish Peace Fellowship, opposed the draft of chaplains and asked for a civilian chaplaincy supported by Jewish funds. He urged the community to give sanctuary to men resisting the draft. One chaplain had explained what it meant for a rabbi to be there ready when a Jewish GI was brought in unrecognisable as a human being. Robinson put it harshly, "One thing is much more effective than holding the hand of someone burned by napalm and that is to stop napalm being used."

The students themselves pressed for a voluntary chaplaincy. "Whether hawk or dove we are united in asking for a voluntary chaplaincy because we are capable of making our own moral decisions."[34] Following long debate at the Conferences of 1968 and 1969 the drafting of military chaplains was abolished.

Michael Robinson raised the underlying problems of putting rabbis into uniform at all. He put it quite bluntly that the CCAR must disassociate itself from a system that tells us to kill. The Army Field Manual proved his point. "To lead men to God and bring God to men is an even more basic requirement in combat than in garrison. Nothing reinforces the combatant more than to know that he is at peace with God. Spiritual stamina is the only dependable support for training, spirit and morale."[335]

Robinson's view is substantiated by Herr's description of the role played by religion in the army, "In woodpanelled, air-conditioned chapels in Saigon, MACV padres would fire one up to sweet muscular Jesus, blessing ammo dumps and 105s and officers' clubs. The best armed patrols in history went out after services to feed smoke to people whose priests could let themselves burn down to consecrated ash on street corners. Deep in the alleys you could hear small Buddhist chimes ringing for peace. .... Sermonettes came over Armed Forces radio every couple of hours, once I heard a chaplain from the 9th Division starting up, 'Oh Gawd, help us to learn to live with Thee in a more dynamic way in these perilous times, that we may better serve Thee in the struggle against Thine enemies ....' Holy war...."

Serving rabbis reporting to the CCAR had emphasised that army chaplains ministered to the GIs, the enlisted Jews. Robinson countered by reading from the Army Manual that "religious services are to be conducted by the chaplain in order to keep the men in fighting condition." He pleaded instead for risks to be taken on behalf of stopping the war, for draft counselling at every synagogue. It was a risk. Draft counselling was illegal. Two Reform rabbis at Sinai Congregation, Washington, met vociferous opposition when they tried to counsel conscripts, even though, they explained, they gave information without advocating a point of view.

Gabriel Kolko describes the anti-war movement as inchoate but real opposition. There was no one movement.[36] Many of the peace organisations which emerged as Draft Resistance were not pacifist; like the non-orthodox rabbinate, they were opposed to the war in Vietnam. Jewish attitudes reflected American opinion. Jews condemned the Vietnam war but not wars of defence either in the States or Israel. Regardless of the law, American objection became selective. In 1967 Robert Levy, an orthodox Jew, a volunteer soldier, demanded selective objection, "As an expression of my religious conviction as an orthodox Jew, I break the law of the United States and refuse to remain a soldier."[37]

1967 saw the biggest American land offensive of the war along the Cambodian border. By the end of the year there were 485,300 American military personnel in Vietnam. In a close vote the CCAR supported selective conscientious objection to the draft. The Selective Service System Form 150 asked in the present tense about opposition to the present war. It was not necessary to commit oneself to opposing all wars in all circumstances.[38] In January 1970 the American Jewish Congress asked the United States Supreme Court to allow Selective Conscientious Objection.[39] Jews began to examine in Jewish terms other issues related to draft resistance: non-violent protest, and civil disobedience.

The American selective draft system had continued since the Second World War. From July 1948 men were obliged to register with the nearest draft board within five days of their eighteenth birthday. There was deferment for high school or university students. There was also deferment on grounds of hardship for those with dependants. There was exemption for ministers of religion. No classification was permanent, and there was appeal against board decisions at both state and national level. Conscientious objectors could take a stand at an early stage by refusing to register. Those who registered were allowed ten days to fill up a form on which they could claim to be a conscientious objector either by religious training or belief.[40] The classifications allowed to conscientious objectors were IAO, an objector available for noncombatant (usually medical) service, and IO, an objector available for civilian service only.[41] The deferments meant the draft fell most heavily on those with the lowest educational achievement, blacks, ethnic minorities and the poor, the very groups who were under-represented on the draft boards. Some individual Jewish students and student rabbis turned in their draft cards in sympathy, and some were then punished by forfeiting deferment.[42]

Resisting selective drafts was part of Jewish history, both in Russia and western Europe. Napoleon had used a lottery system to select conscripts. In Alsace, Jews and Catholics alike devised popular rituals intended to influence the draw. There were Hebrew prayers and psalms to be recited, oil lamps were lit, coins were given, and the souls of charismatic rabbis were invoked to intercede. For those unlucky in the draw, their Judaism, like Catholicism, was a source of moral support and of physical protection. Tefillin (Phylacteries), amulets, and prayer books went to war with the Jewish soldier to keep him from harm.[43] It was the same in Vietnam. "Flip religion, it was so far out, you couldn't blame anybody for believing anything. .... They carried around five pound Bibles from home, crosses, St. Christophers, mezuzahs, locks of hair, girlfriends' underwear, snaps of their families."[44]

In 1966 the American Reform Rabbis spelled out their dissatisfaction with selection for the draft. "The right to dissent, so essential to democracy, must not be infringed by the manipulation of Selective Service as a means of punishing opponents of government policy. .... Men must never be chosen for duty on the basis of opinions, economic status, color or anything other than an objective and relevant set of standards."[45]

The burning of draft cards had been made an offence (the penalty was five years in prison or $10,000 fine) and on the West Coast a Quaker-led Committee for Draft Resistance called to those over 26 years to help draft resisters. Anti-draft unions and "we won't go" groups began to proliferate.[46] By 1968 the Central Conference had intensified its opposition. They suggested that alternative methods should be found of securing the military manpower without resort to conscription or universal military service.

Draft Resistance was widespread. 3,250 men went to jail as conscientious objectors. 250,000 avoided draft registration and one million committed draft offences with only 25,000 indicted.[47] Meanwhile the Jewish Peace Fellowship provided guidance on the draft procedure and helped conscripts understand the basis of Jewish religious objection. Its pamphlets from the Vietnam period provide an invaluable source of Jewish teachings on pacifism. Rabbi Everett Gendler translated and re-published Tamaret's writing on Jewish non-violence.[48] Supporting Robert Levy's objection, he put selective objection at the centre of the Jewish tradition. Judaism does not absolve the individual from responsibility for his own acts. Any individual may challenge the authority of those who order him to fight.

Both Gendler and Reuven Kimelman writing on *Non-Violence in the Talmud* quoted the only woman teacher in the Talmud, Beruriah, whose few words recorded from the second century CE are a poignant reminder of a brilliant and frustrated woman. Her husband was praying for the death of some highwaymen who had caused him trouble.

His wife, Beruriah, said to him: "How do you make [such a prayer to be permitted]? It is written: 'Let sins cease.' Is it written sinners? [No!] It is written sins. Further look at the end of the verse (Psalm 104:35) 'and let the wicked men be no more.' Since the sins will cease, there will be no more wicked men! Rather pray for them that they repent, and there will be no more wicked." He did pray for them, and they repented.[49]

Non-Jews are sometimes disconcerted by the way traditional sources can be cited to justify mutually exclusive courses of action. Beruriah took a verse which appears to call for the destruction of the wicked and by incisive textual analysis insisted (as Sereni did in very different terms) that it was the action, not the man, which stood condemned. Jews opposed to the idea of Jewish pacifism complain that pacifists ignore traditional readings. But Rabbi Gendler and Rabbi Axelrad deny that sources are quoted in an arbitrary manner.[50] The pacifist rabbis in America evoked a long-running non-violent tradition in Judaism, one of total Jewish validity.

In 1969 the JPF appointed Allan Solomonow as its first National Program Field and Youth Director. Solomonow was a young political science graduate from Berkeley who had spent ten months in Allenwood Pa. Prison Camp after tearing up his own draft card. While in prison he became involved in non-violent protest against the moving of one objector, David Miller, to a maximum security prison. Solomonow found that, as in so many wars, the objectors in prison were politically uneducated, outside the Anti-war movement.[51] The JPF needed field secretaries in the major Jewish areas to counsel Jewish objectors. In May 1969 Senator Charles Goodell and Representative Allard Loewnstein called on the Selective Service System "to issue new guidelines to correct the widespread practice of denying Jews Conscientious Objector status."[52] Jewish objection rose. In November 1968 there were 28 objectors in the Alternative Service program of the Selective Service System; by September 1969 there were 73, a year later over one hundred, and the JPF began to help absolute objectors as well. The JPF budget rose from $1500 p.a. to $125,000. Previously they had received one hundred enquiries a year, now they counselled 200 a month. The JPF took its place as part of the American peace movement and in July 1969 it sent two delegates to the meeting of the National Anti-War Steering Committee.[53]

Meanwhile, resisting the law had become an issue. In November 1969 it was revealed that American troops had massacred villagers at My Lai, apparently obeying orders. The issue of 'illegal' orders is a sensitive one for Jews because Nazis had claimed that 'obeying orders' exonerated them from guilt of war crimes. American orders might have to be questioned. In 1973, the year in which American troops finally left Vietnam, Axelrad wrote, "The ultimate responsibility and therefore allegiance of the Jew, both as a people and as individuals, is to God. To be sure, the Jew is to be a loyal and law abiding citizen of the state. It is only when the State violates the supreme Law of God that the Jew, caught in a bind of conflicting responsibilities, is to opt for the Law of God. Such a perspective then puts the acts of draft-resisters in the Vietnam war, for example, in a religiously heroic light."[54]

But what was the Law of God? Rabbi Leo Landman argued that Jewish Law could not determine whether or not the Vietnam war was or was not immoral. Each individual had to come to a conclusion based on his own powers of reason and conscience. All law, both religious law, and 'the law of the land' (which religious Jews were enjoined to obey), could be over-ridden by individual conscience.[55] Other Jewish writers strongly disagreed but the CCAR and individual Reform rabbis engaged in acts of non-violent civil disobedience, withholding war taxes and taking part in religious demonstrations during the closing years of the war. Zeplowitz feels that, in the light of the Holocaust, Jews seem to have felt a collective guilt for what had happened in Vietnam and that to remain silent was itself a crime. As Rabbi Abraham Feinberg from Toronto had said on returning from an illegal trip to North Vietnam, "I carry on for self-respect, for sovereignty of the individual conscience." ... "Dissent is my tribute to intellectual honesty; this disobedience is recognition of God."[56]

War resisters claimed there were 25,000 men in army prisons and that in 1968, the worst year, 20,000 men left for Canada to evade the draft. The anti-war movement was presenting problems for the very reason that it was beginning to represent a sizeable part of American opinion. The public would no longer tolerate the number of lives being lost. General Westmoreland required 500,000 men to pursue the war. As a result the deferment of college students was removed and from 1968 the draft affected articulate, middle class families. In January 1969 there were 542,400 U.S. military personnel in South Vietnam, the war-time peak.[57] Opposition to the Vietnam war peaked in Spring 1970 with 2 to 1 against. There were unprecedented protests against the invasion of Cambodia. When the National Guard opened fire on students at Kent State University, three of the four killed were Jews. That Summer the Jewish Peace Fellowship reached its highest membership of 1,250 members with 2,000 additional supporters. Allan Solomonow estimated that the JPF counselled 8,000 men overall. Figures for 1972 suggested 8,000 of the 30,000 draft resisters in Canada were Jews.[58]

It has been argued that Herberg was wrong to identify American religious structures so closely with the state, that mainstream America offered no sense of belonging to Afro-Americans and other minority ethnic groups who were struggling for a valid identity within society. Zeplowitz has pointed out that American Jewish opinion was as polarised over Vietnam as American opinion in general. Jews were more likely to have opposed the war than those with Christian affiliation. One explanation may be that Jewishness had become a secular identity, and the mass peace movement was largely secular. In a survey of 1970 Richard Neuhaus found only ten per cent of Christian clergy were members of a peace group and only five per cent active in it. For Jews it was probably the same or less.[59] The religious peace movement was as usual a minority cause. But inter-faith opposition to Vietnam suggested that Herberg had hit on an underlying American religious consensus which meant that minority members of the three faiths co-operated as fellow Americans to dissent from government policy, even as the American majority combined across religious groupings to support the Administration.

Heschel put it like this,

A sense of moral integrity, the equation of America with the pursuit of justice and peace has long been part of our self-understanding. Indeed, for generations, the image of America has been associated with the defence of human rights and the hope for world peace. And now history is sneering at us. A ghastly darkness has set in over our souls.

He offered a religious answer.

> The encounter of man and God is an encounter within the
> world. We meet within a situation of shared suffering or shared
> responsibility.
>   This is implied in believing in One God in whose eyes there is
> no dichotomy of here and there, of me and them. They and I
> are one; here is there, and there is here. What goes on over
> there happens even here. Oceans divide us. God's presence
> unites us and God is present wherever man is afflicted and all of
> humanity is embroiled in every agony wherever it may be.[60]

1967 represented the beginning of the peak of the Vietnam War. It
was the year in which Heschel's protest was published, the year of
the massive anti-war march on Washington when American opinion
seems to have been equally divided. Yet for Jews in the peace
movement this crisis period for America embodied another crisis:
June 5 – 11, 1967, Israel was at war.

In May 1967 President Nasser of Egypt ordered the United
Nations Peace-Keeping Force out of Sinai and remilitarised the
area, bringing in 100,000 men. He closed the Tiran Straits to
Israeli shipping, and signed a military agreement with King Hussein
of Jordan where Iraqi forces were drawing up on the Israeli border.
Israel launched a pre-emptive strike which destroyed the Egyptian
air force on the ground. When Jordan and Syria entered the war on
Egypt's side, Israel achieved rapid military control of the Left bank,
the Golan Heights, East Jerusalem and the Sinai. This was the third
time that Israel had anticipated a military attack. Pre-emptive strike
was redefined as a War of Defence.[61] With hindsight, it has been
argued that Israel was not as vulnerable as she perceived herself to
be and a peace process was possible. But in 1967 the Arab threat to
Israel was seen by Jews in terms of another Holocaust. Arab
objectives were the obliteration of Jewish life in Israel and the
destruction of the state.

Many Jews who had refused to fight in Vietnam or who had been
active in the American peace movement altered their position when
the future of the state of Israel was at stake. The Jewish war of self-
defence was a compulsory war as set out by Maimonides,[62] and Jews

who had opposed wars struggled with their theology and their Jewish loyalties.

Rabbi Jacob Weinstein, who had spoken about Tic Nat Hanh at the National Inter-Religious Conference on Peace the previous year, once again addressed the CCAR as President. Making a clear legal distinction between the war in Vietnam and that in the Middle East, he said,

> We must not be embarrassed by the charge that we are doves on Vietnam and hawks on Israel, that we believe in universal truth and international co-operation until our tribal interests are touched and that then we become as parochial and self-centred as any other nationalistic group.

The survival of Israel demanded and had received an immediate response.

> Shall we see this amazing response as recognition of our identity as people, no longer thanks to Israel a weak and always maltreated people, but a people with the courage to fight and the genius to prevail against mountainous odds. Shall we see this as the answer, the only adequate answer to Auschwitz – the collective contrition of the Jewish people for so falsely reading the heart of the non-Jewish world, and the partial atonement for our complicity in a civilisation that could permit so heinous an act of genocide?

He recognised the dangers of Zionism.

> Nationalism is the reigning religion of our time. And we Jews are caught in this ambivalent current: that for our survival we must secure Israel, while for the world's survival we must at the same time contend against the idolatry of nationalism.[63]

The principle of the 'Just War' in self defence was very attractive to Jews. Because the United States objection form did not enquire about attitudes to past wars and required no undertaking not to fight in the future, for example, if the United States was invaded, Jews who had refused to serve in Vietnam felt able to make out a special case for serving in the Israeli Defence Force. A few years later in 1971 the Supreme Court established that the objector "must object to participating in any war and all war". But it was still acceptable for a conscientious objector to use violence in self-defence or defence of his family or friends.[64]

The Jewish situation seemed to the Jews unique, because it was a religious as well as a national dilemma. Leading Holocaust theologians (and most markedly Emil Fackenheim) equated Jewish non-resistance with a posthumous victory for Hitler. The survival of the Jewish people had become the only imperative.[65] While conceding that the Holocaust was a trauma particular to the Jews, and that anti-Semitism before and since creates a unique psychological response, it is worth saying that many declarations of war have been dignified by moral purpose. Nor are the problems of remaining pacifist in wartime unique to Jews. Jessee Macy, a Quaker from Iowa, had opposed slavery but he was a Quaker and therefore constrained from fighting even in the Civil War; his autobiography recorded his agony over the question.[66]

In *Israel an Echo of Eternity* (1967,68 and 69), written at the invitation of the Anti-Defamation League to explain the Israeli war of 1967 to the Christian community, Heschel attempted to reconcile his religious devotion to 'peace' with the passionate Jewish concern about Israel which he was bound to convey. He argued that war was a crisis and in May 1967 the Jews were in crisis, that there was a war of self defence forced on the Jews. He continues to insist that war is evil and all death in war is bad. Yet the survival of the Jewish people is a top priority and the survival entails armed defence. Defeat is equated with Auschwitz, the Holocaust with a military defeat.

Heschel blurs the dividing line between the actual social, historical situation and the religious. He talks in religious terms of the personal involvement of every Jew in the Land of Israel. The State of Israel is not a colonial situation but a return of the Jews to their land. He contrasts the true spirit of the Jewish people with that of the Arabs, led astray by their own leadership or themselves creating a refugee problem. The split in his historical analysis seems to bear out Arthur Cohen's dictum that Jewish and Western history do not fit together. That is a Jewish theological perspective. Jewish and non-Jewish history are played out on the same stage and interact one with the other. The marked difference is one between Jewish and Christian interpretations of history. "The Jew is powerless but endures, the Christian is powerful but has not yet triumphed," wrote Arthur Cohen.[67] In 1967 for the majority of Jews that no longer rang true; Jewish endurance appeared to depend on power.

Jews were stimulated by the juxtaposition of the two wars to re-examine the whole question of war and peace in normative Judaism. Essays and articles ranged from traditional rabbinic responsa to radical books on the morality of warfare.[68] Michael Walzer, Professor of Government at Harvard, explained, "I still want to defend (most of) the particular arguments that underlay our opposition to the American war in Vietnam, but also and more importantly, I want to defend the business of arguing, as we did, and as most people do in moral terms." .... "I want to recapture the just war for political and moral theory. My own work, then, looks back to that religious tradition within which Western politics and morality were first given shape."[69] Jewish writers reacted to 1967 and to Israel's later invasion of Lebanon, by re-asserting the right to defend oneself. The Yom Kipur war of 1973 when Israel was taken by surprise seemed to prove the point. Self-defence justified pre-emptive strike, or initiating war. The religious arguments and proof texts which had sustained Jews in peace movements were now used to legitimise war instead.

One leading Jewish pacifist was incensed by what he saw as the misuse of Jewish argument.

> I suggest that the relationship between religion and peace is that, not only when it fits into the political plans of our government, nor only when it is socially safe to talk about it, nor yet to the degree to which this seems practically prudent and promising of results, but under the irresistible command of God, always, everywhere, in every way and totally, religion must insist on, explore and practise the ways of peace toward the attainment of peace. [70]

Rabbi Steven S. Schwarzschild, distinguished editor of the periodical, *Judaism*, and Professor of Philosophy at Washington University, Missouri, remained pacifist even after 1967.

Wherever Jews have lived in close contact with non-Jewish civilisations, Jewish ethics have been subjected to searching philosophical analysis. Judaism was underpinned by reason long before the philosopher Kant talked of "the imperative of practical reason", and Kant was attractive to Jewish philosophers of the enlightenment because he brought together the two sources of our understanding of reality: something construed by reason as well as experience. He recognised our need to find explanations which unify and systemise the entire human situation. Because Schwarzschild was a Professor of Philosophy, and participated in the contemporary development of religious philosophy, he places the Jewish commitment to peace within a sophisticated intellectual discourse.[71]

Schwarzschild's pacifism predated the Vietnam war. In an address to the World Union for Progressive Judaism in July 1949 he challenged his rabbinic audience by asking whether anyone had really wished to prevent war in 1939? "We had therefore to consider the question as to whether we wanted to prevent war, not in any theoretical or abstract way, but in connection with the real situation in the social and political world." "Man's desire for peace could not be realised by opposing it against the powerful forces that made for war." The only way to prevent wars was to refuse to fight them. He spoke of an unpolitical, moral insistence on peace.

He warned that religions degenerated into instruments of political interest. "We had to become aware of the danger of a nationalised Church with the establishment of the state of Israel." Within a year of the founding of the State of Israel, he asked, "Would every war that the state of Israel might have to fight be declared by Judaism to be a holy and righteous and defensive war, while every war that its enemies might wage would be a wicked and oppressive one?"

This, he urged was not the proper role of religion. Religion had to exercise its function of judgement and criticism. The prevention of war was the business of religion. And even at that early date, speaking fresh from his experience of post-Holocaust Germany, he spoke of the Messianic age as a possibility for the present. Not the remote future but soon and in our days.[72]

Steven Schwarzschild was born in Frankfurt and escaped as a refugee from Nazism in 1939. He was trained and ordained in the United States, and after the war went back to Germany as a Reform Rabbi in Berlin. After two years he opted instead for an academic life, independent of rabbinic structures. He died at the age of sixty-five at the end of 1989, notable for the long time span over which he had been a pacifist, and for the consistency and dignity of his work.

Schwarzschild entered the clerical debate over nuclear weapons in 1961, before the Vietnam war.[73] Jews have been prominent in campaigns for nuclear disarmament and there have been specific Jewish movements for nuclear disarmament, for instance JONAH, Jews Organised for a Nuclear Arms Halt, in the United Kingdom. The implication is that conventional (limited) warfare is acceptable. Schwarzschild disagrees; he points out that limited wars were the only sort of war known to either the Talmudists or to Maimonides. The limits were laid down in Jewish Law. All women and children must be spared, as must fruit trees and water springs. The enemy must have a line of withdrawal.[74] None of these *mitzvot* can be observed in modern warfare. Indeed it is the depersonalized aspect of mechanised combat which has provided orthodox Jews with grounds for question. Missiles do not spare women and children, nor trees, nor produce and it is therefore impossible to press the button without infringing the *halakha* on warfare. But Schwarzschild dismissed their notion of limited war and bitterly attacked the theologians who used biblical categories to justify war of any kind.

Schwarzschild's pacifism was attached to a frank admission of the gloomiest prognosis: the decline of the quality of life, and the likelihood of nuclear catastrophe. For Schwarzschild, social and ethical commitment do not depend on the expectation of success. The Holocaust furnished him with the unshakeable conviction that war of any kind is wrong. "Out of the unpromising, desperate struggle against Nazism in occupied Europe and in the concentration camps – if for no other reason– an ethos has arisen in our time which practises morality as an *acte gratuit*: you do what you believe to be right or what you wish to be right not because you necessarily expect to succeed but because doing it is the only way of being a truly human being." Schwarzschild suggests that this is sufficient basis for both personal and social morality, whether one be a believer or an atheist – and he says that the difference between the two is not so clear any more at a time when a 'God is dead' theology spreads. He adopts the words of Martin Luther King, "All last night I had been agonising. I made my choice. I have decided it is better to die on the highway than to make a butchery of my conscience."[75]

For Fackenheim, Buber and Heschel, Jewish survival is the imperative. Schwarzschild contradicts, "What is being asked is the quality rather than the quantity of life." He relies on the same sources as Magnes. Jewish law insists that there are things one may not do even to save one's own life. One must not kill. Death cannot become a means to life. "Each day's quality is its divine nature."

Is it hopeless? he asks, this task of Holiness imposed on us by scripture? How may we act in the face of death? He elucidates by using ideas of Herman Cohen who, like Schwarzschild himself, was German by birth, and a professional philosopher as well as a religious Jew. Schwarzschild pays tribute to him as "the last great rationalist in Jewish philosophy," and reason, for Schwarzschild, is a vital element in religion. Existentialism, personal experience or conviction is not enough. "Suppose one has not had the experience which Buber and Rosenzweig simply assert?" he asks.

Without going into the perplexing constructs of religious philosophy, one can recognise that with Heschel and Schwarzschild Jewish pacifism became part of modern theology. Hermann Cohen (1842-1918) revitalised Jewish philosophy by re-interpreting Kant's idea of God and applying it to Judaism. The one and unifying God of Jewish monotheism has always had an ethical significance. For Cohen, God was an essential idea, and one which centred Judaism in a moral way of behaving. How we behave is as important as what we know.[76] Schwarzschild relates the idea or ideals of God and morality, to the empirical goals for which we are bound to work. But he seeks to "recast rationalism". Theology itself is real, one of the facts of life. "We must indeed go forward to a more wholehearted submission to the historical realities of Jewish history and established law and doctrine and to the theological realities of God and Revelation." We have to get rid of what he calls "the outward distinction between rationalism and mysticism". Truth is an ought, not an is. It is God's promise and purpose that makes the struggle for peace and social justice maintainable.[77]

One can define a good action by saying that it will be appropriate both for the hastening of the Kingdom in time and within the Kingdom itself once it is established. In Judaism the ultimate end, the reign of peace, of human dignity and justice, of meaningful activity, can only be achieved through those means. The *mitzvot* of divinely commanded deed must be of peace not war. Any other action leads away from the destination.

The Necessity of the Lone Man appeared in the May 1965 issue of *Fellowship*. Like Gendler, Schwarzschild points to the biblical life-sparing exemptions "and the sending home all those who declare, not that they have scruples against bearing arms, but that they are afraid!" "Who is not afraid?" he asks, implying that, since fear is unavoidable and universal, it follows that religion should not call on a single man to fight. Speaking at the National Inter-religious Conference on Peace, he said,

> We do not realistically expect ourselves or society to be capable of immediately and completely obeying the Divine command to peacefulness .... but what is wrong is for religion to be used to justify the proximations and compromises we make in obeying God's call. .... The social role of authentic faith is not to be accepta`

Schwarzschild's image of the Lone Man was linked to his rehabilitation of the concept of the Messianic age, that eternal Sabbath of worship and study in which we shall be cut free from physical demands. Elsewhere he was to speak scathingly of people who regarded Isaiah Chapter II as an "indefinitely postponed dream rather than an immediate Messianic action programme."[79] In Schwarzschild's thought: the Sabbath experience is a-social, "lone"; society, community, and collectivity fade into the background. Labour socialises man. Leisure isolates and individuates. Schwarzschild calls for the 'ability to live by oneself.' Both individuals and societies must determine their own actions. "Freedom and dignity are products of man's relationship to the transcendent personal God and no one nor anything can take over this function from him."

Schwarzschild was calling for individual acts of pacifist conscience against the war in Vietnam. Yet his article is demanding to read; he was not afraid to quote Kant, Rosenzweig and Whitehead along with the Talmud. His work was an answer to those who (in his own words) regarded pacifists as "small sentimental fools."[80] Schwarzschild was intellectually equal to any of the scholars who were paying such meticulous attention to Jewish attitudes to warfare, and he had the scholarship to answer their points on behalf of the uneducated and inarticulate objectors who never spoke for themselves.

Schwarzschild deplored the passing of an age when Judaism had been ethics rather than ethnicity, when the historic values of classical Jewish culture had been "humanism, cosmopolitanism, the rule of reason, intellectualism, peacefulness, if not pacifism".[81] He admitted that pacifism no longer represented majority opinion in Judaism, but, not content with writing for the small number of pacifists, he continued to address all Jews, pleading for a scrutiny of the issues involved in the Middle East, a true soul searching by Jews in the light of their own tradition. "I believe, on the basis of intense, lifelong and professional studies, that pacifism is the best, the most authentic interpretation of classical Judaism."[82]

Schwarzschild had important things to say about the relationship between Jewish theology and issues of war and peace. For forty years he never lost faith in "the radical imperatives of Judaism", nor tired of speaking for that minority of Jews who, he says, will continue to dissent from growing Jewish conservatism and conformity.

They can and must study the implications and demands of authentic, classical Jewish culture. They will order their own lives increasingly in keeping with that culture and tell the truth as they see it about Judaism, the world and themselves – with a due sense of self-preservation and in the vestigial hope of getting their point across here or there.[83]

Chapter 9
Natan Hofshi and Pacifism in Israel

"Zionism," wrote Sereni, "aspires to the *normalisation* of Jewish life and is in this the heir of emancipation and assimilation."[1] The establishment of the state of Israel in 1948 had normalising effects rather different from those foreseen by the early Zionists, and came as a severe shock to many Jews.

Jews had always been characterised both by themselves and others as different. It was the difference which was emphasised, whether imagined or real. Anti-semites feared the difference of Jews, and conversely in religious terms Jews adhered to their own difference, a separation which was reinforced by their different social conventions and diet. On an objective level Jews are rendered different by Jewish history: the experience of persecution, or discrimination, by the psychological effects of marginality and of emancipation which stimulated a significant Jewish intellectual contribution to modern thought. Jewish difference or 'superiority' sometimes provided a rationale for pacifism as well. Jews were pacifists because they were not like unto the nations, as Judah Magnes put it. And when it came to recognition of the State, Israel was different again. For Jews even wars were different.

Normalisation was attached to the occupation of land, whether one regarded it in a religious sense as 'given' or in a political sense disputed. The existence of Israel greatly reduced previous Jewish opposition to the idea of a Jewish state. A state recognised in international law put Jews in charge of their own security. Their right to exist was no longer dependent on the favour or fortune of a non-Jewish government. Most Jews, whether orthodox or Reform, religious or secular, now endorsed the state, identified with it and assumed there was a religious duty to defend it.

The moment one experiences the physical and psychological reality of a Jewish state, it becomes hard to surrender. Judaism has existed as an invalidating presence within Christian society, and society reciprocates by invalidating Judaism. Most Jews live in a pervading culture which disparages Judaism. In the popular mind, not just Jews themselves but Jewish symbols and rituals were stigmatised; Hebrew itself was suspect. What Ahad Ha-Am could not foresee was the radical alteration made by the declaration of the State of Israel. Having a Jewish state where the language is Hebrew, where all institutions are Jewish in character, where Jewish is the norm, disproved at a stroke the contentions of Magnes and Buber that a Jewish majority was not important. After forty years Jews are no longer enraptured by the idea of a bi-national state in Palestine. A minority Jewish community in Palestine would be no different from any other minority Jewish population in the Diaspora.

The shift in self-perception given to Jews by the United Nations resolution was inconceivable until it happened. As soon as the Jewish state existed in international law, if not in undisputed moral right, Jewish pacifists were forced into an uneasy position. A pacifist objection to defending the state was interpreted as a religious offence or a denial of the legitimacy of the state.

Some Israeli pacifists would go along with this. Uri Davis found that his youthful pacifism eventually brought him to logical and inevitable alignment with the Palestinians. He has published a fierce critique of the discrimination and lack of rights in Israeli society.[2] But, in spite of the problems, some pacifists remained greatly attached to the Jewish state as a moral as well as a physical entity.

As Israel took its place as a normal state, so its artistic, intellectual and academic life also became normalised. Israeli intellectuals functioning as Jews (rather than say as American or German academics) are dealing with Israeli and Jewish material on the same footing as their colleagues from abroad. This might be considered a real emancipation. Jewish intellectual life previously existed only in the enclosed rabbinic world, isolated from other cultures, or by assimilating in the universities of the Diaspora. For the first time Jewish academics function as Jews closely in touch with current developments in their own fields. It has become possible for academics to apply the current ideas of political geography to Jewish territorialism or for political theorists to describe the development of civil religion in Israel. One problem for Jewish pacifists is that to abandon the state would be to relinquish the concomitant developments.

Christian pacifists make unfair demands on Jewish pacifists if they expect the refusal to fight for Israel to entail denying Israel's right to exist. The Israeli pacifist, Natan Hofshi, was deeply distressed by pressure from anti-Zionist colleagues in the War Resisters International and pleaded for "this Jewish pacifist Zionism, which has instilled in me and my fellows the fire of faith and yearning for Zion of 'the end of days'".[3] Conscientious objection to war does not normally involve denying the legitimate existence of one's own country.

To live as a Jew under a Jewish government is not necessarily to support that government. With the normalisation of the Jewish parliamentary democracy and its religious identification there came the normalisation of opposition parties and of minority groups and sub-cultures within Israel itself. Pacifism is met with widespread denial within Israel and in many Diaspora communities. Beata Lipman, a Jewish journalist, who went to Israel to interview Jewish and Arab women for her book *Israel: the Embattled Land* says, "I met no Israeli pacifists and no one whatsoever their political view, who did not believe in the necessity of a system of defence." Even in Christianity, pacifists are a tiny minority. In Judaism it is the same. Israeli pacifists survive within Israeli society as a tolerated if de-legitimised minority.

Israeli pacifism is home grown and the name of its mentor, Natan Hofshi, is virtually unknown outside Israel. He wrote no book. His journalism and some of his letters were privately printed by friends and presented to him on his seventy-fifth birthday. He was honoured in this way and is still cited by pacifists in Israel because he demonstrated that a Jew could be a pacifist in a Jewish state.[4]

Hofshi provides a Jewish approach to questions which beset all pacifists. He wrote in Hebrew, and this, with his access to the Hebrew religious sources, gives a beautiful religious dimension to his work. It is not easy to pick up in translation, but for anyone familiar with the Hebrew text, Hofshi's writing reverberates with echoes of, or alterations to, a familiar Biblical word or phrase. During his childhood in Poland he was given the normal Jewish education but from his father he learned to enjoy reading and to study the Bible, particularly the later prophets who are neglected in traditional Talmud-based study. Hofshi was unusual; he said he knew most of the Bible by heart. He uses it to startle or to make a point.

For Hofshi there was something very special about being Jewish. In his teens he discovered that he could not reconcile his socialist activity in Poland with what he read in those later prophets: Isaiah, Hosea and Amos. He was almost a pacifist already.[5] His father was a professional man, a leader of the local community who spoke

Polish and German. The spoken language of their orthodox community was Yiddish but Hofshi also learned surreptitiously to read and discuss in Hebrew, preparing himself for 1909 and his arrival in Palestine, aged twenty, part of the prestigious second *aliyah*. Once in Palestine, he worked as an agricultural labourer, moving from place to place: Rehovot, Petah Tikvah, Huldah. Wherever he worked, he found that he made friends with Arabs; there was no personal problem between him and them.

One of Hofshi's contemporaries, the secular Israeli pacifist, Joseph Abileah, has said the same. He arrived with his family in 1926 at the age of eleven and grew up part of a well-known family and mixing with Arabs. The old Yishuv, the old settlers, knew Arab social conventions and took care to abide by them. Even at moments of communal tension, they met with Arabs, ate with Arabs, did business with Arabs and trusted them. Trust was given in return. Jewish pacifists in the thirties and since have always mentioned the work of those animal behaviourists who demonstrate that animals will not kill unless they feel threatened.[6] Asked what made him a pacifist, Abileah described an incident in 1936 (a period of great unrest) when at the age of nineteen he was out hiking and found himself threatened with death by a group of Arabs. Abileah tells the story of how he himself walked to the well where he was to be killed. No one was willing to take the final step and throw him in. Instead they offered him the chance nominally to become a Moslem. He remembered how he had walked alone in the deserts of Trans-Jordan where the Bedou had fierce dogs. At the approach of a dog, he would always sit still. It is fear that provokes violence. So, too with the Arabs, he made the submissive gesture. The way to achieve peace with the Arabs was to live in peace. Abileah makes out no case for distinctive Jewish pacifism. Judaism is not completely pacifist, any more than Christianity or Islam. But all three religions have a common ethical ground for peace. Non-violence cannot be used as tactics, just because it is expedient, he says. It must be a way of life, arising from conviction.[7]

In 1921 Hofshi joined the secular *moshav* (co-operative) of Nahallal near Haifa which was also the home of Moshe Dayan, later General and Minister of Defence. Hofshi's membership of this communal settlement associated him with the Labour élite who were to form the socialist governments. Pacifist though he was, he was part of the Israeli establishment and his influence was commensurate. He was a member of *Brith Shalom* and later of *Ichud.* In *Looking Inwards* (undated), surveying fifty years of life in Israel, he described the growth of violence throughout every nation and land, including the land of Israel. "Not only between Jews and Arabs but between the Jewish people themselves. And you stand and see how people with fine minds, people with feeling hearts, people of learning and culture, gather all their strength to kindle the fire, to stimulate all the instincts that drive brothers to fight between themselves." Anthony Storr, the psychologist, concludes that aggression is natural to man; that hostility against competitors for land and food has a normal social function in preserving the group.[8] Joseph Abileah works on the same premise: animals use violence only for a reason. Human beings go further and take risks, make sacrifices for the group which animals would not. Religious and ethical guidelines on inter-human relations are directed to the personal. They need to be applied to relationships between groups. We have to insist that peace is possible.

As a Zionist, Hofshi makes moral demands both on the political situation and on people. "There is only one way, one truth, the living truth and one should not contradict or hide the living truth, that the only rule one should live by is, 'What is hateful to yourself, you should not do to your fellow man'."[9] For Hofshi the fellow man and woman is not restricted to other Jews. The rule must be carried out "in daily life, in relationship to your community, because this is the only righteous way; and this safe and solid way provides a strong basis for a new life which will guarantee the security and success of our Zionist enterprise."[10]

Hofshi's very Jewishness carries within it a biblical universalism. His grandfather had been a farmer in Poland and, as a boy, Hofshi had mixed freely with the non-Jewish peasants. He did not distinguish between Jew and non-Jew: all men and women are created in the image of God and the voice of God is within us. All men and women are brothers and sisters; in a paper of 25 February 1940, he refers to us as the children of Adam and of Eve. Jews often use the phrase 'children of Adam' to mean all mankind, but Hofshi gives the woman Eve an equal place in the idiom. The Jewish conviction that brought him as a socialist settler to Palestine to create a new society, taught also that all men and women are our sisters and brothers whose blood we must not spill. "My Zionism and my resistance to war and violence – both are grounded on religion and conscience."[11]

Hofshi asked his fellow Jews to confront the sad and painful fact which demanded reparation: that during fifty years of living and working in the land, Jews had failed to make friends with Arabs, either in cities or in the villages. There was no simple human contact between our workers or between Jewish farmers and Arab farmers. Hofshi saw what troubled few: the apartheid in Israeli society.

> There is only one sun that gives light to all of us without differentiation, and the same mother earth supports or deprives us of harvest and blessing. .... And the question is how much did we do either as individuals or as the organised public, what did we do all those years we worked in the land to improve or create friendly, truthful relationships – trust in each other – trust between us and the Arab people, that trust which would have avoided the sickness of hatred and riots?[12]

Hofshi asks whether this Jewish failure does not shed a different light on questions of majority/minority rights, questions of self-defence and all the other problems which follow in its wake?

Hofshi challenged the Israeli emphasis on self-defence. He was making an important point. Maimonides would have said that the enemy had actually to be intruding on one's own soil before he could be repelled. From 1938 some Jewish self-defence patrols under the mandate had gradually adopted a policy of retaliation and reprisal, "*Yetziah minn ha'gader*" going beyond the hedge, what was known as aggressive defence.[13] If it is legitimate to defend existing frontiers, the implication is that the refusal to surrender the status quo takes moral precedent over the 'attacking' force that calls it to question. The irony is that in the context of the Mandate the Arabs might be said to be defending the status quo. Insisting on the legitimacy of the existing situation seems an unreliable principle, and highly theoretical. Historical reality suggests that change is an unavoidable and universal fact of life. This 'moral demand' for something different provided the Zionists with their rationale and justification for demanding a new Jewish state or at least a geographical location where one had the liberty to be a Jew.

Some Jewish pacifists disconcerted their Christian colleagues by insisting that it was a Jewish duty to defend this liberty. Even within the Jewish Peace Fellowship the view is expressed from time to time; in *Shalom*, Autumn/Winter 1987, Rabbi Philip Bentley, President of the JPF, refused to disguise the problem. He looked for ways to reaffirm Jewish pacifism without the implication that pacifists advocated Israeli surrender. Rabbi Albert Axelrad whose indispensable book on Jewish pacifism, *Call to Conscience*, provided American Jewish objectors with a comprehensive guide to their legal and religious position, coined the term "Pacifoid" to explain his continuing search for peace, and desire to be regarded as part of the American peace movement even though he endorsed Israel's right to defend herself.

Israelis, if they are to be pacifists at all, have to be pacifists in a war situation. Yeheska Landau, an articulate spokesman for the Jewish Vietnam objector, initially refused to serve in the Israeli Defence Force. But eventually Landau agreed to do annual military service even though he continued to work for the orthodox peace movement, *Oz v'Shalom*, (Strength and Peace), to devote himself to reconciliation with Palestinians, and to introduce himself as a Jewish pacifist. For *Oz v'Shalom*, that qualifying word 'Jewish' meant that although Jews must strive for peace they must none the less be prepared to use physical force in self-defence.[14]

Landau's position exemplified another problem in defining Jewish pacifism. Normative Judaism is not pacifist in as much as the Jewish law provides no definite injunction not to resist, but the notion of peace (*shalom*) is central to Judaism. We constantly pray for and idealise *shalom*. It is extolled by the later prophets, valued throughout the Rabbinic period, insisted on in Jewish liturgy. Sometimes the Hebrew word *shalom* is translated as completeness rather than as peace. But the popular equation of *shalom* with its usual translation "peace" is so taken for granted, that Jews compete for the peace position. Thus *Oz v'Shalom* works for peace without being pacifist. Indeed many people in peace movements in Israel would argue that pacifism is not possible.

Hofshi was once asked how it was possible for someone who had lived in the State from the beginning to be a pacifist.[15] He said it had been bothering him too. But equally an Arab had asked him how he could be silent in face of the Arab refugee problem? Hofshi said that "we are responsible for our situation as opposed to the situation being thrust upon us." Fatalism is wrong. 'The situation' can be used to justify anything. Instead of looking at the situation,

Hofshi begged Jews to look at the argument between themselves and the Arabs. "We have a historic claim to the land of Israel and by virtue of these claims I and my friends returned here in 1909. But when we came here we stumbled on the Arabs who had lived here for 1300 years without knowing about Zionism or our claims. And it was no sin on their part that generation after generation was born here. We lived here and regarded the Arabs as something historical that would pass."

Hofshi understood the magnetic appeal of heroism. Jabotinsky had said, "Our youth should learn to fight .... a people in our situation must know the new alphabet, the psychology of fighting, the longing to fight – all these are important."[16] His religious fervour was unmistakable. In 1939 Hofshi warned that the Jewish Legion had all the attractions of a false messiah. Later, he was appalled by the militarisation of Israel. The Left which had professed peace was in power, yet they fought for a Jewish state in a land that was predominantly Arab. He was dismayed to think they had created the refugee problem and had a negative approach to the Arab minority that remained. In his view, the Left went back on the principle of not doing things by strength and might.

Hofshi had never denied the pull of the land. But he knew it had a price on it. However great our love of the land, it can go beyond all bounds, he warned. "Will we not find the inner strength at this point to turn aside from the way of death and beat our swords into ploughshares?" He denied that pacifism arose from cowardice, Everyone was afraid of war, even soldiers. "Everyone fears the consequences of war but they do not ask one very serious question which is how can we rise against our fellow men and murder other human beings who were like us created in the image of God?" The word he uses for 'murder' is taken straight from the Ten Commandments. "How can we turn into murderers?" he asks. Hofshi does not try to explain away that awkward Commandment, "You shall not kill". He does not claim that "murder" does not apply to military service. For Hofshi war is murder. "How can we bear the mark of Cain for the rest of our lives for which we cannot atone?"[17]

As a religious pacifist, it is not surprising that Hofshi lamented the changed identity of Judaism. In Israel religion reinforced and dignified army service. It is worth pointing out, as notable Israeli scholars have done, that however unique Jews may seem both to themselves and others, the development of civil religion in Israel follows the normal pattern. Judaism which had been an invalidating presence within Christian society has adapted to being a legitimising presence in the Jewish State.[18] Classical sociology regarded religion as providing a social cement. Contemporary political theorists may go further and suggest that it is ideology which alone creates the identity of modern nation states.[19] In Israel the State embraces and embodies the externals of Judaism. A combination of religion, myth and popular Jewish culture integrates and legitimises the nation. As a result, it is difficult for non-Jews to identify or be identified with Israeli values. Equally it makes it harder to express religious dissent; pacifism is made to appear un-Jewish. Army recruits are sworn in at Masada with the vow that Masada shall never fall again. The army has its own rabbinate and its Chief Rabbi with the rank of General. *Tefillin* (copies of the Shema with leather straps to be bound to the head and right arm) are army issue in khaki bags. Each conscript is presented simultaneously with his rifle and a bible.

Reading Hofshi's impassioned journalism one could be misled into thinking the history of Israel was a series of Jewish atrocities. Not so, but Hofshi did not take it upon himself to reprove the Palestinians for their violence. His task was to address the shortcomings of his own people.[20] At Kafr Kassem in 1956 Israeli soldiers slaughtered peaceful Arab villagers. The massacre filled Hofshi with fears for the future. Zionism had been transformed from a religious and humanitarian movement of the people, into a swaggering Judah returned in blood and fire. Shaken by the "nightmare results of leadership which believed salvation could come from the angel of death, of blood and fire," he called on Israelis not to abandon their inheritance: "Not with heroism and not with strength but with My spirit."[21] The Bible text is inserted into his journalism without embarrassment because Hofshi's protest is about Israeli society itself. "The three qualities that mark out a Jew: humility, pity and the act of charity, have been taken away by a strong hand." The strong hand of power, perhaps, but in biblical Hebrew the hand of power is the hand of God. Hofshi says that if the soldiers from the frontier slaughtered Arabs, then that was symptomatic of Israeli society; they did so only out of allegiance to the word and spirit of their military oath. "I swear to take on myself without any reservation, without any conditions, the yoke of the authority of the Army of Israel, to obey all orders that are given by the commanding officers."[22] This was the oath that Uri Davis refused to take.

Hofshi says that the military oath and the procedures which are today called training in killing people, destroy the voice of his conscience in each human being, in each soldier, the liberty of self-judgement. Hofshi is unusual as a Jewish thinker because he unashamedly puts individual conscience at the religious centre of one's life. He uses the modern Hebrew word for conscience: *matzpun*. It comes from the biblical Hebrew, *zapan*, meaning what is hidden or treasured up, what is in one's own keeping. No authority, whether religious or secular, can usurp the responsibility of the individual Jew in following his conscience.

The perpetrators of Kafr Kassem were court-martialled and the Appellate Military Court hearing their appeal established a principle that Israeli soldiers were to disobey any obviously illegal order.[23] Dissent over the 1982 invasion of Lebanon and over the suppression of the Intifada in the occupied territories still centres on the question of law. Lieutenant-Colonel Dov Yirmiya is quoted by Amnesty International, "During the Lebanon war I thought that refusing to serve was wrong. But the illegal orders given by Defence Minister Rabin at the start of the uprising showed me that I was mistaken. So I called on other soldiers to refuse to carry out war crimes by breaking bones, killing civilians and trampling on human dignity." Lieutenant Colonel Yirmiya was charged with incitement to mutiny.

The constant resort to legality and the application of *halakha*, Jewish law, create the feeling that Jews are peculiarly deprived of choice. Jews may feel forced to conclude that the War of Defence is incumbent on them as Jews. They ask Christian pacifists to understand this dilemma. Christian pacifists on the other hand will recognise that going unwillingly to war, 'having no choice', is part of a general human pattern; nineteenth century British music hall audiences sang, "We don't want to fight but by Jingo if we do, we've got the ships, we've got the men, we've got the money too."[24]

Buber had said that "Whoever considers war to be inevitable collaborates, willingly or unwillingly, consciously or unconsciously in bringing about war"[25] But Buber also said "I am no radical pacifist: I do not believe that one must always answer violence with non-violence : when there is war, it must be fought."

This elliptical argument was not good enough for Hofshi:

> The main problem is that people are unable to see the truth for what it is and that is why war is inevitable. You have to look at what is going on and you will see war being created. Every morning millions of brothers leave the shelter of their families with affectionate looks towards their wives and their children who are playing, and go off to their 'holy work' of preparing murderous weapons of slaughter and destruction, armaments of great sophistication. They have done this and will do so for years. This is how they support their families, by working in this terrible industry which spells catastrophe and massacre for millions of much-loved families, including those of the very men who do the work. No one, Christians, socialists, Non-Jew or Jew – sees anything wrong with this; it is making a living.[26]

The arms industry has a logic all of its own. He asks what we Jews would have called people who supplied arms for White Russian Pogroms. Would we have found some excuse for them in terms of social structure or economic need? "Am I alone in thinking this unacceptable?" he asks sarcastically. "Practical and intelligent people see business opportunities and don't enquire further."

Unlike Sereni and the Marxists, Hofshi did not accept that we are the victims of our situation. We cannot blame the government or capitalists for the ills of war. He said the colour of the government had nothing to do with it; it was not the government that was monstrous. Hofshi harked back to Tolstoy and Gandhi. It was the fighting of wars by individual men and women that created war. "What strength does a government have without tens of millions of people who do its works and guard it with weapons? Hitler and the other great dictators of history would be nothing without the narrow mindedness and stupidity of the masses who go off to their Holy Wars, caught up in a compulsion against the bonds that they have actually fashioned for themselves." Hofshi will not allow the people to blame the government for everything.

The people participate in the arms industry and it is they who blame the authorities for war until the moment comes when they are ordered "to murder for the sake of their birthplace, for the sake of their homeland, for the sake of culture, freedom, race, and class and peace." It is not the structure of society, it is individual men who glamorise war "the greatness of might, the flags fluttering and waving, the intoxicating rhetoric of war which treats the death of young men in literary and poetic language."

Because Judaism asks what is the law, Jewish conscientious objectors tend to deal with particular situations, rather than with "war" in the abstract. Their pacifism is sometimes not recognised as genuine by non-Jewish peace movements since it fails to conform to Christian patterns. Far more widespread in Israel is the type of objection which Amnesty International calls 'partial objection', and which began within the army among the men who were actually called upon to do the fighting. The organisation, Peace Now, is not pacifist. It was a pressure group set up in 1979 to press for a peace agreement with Egypt at the Camp David talks. One of the largest Peace Now demonstrations drew 100,000 people in Tel Aviv on 7 July 1979 and the demonstrations led to the formation of soldiers' groups, the best known of which was Soldiers against Silence.

The movement, *Yesh G'vul*, there is a limit (or, punning, there is a frontier), was originally a protest movement of 86 reservists refusing to serve in the Lebanon. The army prosecuted and imprisoned those who refused to serve. 3,000 men signed the protest; fewer than 200 soldiers went to prison. Now *Yesh G'vul* supports soldiers refusing to serve in the occupied territories. Yet because they don't want to be accused of cowardice, they emphasise their past achievements as paratroopers. They are conscientious objectors who insist on seeing themselves as members of a military élite.

The military profile of some Israeli prisoners of conscience alienates non-Jewish peace movements who find it difficult to equate military rank with pacifism. Looking through the Amnesty list of prisoners one is struck at once by the fact that many of these objectors are sergeants and captains and privates. But this is not because the peace movement in Israel is militaristic. It is because Israel itself is synonymous with its army. Everywhere one goes in Israel there are soldiers. Every child goes through school anticipating his or her own military service. Boys aspire to serve in high prestige units, crack tank regiments or paratroops. Military service provides the entrée into Israeli society and has proved also the melting pot for the integration of immigrants from diverse cultural backgrounds, African, Middle Eastern or Central European. Many objectors are or have been part of the army too.

Their personal identification with the Israeli Defence Forces is yet another expression of that Jewish reaction to the Holocaust which places so much emphasis on resistance. The extermination of the Jews underlined yet again the bitter truth that Jews may exist only by permission of the non-Jewish society of which they find themselves part. That feeling of vulnerability has been reinforced by Israel's isolation in the international community, by the lack of recognition and at times the failure of miltary assitance. Reacting against this insecurity, Jews in Israel saw their own empowerment in military terms.

The Intifada changed the profile of the Israeli objector. Some school-leavers were unwilling to serve in the administered territories and a new generation of pacifists has refused military call up and gone to prison without going into the army at all.

Jews who have been and are so much discriminated against find it hard to advise other oppressed people not to use force to endeavour to improve their situation. Nor is it easy for Jews to see themselves as oppressors. So during Vietnam and since, Jews have opted for selective conscientious objection. Jews have gone to prison rather than serve in the South African army. Likewise in Israel objection on the whole has been selective (Partial Objection). A great many Israelis, and the number has been put as high as 25,000, have evaded military service, many by leaving the country.[27] Other families are deterred from settling there by the prospect of military service.

Most selective objectors refuse to serve in the territories or Gaza because they support the Palestinian claim for civil rights and self-determination. They sympathise with the Intifada.

Liberation theology exercises a great pull at the moment. Marc Ellis has argued that Jewish theology should emulate Catholicism and endorse the liberation struggles of other peoples.[28] The Holocaust seemed to imply a duty to defend the underdog, the victim. After the Six Days' War, a young Israeli put it like this, "There are some people who claim that war – any war – is opposed to justice and that there is an exact mechanism for recognising the one who's in the right: he's the one who loses .... as if this were the rule of justice, the opposite of "might is right". .... Sometimes it even stems from the desire for national suicide which is so deeply implanted in us just because we are the children of Jewish history and are perpetuating its negative aspects."[29] Challenged by such arguments, Jews are justified in asking what is meant by liberation and how far religion can become synonymous with politics. Jews need to remind themselves too that some Christian liberation theologists remain pacifist. One of them, Dom Helder Câmara, provides a critique of violence. He asks whether there is

anywhere in the world which does not know injustices, inequalities, division? Is there anywhere where injustice does not constitute the first violence, the violence which begets all violence? Where violent protest against injustice does not threaten public order and the security of the State? And provoke violent repression by the Authorities?

He recognises the attractions of a violent solution to the problems of oppression.

Everywhere there are people, particularly young people, who come to believe that the only way to remedy injustice is to stir up the victims of injustice. ...

But [Câmara says] there are also many who want a juster and more humane world but who do not believe that this can be achieved through force and armed violence. Even without resorting to religious or ideological arguments, those who choose active non-violence, that is the violence of pacifists, know that today the world is dominated by a complex alliance of economic, political, technological and military power: how can one imagine that armed struggle will succeed in defeating the rulers of the world who have the arms manufacturers and instigators of war on their side?[30]

Hofshi said something similar about the Arab/Jewish conflict, warning that neither side would seek a peaceful settlement if they assumed that, with power, they could impose a military solution.

The flaw in Liberation Theology is the assumption that the oppressed will win, and that their victory will be final. Empowerment becomes everything.

Self-determination was not new to the Jews. Under the Turks in Palestine and within the European ghettos Jews had exercised a degree of self-government, severely limited by the authority of the controlling non-Jewish society. In this sense Israeli self-government resembles ghetto life. Jews live in a majority Jewish society but their freedom of action is limited both by the character of orthodox Judaism, and by Israel's economic and political setting in the wider, dominating, non-Jewish world.

> All our lives we've been educated against war and we've fought against the whole idea of war; and you can see that it doesn't help. Even now we're already saying, 'The next war, the next fight'. You can see it doesn't help, it's something forced on us. We're even forced to want it. .... Sometimes I really had rebellious thoughts – in the shelter, for example as I held my two weeks' old baby in my arms, I wondered whether this war was really necessary. Was it vital that we could or couldn't sail through the Straits of Tiran? Now, as I analyse it, it's clear that everything was absolutely necessary and completely justified. But even then if Giora (her husband) hadn't come back perhaps I wouldn't have been able to come to that conclusion.[31]

The Six days' War ended in victory. The command to defend oneself assumes that one will be successful.

But even victory left some of the participants asking questions. The same girl of nineteen from a Kibbutz wrote in her diary,

> And they tell me it's not over; they say it's only the beginning. 'Look here, girl, you've got to understand .... there's no choice,' they say.
> But I don't want to understand that there's no choice; that people should get angry with each other, that they should slaughter each other, and that while it's not exactly nice, there's still no choice ('and anyway it's time you understood that not everything in life can be controlled, and that everything isn't always nice...').[32]

When previously pacifist Christian aid workers support liberation struggles, and in particular the struggle of the Palestinians against Israel, Jews are justified in asking how it was that when Jews were exterminated these same pacifist groups were not willing to fight Hitler. Israeli pacifists may sympathise with the Palestinian demands for civil rights in Israel and self-determination outside Israel but they do not support the use of violence by anyone.

Amos Gvirtz has been a secular pacifist all his life. His pacifism is in the Zionist tradition of Hofshi, Abileah, and the early socialist settlers who purchased land in Palestine, lived side by side with Arabs and attempted to live with them in peace. Contemporary Israeli pacifism, simple in style, has much in common with Quaker pacifism. It rests on respect for one's fellow men, the need to co-operate and not to compete, to treat all people with equal respect regardless of their religion or colour or race. Gvirtz sees this as an imperative for Jews who have suffered so much from racism themselves. He emphasises the need to work constructively for peace by tackling the grievances which provoke violence and terror, and by supporting what he calls "constructive" i.e. non-violent forms of protest instead. Israeli pacifists do not endorse the violence of the intifada, even though it may be limited to stone throwing. They condemn the use of children whose lives are at risk when they are used as the 'front line' in a national struggle.[33]

Jewish self-government does not guarantee civil rights even to all Jews and some small leftish parties in the Meretz group are fighting to have this redressed. The State recognises only orthodox Judaism. In accordance with orthodox rabbinic law, there is no secular or non-orthodox Jewish procedure for marriage in Israel. Secular burial was regularised in 1992. There is no freedom of conscience in Israel for Reform, Liberal, Reconstructionist and Conservative Jews whose rabbis may not legally officiate in marriage, divorce, and conversion, and are not exempt from military service.[34] The human rights currently denied in Israel include a right to exemption from military service on grounds of conscientious objection.

Israel has universal military conscription for men and women at the age of eighteen. Israeli Arabs and Druze women are excluded from compulsory military service. So are observant orthodox women if their religious practice prevents them following normal army life or leaving their domestic role. Men studying in *Yeshivot* (orthodox religion schools) are also exempt or have their conscription indefinitely deferred. After leaving school men serve three years and women two years in the regular army. They must continue to do reserve duty for one month every year until the age of 54. (The length of reserve duty was increased to 60 days in 1988).

The whole community is permanently involved with the army and the army constitutes the social world in which each individual finds himself. Reserve units tend to stay together year after year, under the same officer. The solidarity of the peer group constitutes a bond from which it is difficult to disassociate oneself. Disciplinary problems within each unit are handled by its own commanding officer, thus intensifying the sense of family. A CO may try to find noncombatant work for a pacifist, or even send him home in order to keep the problem within the group. But this means objection is looked on as a luxury, shirking a chore which the rest of the citizen army have to endure.

Hofshi protested about compulsion in 1941 when the Hebrew University was closed. He asked whether it wasn't a contradiction in terms, forcing people to fight for freedom? He asked how one could have democracy and compulsion in matters of life and death. It was full of contradictions, that in the name of democracy and freedom, people should be deprived of the right to earn their living. He saw it as a victory for Hitler in life and soul. Army service was not a summer holiday camp. Military service entailed mass murder and things should be called by their proper names.[35]

Under the Defence Service Law, cases of conscience are dealt with by disciplinary and military courts. Military courts have a judicial process and defendants may be represented by a lawyer. Legal remedies include appeals to higher courts. In 1980 the army was criticised by the High Court for not having "a clear and non-discriminatory policy regarding requests for exemptions from military service for reasons of conscience".[36]

As there is provision for religious conscientious objection for women, women in the peace movement may appear before an Exemption Board. Boards which may include a Rabbi, psychiatrist, army officer, woman soldier, or member of the public, will not necessarily grant exemption to a pacifist. Men may not seek exemption on grounds of conscience. They can ask to be excused on grounds of unsuitability and their cases are dealt with not by an Exemption Board but individually by the conscription unit.

The government handles cases on an individual basis. There is no consistency and much is left to the discretion of individual commanding officers. Some men are offered alternative service either within the army or in hospitals or schools. Some rare pacifists are excused altogether; some are penalised. Each Israeli has a Profile number indicating his category for military service. The higher the number, the fitter the man. Those with numbers over 45 do all their service. Numbers in the 20s are bad. The authorities in Israel, like those elsewhere, may discredit those who question them, by requiring an objector to undergo psychiatric treatment. He may then be discharged with Profile 21, psychologically unfit to serve, which will remain with him as a social stigma. It suggests that he may (for instance) be unbalanced or a drug addict, and may make it difficult for him to pursue his profession or find employment. By dealing with each case on an ad hoc basis according to its own merits, the authorities deprive objectors of mutual support, reduce their credibility and have inhibited the development of one unified peace movement.

The nature of pacifism in any particular country seems determined by the character of that country's laws regarding conscientious objection. Where the law establishes a clear definition of pacifist objection, one finds pacifists banded together in more or less homogeneous groups. In Israel there is no legal provision for conscience. It is up to each individual objector to decide at what point he will refuse to obey a military order. Each individual has to negotiate annually what seems to him a geographically acceptable posting and perhaps a noncombatant function which does not offend his religious or ethical convictions. This has the effect of fragmenting the Israeli peace movement. No one has agreed on a standard procedure.

An Amnesty International summary of October 1988 says that "in practice accommodation is often achieved between the military authorities and pacifists who completely refuse to serve in the military". This seems a sanguine view. Amos Gvirtz has described the problems he experienced, his isolation and his problems with different military authorities and the on-going tension over his reserve duty.

> I wanted to do civilian not military service. The army compromised but I still had to do my service within the army. .... After seven years we finally agreed. .... I served my reserve duty on condition that I didn't handle weapons, that I didn't wear a uniform and that I didn't have to serve in the occupied territories. Unfortunately the army and I have differences in

understanding the agreement. Personally it was a very hard time. ...

I was very lucky compared to some other conscientious objectors here. I do know people who were thrown into prison and broken there, and as a result they finally agreed to serve.[37]

Hofshi knew the utter despair that came from this kind of isolation. "I have no way of publicising my views and I cannot look on and be silent. Therefore I have poured out my feelings to you in the hope that you will understand," he wrote on 5 July, 1941. When an article he had sent to the famous journal *Moz Naim* was turned down in September 1939 he wrote that he felt like a voice in the wilderness. He wanted to know that he was not alone. He cried out, not because he was surprised by the mass murder they call war, he had warned against it. He stood with those that had refused in other countries. Writing in a literary style, he creates a terrible imagery. He speaks of the fear you feel when waiting for the blow to fall. He spoke of the sickle in the hands of his brethren falling on their necks "and I cried out as if it were happening to me".[38]

It is an offence under Israeli law to help a conscientious objector avoid military service or to encourage refusal of service. Hofshi said he was very careful not to give advice to people about conscription. A young man had once asked his advice about whether or not he should go on military service and Hofshi had replied, "If you are asking, that is a sign you should go." The young man joined up and was killed. Hofshi said that when he heard about his death, he remembered their discussion and knew that he could not have answered in any other way. A pacifist would have been able to explain his point of view. Hofshi could not force his opinion on another man. Hofshi is defining conscience as an inner conviction, not something directed by a teacher or leader.

Ernst Simon had written to Hofshi and raised the question of whether it was right for an individual dissenter to continue to object to the decision of the majority. Hofshi saw no difficulty in allowing minority pacifism in a Jewish state. In fact he reassures the authorities,

In this way there is no room for the fear that all the children of the land will be conscientious objectors and that our enemies will therefore destroy us.

Though [he added] if the day did come when everyone refused military service, that would be a miracle, and we would come very quickly to an agreement and peace with our Arab neighbours on the basis of humanity. Nineveh would repent as in the Jonah story and there would be great hope for Jacob and Israel.[39]

Hofshi saw that hope for the future depended on educating the children. His expression, "I believe in perfect faith", echoes Maimonides speaking of the Messianic age.

I believe in perfect faith that the days of peace and brotherhood will come only as a result of a new form of education in school and home whose central feature will be 'Man was created in the image of God.' Everything that is taught to children, young people and adolescents will be subordinate to this one principle.

Hofshi understood that communication is vital for improving the long-term relationship between Jew and Arab. He saw that segregated education in Israel reinforced the division between the communities: the Palestinians fear Jews and Jews fear Palestinians, for neither knows the other. Responding to this in recent years, the peace movement has fostered contact between Jewish and Palestinian children: in the inter-communal village of Neve Shalom, in youth clubs in the mixed city of Haifa, in education projects and language teaching schemes. Young Jews who have Arab Israeli friends are sensitive to the issues. School leavers have begun to protest about military service and there is a new generation of young objectors in Israel who have never served in the army at all. Their imprisonment and re-imprisonment by the Israeli government constitutes real hardship. They have no military pretensions and are much more like their opposite numbers, conscientious objectors in Europe and America.

Anthony Storr describes the way primitive societies deny status to the man who has not killed. He is a worthless man, whose wives and property may be taken from him.[40] Hofshi faced up to this denial of status. Pacifists would not be deterred when their opponents called them herbivores, cranks or nut eaters.

Because pacifists lack authority and credibility within society, they seek support and encouragement from fellow pacifists both at home and abroad. Hofshi was a member of War Resisters

International. Israeli pacifists who succeeded Hofshi, Jews and Palestinians together, formed a Jerusalem branch of the International Fellowship of Reconciliation. Before the Intifada, members of this group were exploring the relevance of Gandhian non-violence to their own situation. They attempt to lead a life of peace on both personal and political levels. They encourage individual contact between Jews and Palestinians, and several work in the caring professions which cross communal boundaries. Israeli pacifists align themselves with many non-pacifist peace groups, and play an active role in the political peace process, maintaining contacts with Palestinians, both Moslems and Christians, and trying to mitigate divisive social problems.

Israeli religious pacifism draws directly on the American tradition of tolerant religious pluralism. Conservative Rabbi Jeremy Milgrom found that years of military duty bore in on him the innate contradiction between the Zionism he preached and what he did when he picked up a gun. The covenant should not be used as an excuse for chauvinism. It does not confer privileges which can be established by force of arms. On the contrary, it makes positive demands for truth, justice and peace. Jews must not only refrain from war, they must create Peace.

That was what Milgrom was attempting when with Palestinian and Jewish friends in the Committee Against Racism he took part in a rally to protest against the establishment of a Kahane-inspired office for Arab emigration at Um El-Fahm. In the demonstration, his *kippah* (the small skull cap worn by many rabbis and observant Jews) was lost. Without this badge of identity, he was not recognised as a rabbi by the police and was thrown into prison.[41] The experience of being beaten by the Israeli police was traumatic. Totally powerless in prison and cut off from the outside world, he realised that Jewish communal values which had survived the tribulations of the Diaspora had given way when Jews themselves were called upon to exercise power. The mission of the Jewish people is not to secure their own survival at any cost, but to serve God through observing Torah. The *mitzvot* have a spiritual function in imposing a moral standard on every individual Jew. The true defence of Judaism is to insist that ethical standards should apply to the state as well as the individual. This type of religious pacifism is far from being a watered down version of Christianity. It is Jewish in character and origin.

But for pacifists like Milgrom and Schwarzschild, Jewish pacifism has involved a painful process of recognising and condemning the un-pacific, the militant, in our own religion: its exclusivity, intolerance, and nationalism. Being a critic of one's own tradition is not easy. When General Harkabi wrote on the antagonisms perpetuated within Jewish liturgy, even Reform Jews were unwilling to put his views into print. Non-conformist Jews are called 'self-hating'. Like John Harris, today's pacifist rabbis are reprimanded, ordered to be silent or risk the termination of their contracts.

Jewish pacifism, like Judaism itself, is pragmatic and practical. Its justification is that it is in the long term interest of the Jewish people; non-violence and reconciliation provide more security for the future than the Israel Defence Force. Hofshi refused to become helpless or hopeless in the political circumstances. He insisted that "our moral freedom lies in our taking responsibility for our situation".

Some of the extracts from Natan Hofshi used in this chapter date from the thirties and forties and refer to the war against Hitler. Other passages were written in Israel in the fifties and sixties. Significantly, it is difficult to distinguish between them. His pacifism was adamant. When people said it was not realistic, he disagreed. He said that conscientious objectors acted in a straightforward manner. They didn't just dream about peace; they created it in fact. Men were created in the image of God. Hofshi saw himself as someone who for this reason wanted to live a pure life (although, he was the first to admit, we're not angels). Conscientious objectors had a religious faith in the holiness of life, in the hidden voice of humanity. "One can fail," he said. "But one does one's best."[42]

One notices when studying Jewish pacifists how many in the end despair of politics and define the Kingdom of Israel as one of the spirit. In contemporary terms they renounce the Jewish state and often become anti-Zionists. In Israel, Judaism comes up against the problem which also faced the first Quaker state in America. When one has political power, the exercise of pacifism and the preservation of the religious state may be incompatible one with another. Yet to say that *realpolitik* and religion do not mix is not an inevitable response. As the *halakha* regulates our relationship with other individuals, and with the practicalities of life, there is no indication that it is not also to regulate relationships between groups.

Rabbi Glustrom has retold a Talmudic Midrash. "When the Israelites were assembled at Mount Sinai, an apparition of *The Book* and *The Sword* appeared before them. A heavenly voice demanded that they make a solemn choice: 'You can have one or the other but not both. If you choose *The Book* you must renounce *The Sword*. Should you choose *The Sword* then *The Book* will perish'."[43]

The original Midrash puts it in more neutral terms: "Rabbi Eleazar said that at Sinai, the Book and the Sword came down from Heaven wrapped together. God said to Israel, If you observe what is written in the book then you will be saved. But if you refuse to obey it, then the Sword will destroy you."[44]

Again we have this bizarre, surrealist vision, an incongruous coupling which apparently suggests that there is a choice between Judaism and military destruction. The men who figure in this book did indeed believe that, and devoted their lives to the principle. But when all is said and done, what do they count for? One concludes that all were in some way marginal to the Jewish community and apparently without political significance or hope of success.

Hans Mommsen who describes the small group involved in the July 1944 plot against Hitler as similarly marginal, with unrealistic plans and little hope of success, makes this observation. "It is not an easy matter to admit that National Socialism, or at least some of the aims for which it stood, had taken such root in the minds and behaviour of the mass of Germans that any will to resist it could only have been mobilised on the basis of ultimately utopian and deeply religious convictions, while capable, pragmatic politicians ... resigned themselves to complete passivity or believed there was absolutely nothing that could be realistically done in the situation."[45]

Since 1944, again and again, in the former Soviet Union, in the West, in the Middle East, violence itself has been sustained by ideology and often by religious conviction as well. One could suggest that the book and the sword come bundled together because in life too they are inseparable. There is no war which is not blessed with a moral purpose nor fuelled by ethnic and religious attachments. Religious fundamentalism and ideologies of violence can only be challenged by alternative moralities and ideals. There are Jews who have obstinately clung to that alternative view, and their courage and inspiration to do so come from the Jewish tradition.

Appendix
The Religious Basis of Jewish Pacifism

The classic texts of Judaism are not readily accessible to the average reader. The convoluted argument of the Talmud and the sheer quantity of material are a bar to reading the original. So for reference there follows a short selection of texts which are either discussed in this book or which are relevant.

The Talmud

There are two versions of the Talmud, the Babylonian Talmud (available in English), completed about 600CE and the Jerusalem Talmud, about 400CE. Both have at their centre versions of an earlier biblical commentary called The Mishnah.

The Mishnah, dating from 200CE records an oral tradition going back to 200 BCE.

In the Talmud, each section of Mishnah is followed by a further commentary called the Gemara. The Babylonian Talmud, the longer and the one in most common use, is divided (like the Mishnah) into six parts or Orders. Each Order is subdivided into Tractates which in turn are made up of chapters.

Babylonian Talmud references are given by Tractate and a standard page number, either a or b. Bab. Talmud, Shabat 31a. refers to Tractate "Shabat" page 31a.

> What is hateful to you, do not do to your fellow man; that is the essence of the Torah. The rest is commentary: go and learn.
>
> Hillel (1st c. BCE) Bab. Talmud, Shabat 31a

Bible quotations

Hebrew Bible references are given by Book using the English names. Chapter and verse divisions are of Christian origin, but are commonly used by Jews.

> Whoever sheds man's blood, by man his blood shall be shed; for in the image of God made He man.
>
> Genesis IX 6

This is one of the commandments given to Noah. These commandments predate the Covenant with Abraham and Jews therefore regard them as a universal moral code. This commandment is understood by pacifists to reinforce the injunction against taking human life, but it has also been used (as by Rashi, the French medieval commentator) to justify capital punishment.

Midrash

The Rabbinic Bible Commentaries called Midrash come from the same period as the Mishnah and Talmud. Midrash provide a free ranging and spiritual discussion of the inner meaning of Bible texts. Their chapter divisions do not coincide with the Biblical division of chapter and verse. References in this book are largely to *Midrash Rabbah* (The Great Midrash).

Midrash Genesis Rabbah XXIV discusses the meaning and relative importance of two Biblical commandments: *Thou shalt love thy neighbour as thyself* and *This is the book of the generations of Adam*.

Compressed though it is, the discussion encompasses both the question of what is meant by one's neighbour, and the idea that God is present within every human being.

> Ben 'Azzai said: *This is the book of the descendants of Adam* is a great principle of the Torah. R. Akiba said: *But thou shalt love thy neighbour as thyself* (Lev. XIX 18) is an even greater principle. Hence you must not say, Since I have been put to shame, let my neighbour be put to shame. R. Tanhuma said: If you do so, know whom you put to shame, [for] *In the likeness of God made He him.*

In an earlier book of Midrash, Sifra on Deuteronomy, Perek 4, the order of the statements is different.

> *You shall love your neighbour as yourself* and Rabbi Akiba said, this is the greatest of all commandments. Ben 'Azzai said, *This is the book of the generations of Adam*, this is the greatest of all.

Whereas one's "neighbour" could be interpreted as a member of one's own community, "This is the book of the generations of Adam" leaves us in no doubt that our duty in Torah is to all descendents of Adam, the first man. All men are created in the image of God and in shaming them we shame God.

For Jews, God's image in man extended to the human body. A dead body must be buried out of respect for God in whose image it was made.

War and Arms are incompatible with religion

> For out of Zion shall go forth the law, and the word of the Lord from Jerusalem.

> And He shall judge between the nations, and shall decide for many peoples; And they shall beat their swords into ploughshares, and their

spears into pruning hooks; Nation shall not lift up sword against nation, neither shall they learn war any more.

Isaiah II 3-4

A man should not go out on the Sabbath wearing a sword. Rabbi Eliezar said [it is permitted] as a weapon is a personal ornament. The rabbis said, on the contrary, it is a mark of disgrace as it says (Isaiah II) they shall beat their swords into ploughshares ... nation shall not raise a sword against nation.

Mishnah Shabat 63a

And there shalt thou build an altar unto the Lord thy God, an altar of stones: thou shalt not lift up any iron tool upon them.

Deuteronomy XXVII 5

Commenting on this verse, Mechilta Yitro, (Midrash on Exodus) explains that the altar was created to lengthen man's days, and iron (weapons) to shorten them. Therefore iron implements must not be used to build an altar.

And David said to Solomon, My son, as for me, it was in my mind to build an house unto the name of the Lord my God: but the word of the Lord came to me, saying, Thou hast shed blood abundantly, and hast made great wars: thou shalt not build a house unto my name, because thou hast shed much blood onto the earth in my sight.

Behold a son shall be born to thee, who shall be a man of rest; and I will give him rest from his enemies round about: for his name shall be Solomon, and I will give peace and quietness to Israel in his days. he shall build a house for my name and he shall be my son and I shall be his father.

1 Chronicles XXII 7-10

Saving life is to take precedence over the Law

The circumstances under which the law may and may not be broken are given in the Babylonian Talmud Sanhedrin 74a:

For every law of Torah the rule is that a man may transgress the commandment rather than suffer death, excepting idolatry, incest and murder...Murder may not be committed (even) to save one's life..for example someone came to Raba and told him "The general of my town has ordered me to go and kill a named person, and if not, the general will kill me." Rabba said to him, "Let the general kill you rather than that you should commit murder. Who knows that your blood is redder? Maybe his blood is redder."

God fights for Israel

The idea that God fights for Israel recurs in Jewish sources from Exodus and Judges onwards.

> And Moses said unto the people: Fear ye not, stand (still) and see the salvation of the Lord, which He will work for you today; for whereas ye have seen the Egyptians today, ye shall see them again no more for ever.
> The Lord will fight for you, and you shall hold your peace.
>
> Exodus XIV 13-14

The Hebrew word translated as 'hold your peace' is not *Shalom* meaning peace but *Haresh* meaning to be silent or dumb or speechless.

(F.Brown, S.R. Driver and C.A.Briggs eds. Gesenius, trans. Robinson *A Hebrew and English Lexicon of the Old Testament*)

The Jerusalem Talmud, Sotah VIII, explores the idea that God fights for the Jews, with natural forces.

> It is written (2 Samuel XX 13) *Through the brightness before him were coals of fire kindled* or (Psalm XVIII 13) *At the brightness that was before him his thick clouds passed, hail stones and coals of fire....* it is to face up to their squadrons. They burn to prevent the passage of the enemies' forces. God launches hail against their war machines and glowing coals against their catapults; and finally fire to burn their naphtha. Then verse 14. *The Lord also thundered in the Heavens, and the Highest gave His voice; hail stones and coals of fire.*
>
> He thunders against their flaming torches, he makes himself heard in order to equal the sound of their chariots. *Yea he sent out his arrows and scattered them; and he shot out lightenings, and discomforted them.* He hurls his arrows to divert those of his enemies; *they scatter* these words indicate that the enemy were dispersed by his blows. According to Aba B Cahana, this verse proves that the Egyptians had been deployed in different divisions according to the orders of their leaders. But on the one hand the arrows sent against them by God, and on the other hand lightning striking amongst them frightened them and dispersed them. The lightening was the counterpart of the brightness of their arms.
>
> Jerusalem Talmud Sotah VIII Halakha 3

(References to the Jerusalem Talmud are usually by Tractate, Chapter (*Perek*) and numbered paragraphs (*Halakha*), or occasionally, as in the *Encyclopedia Judaica*, to page numbers in the Krotoschin edition.)

Exemptions from Military Service

The Biblical exemptions from military service are as follows:

> And the officers shall speak unto the people, saying, What man is there that hath built a new house, and hath not dedicated it? Let him go and return to his house, lest he die in the battle, and another man dedicate it.
>
> And what man is he that hath planted a vineyard, and hath not yet eaten of it? Let him also go and return unto his house, lest he die in the battle and another man eat of it.
>
> And what man is there that hath betrothed a wife, and hath not taken her? Let him go and return unto his house, lest he die in the battle, and another man take her.
>
> And the officers shall speak further unto the people, and they shall say, What man is there that is fearful and faint hearted? Let him go and return unto his house, lest his brethren's heart faint as well as his heart.
>
> Deuteronomy XX 5-8

The Tosefta, (referred to in Chapter 4) is a supplementary collection of oral teaching not included in the Mishnah. The Tosefta interprets the exemption of the faint-hearted as a matter of conscience, not necessarily implying weakness of character.

> Rabbi Akiva says, *One who is afraid and soft of heart* is to tell you that even if he is the greatest of heroes and the strongest of men, if he is compassionate, he should return home.
>
> Tosefta Sotah Ch 7.14

The classic discussion of Biblical exemption has not been about pacifism but the issues raised by the rabbis have a bearing on conscientious objection. They deal with the question of why men may be unwilling to fight, the problems of establishing genuine objectors, and the disadvantages of retaining soldiers who are unwilling to fight.

The Babylonian Talmud Sotah VIII discusses the Biblical exemption of the fainthearted. It suggests that the "fearful" are afraid they will be killed in battle as a punishment for sins they have committed:

> And the officers shall speak further unto the people etc. Rabbi Akiba says 'fearful and fainthearted' is to be understood literally viz., he is unable to stand in the battle-ranks and see a drawn sword. Rabbi Jose the Galilean says: 'fearful and fainthearted' alludes to one who is afraid because of transgressions he had committed.
>
> Bab. Talmud, Sotah VIII Mishnah 44a

The transgressions are then listed; they all involve infringement of regulations governing marriage, both of the priests and lay Israelites.

The Gemara (44b) suggests that some sins are so trivial that no man can be regarded as entirely innocent:

> What is the difference between R.Jose and R. Jose the Galilean? -The issue between them is the transgression of a Rabbinical Ordinance. With whom does the following teaching accord: He who speaks between [donning] one phylactery and the other has committed a transgression and returns home under the war regulations?

The Talmudic debate continues

> Our rabbis taught if he heard the sound of trumpets and was terror-stricken, or the crash of shields and was terror stricken, or [beheld] the brandishing of swords and urine discharged itself upon his knees, he returns home? With whom [does it accord]? Are we to say that it is with Rabbi Akiba and not Rabbi Jose the Galilean? In such a circumstance even Rabbi Jose the Galilean admits [that he returns home], because it is written, *Lest his brethren's heart melt as his heart.*
>
> Extracts from Bab. Talmud, Sotah VIII 44b

The Jerusalem Talmud looked at the difficulty of establishing that exemptions were genuine, without requiring men to make a public confession of sins they have committed.

> It has been taught: all the individuals enumerated in the Mishnah as having the right to return home because exempted from service must provide proof of their assertion (prove that they are not lying with the straightforward aim of escaping the dangers of war), except for the man who in a manner of speaking has his witnesses at hand (whom fear and apprehension of danger make to tremble and turn pale in advance). This is in line with the opinion of him who says: that by the "fearful" one means someone who is incapable of standing valiantly in the ranks of the fighters with a naked sword in his hand (his face betrays his lack of courage). According to another opinion, however which says this fear is caused by the sins of which this man is conscious, he should still produce the proof of his assertion (say what the sin is in order to convince that this is not a pretext to escape from danger). That is why the Law grants to these several different categories of people the facility of being able to go back home without fighting, in order to avoid the shame of confessing their sins in public."
>
> The Jerusalem Talmud, Sotah VIII

Sifre, an early rabbinic commentary on the Book of Deuteronomy, suggested that one should avoid public embarrassment for anyone returning home, not only for the sinners, but also the men who were afraid to fight.

> *What man is there that is fearful and fainthearted (20:8): And the officers shall speak further (20:8):*
> Why were all these matters spoken of? So that the cities of Israel should not become desolate; so taught Rabbi Jonathan ben Zakkai. Come and see how considerate God is for the honor of his creatures, even such as are fearful and fainthearted, so that when such a person returns, the others would say, Perhaps he left to build a house, or to plant a vineyard or to wed a wife. Other absentees had to present valid proof, but not the fearful and fainthearted, in whose case the proof is self-evident: he heard the crashing of shields and was terrified, he heard the neighing of horses and trembled, he heard the piercing sound of trumpets and was frightened, he saw the unsheathing of swords and water ran down between his knees.
>
> Piska 192

A little further on the commentary emphasises that the fearful must return home.

> *Lest his brethren's heart melt as his heart* (20:8) Showing that if one of them is afraid because of his sins, all would return home.
>
> Piska 197

(*Sifre: A Tannaitic Commentary on the Book of Deuteronomy* trans and ed. Reuven Hammer. Yale University Press 1986)

Ramban (Nachmanides), the medieval Spanish scholar, describes the "fearful" as men who retain religious scruples despite the reassurances of the religious authorities.

> According to the opinion of Rabbi Jose the Galilean, after the priest had assured them that G-d would help them and that not one man of them would be lacking, it was fitting that the Righteous put their trust in Him. Then, the officers warn those that are afraid [to go into battle] because of the transgressions they had committed. The Torah therefore gave everyone the opportunity of attributing his return home because of his house, his vineyard or his wife, in order to serve as a pretext for those who are returning home because they are afraid of their transgressions. And the meaning of the expression *lest he die in the*

battle [mentioned in each of the three categories] is that he will think so in his heart and he will flee.

Nachmanides analyses the difference between the fearful and the fainthearted, recognising that whether a man is a fighter or not will sometimes depend on his character.

Fainthearted. The meaning thereof is that it is not in his nature to see *the stroke of the sword, and slaughter,* for the *fearful* is he who does not trust and Scripture commands him to return to his home because of his deficient trust. The *faint-hearted* is sent home because of the weakness of his nature, for he will flee or faint.

Ramban (Nachmanides) *Commentary on the Torah. Vol V Deuteronomy* Trans and ed. Charles Chavel. Shilo Publishing House NY 1976

The Talmud discusses whether the exemptions apply to all wars, or to permitted wars but not to a war that is obligatory. (In the context of Torah, 'commanded' in the following passage means 'not forbidden', i.e. 'permitted')

To what does all the foregoing apply? To voluntary wars, but in the wars commanded by the Torah all go forth, even a bridegroom from his chamber and a bride from her canopy. Rabbi Judah says: To what does all the foregoing apply? To the wars commanded by the Torah; but in obligatory wars all go forth, even a bridegroom from his chamber and a bride from her canopy.

Sotah VIII Mishnah 44b.

Is war permitted?

Maimonides' explanation of wars which are obligatory and wars which are permitted (if any) is used by both sides in the peace debate. Maimonides' Mishnah Torah organises the law topic by topic. Regulation of warfare is covered in *The Book of Judges*, Melachim (on Kings and Wars).
Chapter 5 is used by Jews who wish to justify wars of defence.

The primary war which the king wages is a war for a religious cause. Which may be denominated a war for a religious cause? It includes the war against the seven nations, that against Amalek, and a war to deliver Israel from the enemy attacking him. Thereafter he may engage in an optional war, that is, a war against neighbouring nations to extend the borders of Israel and to enhance his greatness and prestige.

(Jews in peace movements object to this argument on the grounds that Maimonides is referring only to Biblical times. See following extracts)

Provisions for offering peace are given in Chapter 6.

1. No war is declared against any nation before peace offers are made to it. This obtains both in an optional war and a war for a religious cause, as it is said *"When thou drawest nigh unto a city to fight against it, then proclaim peace unto it"*. (Deuteronomy XX.10)

This is to say that one does not make war until one has offered peace. Little distinction is made between peace and capitulation. If the enemy accept peace, they must accept also the Noachide commandments and economic and political subjection.

Limits to warfare

Limits to warfare are given by Maimonides in Chapter 6.

7. When siege is laid to a city for the purpose of capture, it may not be surrounded on all four sides but only on three in order to give an opportunity for escape to those who would flee to save their lives, as it is said: *"And they warred against Midian, as the Lord commanded Moses* (Numbers XXXI.7). It has been learned by tradition that that was the instruction given to Moses.

8. It is forbidden to cut down fruit-bearing trees outside a (besieged) city, nor may a water channel be deflected from them so that they wither, as it is said: *Thou shall not destroy the trees thereof* (Deuteronomy XX:19)

10. Not only one who cuts down (fruit-producing) trees, but also one who smashes household goods, tears clothes, demolishes a building, stops up a spring, or destroys articles of food with a destructive intent, transgresses the command *Thou shalt not destroy.*

Moses Maimonides *Code. Book 14: The Book of Judges* trans and ed. A Hersham. Yale University Press 1949

Regulations on war applied only to Temple times.

In one edition of his book on the Negative Commandments Maimonides gives the opinion that the commandments regulating war and warfare are no longer operative.

Now since all these matters are known to most people, every Positive or Negative Command pertaining to the sacrifices or the rituals (in the Sanctuary), or the death penalties inflicted by the Court, or the

Sanhedrin, or the prophet and king, or the obligatory and non-obligatory war, it will not be necessary for me to say concerning them: "This commandment applies only during the existence of the Sanctuary," since this is clear on the basis of what we have mentioned.

Maimonides *The Commandments Vol. II Negative*, 14th Principle. trans. Charles B. Chavel, Soncino Press 1967

Jews must not make war

The discussion which interprets part of the Song of Songs as a prohibition on Israel from waging war in her exile comes from the Babylonian Talmud, The Three Oaths. Jews must avoid war principally to avoid retribution.

I adjure you, O daughters of Jerusalem, by the gazelles, and by the hinds of the field, [that you awaken not, nor stir up love, until it please].

And R. Zera? – That implies that Israel shall not go up [all together as if surrounded] by a wall.

And R. Judah? – Another *'I adjure you'* is written in Scripture.

And R. Zera? – That text is required for [an exposition] like that of R. Jose son of R. Hanina who said: What was the purpose of those three adjurations? –

One, that Israel shall not go up [all together as if surrounded] by a wall,

the second, that whereby the Holy One blessed be He, adjured Israel that they shall not rebel against the nations of the world;

and the third is that whereby the Holy One blessed be He, adjured the idolaters that they shall not oppress Israel too much.

Bab. Talmud Kethubot 111a

The Guardians of the City

They teach that Rabbi ben Yohai said, If one sees ruined cities in the land of Israel, you must know they failed to survive because of lack of schools and teachers, according to (Jeremiah IX 11-12) *Why is the land perished and burned up like a wilderness where no one passes? It is because, said the Eternal, You have forsaken My Law.* Rabbi Judah the Prince instructed Rabbi Hiya, Rabbi Asi and Rabbi Ami to go on a journey to various places in Israel to organise education. They arrived in a town where they could find no trace of teaching. They demanded to be taken to those who were known as the Guardians of the City. And they cried, Are these the guardians of the city? No, rather the destroyers of the city. And they said, Then who are the guardians of the city? And the rabbis said, The writers, the teachers, those who instruct the young.

Jerusalem Talmud. Hagigah, Perek 1 Halakha 7

Notes

Chapter 1

1. *Jewish Chronicle*, 19 January 1917
2. ibid.
3. A survey showed 250 Friends in the armed forces, spring 1915. *The Friend*, 28 May 1915
4. *Jewish Chronicle*, 28 January 1916
5. Jewish Peace Society, *Annual Report*, 1915
6. *Jewish World*, 19 April 1916
7. *Liverpool Daily Post*, 6 April 1916
8. *Jewish World*, 19 April 1916
9. Author's conversation with G.J.Gollin, 1986
10. Letter from H. Endbinder, 8 March 1916
11. Papers of J.E. Hoare, held at Department of Documents, Imperial War Museum, London.
12. Author's conversation with R. Page Arnot, 1985, also *Jewish Chronicle*, 14 July 1916
13. *Jewish Chronicle*, 30 June 1916
14. ibid. 19 March 1915
15. David Hudaly, *Liverpool Old Hebrew Congregation 1780-1974*. 1974
16. N. Kokosalakis, *Ethnic Identity and Religion: Tradition and Change in Liverpool Jewry*, University of America Press 1982
17. In 1915 seven Jewish congregations in Liverpool joined for charitable purposes in a Jewish Communal Council. The two leading synagogues, Hope Street and Prince's Road, held aloof. In July 1916 Prince's Road again refused to join joint fund raising efforts of the Jewish War Victims Relief Committee.
18. Taking the population figures for 1910, of 615,000 Jews, this would seem to be a higher proportion of Jews than in the British army, though one should note that not even the German figure is as high as the proportion of Australian Jews who served, perhaps in some measure due to the wide reaching compulsion imposed in Australia.
19. *Liverpool Daily Post*, 9 March 1916
20. *Jewish Chronicle*, 21 May 1916
21. Harris family reminiscence.
22. *Liverpool Express*, 11 March 1916
23. Michael Adler ed. *British Jewry Book of Honour*, Caxton 1922
24. *Jewish Chronicle*, 3 May 1916
25. *Jewish World*, 5 May 1916
26. *Jewish Chronicle*, 10 March 1916
27. *Jewish Chronicle*, 17 March 1916
28. Letter, 5 March 1916
29. *Jewish Chronicle*, 28 April 1916
30. *Jewish World*, 5 April 1916
31. *Jewish Chronicle*, 4 February 1916
32. Samuel papers.
33. *Jewish Chronicle*, 28 April 1916
34. B. Williams, *The Making of Manchester Jewry 1740-1875*, Manchester UP 1976, points out that Jews were not peripheral in that city.

35. *Liverpool Daily Post*, 7 March 1916
36. Letter from J. Abrahams and others to the Chief Rabbi, 18 November 1917, archive of the Chief Rabbi's Office.
37. See also Hudaly op cit. and Barry A. Kosmin, "Localism and Pluralism in British Jewry 1900-80" in *Transactions, Jewish Historical Society of England* XXVIII, 1984
38. Letter from J. Harris, 26 June 1916, Gaster papers.
39. *Liverpool Daily Post*, 6 March 1916
40. Testimonial from Lily Montagu, 12 September 1916. Harris family papers.
41. Cutting. Harris family papers.
42. Letter, 12 March 1916
43. Michael R. Marrus, *The Politics of Assimilation: A Study of the French Jewish Community at the time of the Dreyfus Affair*, Oxford University Press 1971

Chapter 2

1. Henrietta Szold, 1903, quoted in William M. Brinner, and Moses Rischin eds *Like All the Nations: The Life and Legacy of Judah L. Magnes*, State University of N.Y. 1984
2. *The American Hebrew*, 12 January 1917
3. Stephen Wise, *Challenging Years:The Autobiography of Stephen S. Wise*, East and West Library 1951, and John Haynes Holmes, "Should Jews be Pacifists?", *Opinion: A Journal of Jewish Life and Letters*, September 1940
4. Woodrow Wilson, Address to Congress, 2 April 1917
5. *American Hebrew*, 9 February 1917
6. Melvin Urofsky, *A Voice that Spoke for Justice: the life and times of Stephen S. Wise*, State University of New York Press 1982
7. Stephen Wise, *Challenging Years*, op cit.
8. C. Roland Marchand, *The American Peace Movement and Social Reform, 1898-1918* Princeton 1982. For American pacifism see also Merle E. Curti, *Peace or War: The American Struggle 1636-1936*, Norton 1936, and Charles Chatfield, *For Peace and Justice: Pacifism in America 1914-41*, University of Tennessee Press 1971
9. *American Hebrew*, 20 April 1917
10. *American Hebrew*, 19 January 1917
11. Michael May, *Can Prejudice be Measured*, Institute of Jewish Affairs. Research Report 18, December 1981
12. Letter to his parents cited by Arthur Goren ed. *Dissenter in Zion: From the Writings of Judah L. Magnes*, Harvard University Press 1982, from Norman Bentwich, *For Zion's Sake: A Biography of Judah L. Magnes*, Jewish Publication Society Philadelphia 1954
13. From Goell, *Aliyah* and Bentwich, *For Zion's Sake*, op cit.
14. Opening address, First American Conference for Democracy and Terms of Peace, Madison Gardens, New York, 30 May 1917, in Judah Magnes, *War-time Addresses 1917-21*, Thomas Selzer New York 1923
15. Journal entry, 18 July 1919, in Arthur Goren ed. *Dissenter in Zion: From the Writings of Judah L. Magnes*, Harvard University Press 1982
16. *American Hebrew*, 16 March 1917

17. Address to the People's Relief Committee, Cooper Union, New York, 29 December 1917 in *War-time Addresses,* op cit.
18. ibid.
19. Journal entry, 2 October 1917, in Arthur Goren ed. 1982, op cit.
20. Opening address, The Jewish Labor Congress, Labor Hall, New York, 16 January 1919 in *War-time Addresses,* op cit.
21. "Jews and Pacifism". Journal entry, 2 October 1917, in Goren 1982 op cit.
22. Address to the World Peace Fellowship, Town Hall, New York, 30 November 1921 in *War-time Addresses,* op cit.
23. Opening address, The Jewish Labor Congress, NY 16 January 1919 op cit.
24. Marchand, op cit.
25. *American Israelite,* 7 June 1917
26. *New York Times,* 4 June 1917
27. Opening address Jewish Labor Congress NY 16 January 1919 op cit.
28. "The Rights of Jews as a Nation", address, Conference of American Academy of Political and Social Science, Philadelphia, 21 April 1919 in *War-time Addresses,* op cit.
29. Godfrey Harris, "Our Jewish Soldier Boy" in *Jewish Comment,* Baltimore, 8 June 1917
30. *American Israelite,* 17 May 1917
31. *American Israelite,* 4 April 1918
32. *American Hebrew,* 29 June 1917
33. *American Hebrew,* 2 November 1917
34. Constituent meeting of the People's Council of America, West Side Auditorium, Chicago, 2 September 1917 in *War-time Addresses,* op cit.
35. "For Democracy and Terms of Peace", address New York, 30 May 1917 op cit.
36. CCAR Yearbook 1917. Resolution 3.
37. Irma Cohon, Letter to Harold Reinhart 1917. Reinhart papers.
38. cf Arthur Goren op cit.
39. Judah Magnes, Letter to Israel Zangwill, April 1922, quoted in Bentwich *For Zion's Sake,* op cit.
40. cf. Horace C. Peterson and Gilbert C. Fite, *Opponents of War 1917-19,* Maddison 1957
41. *American Israelite,* 18 October 1917
42. Henrietta Szold, letter to Richard Gottheil 13 May 1917, Central Zionist Archive, Jerusalem, quoted in Zeitlin *Henrietta Szold,* ref. Brinner and Rischin, op cit.
43. Cong. Rec 66 Cong 1 sess., 23 July 1919, p.3065 quoted in Peterson and Fite, op cit.
44. Chicago, 2 September 1917, in *War-time Addresses,* op cit.
45. Address to World Peace Fellowship, 30 November 1921, op cit.
46. *American Israelite,* 9 August 1917
47. *New York Times,* 10 and 11 December 1918
48. For a full account of Magnes and the Kehillah see Arthur A. Goren, *New York Jews and the Quest for Community: The Kehillah Experiment 1908-22,* Columbia University Press 1970
49. July 1920, on a Jewish Defence Committee mission.
50. "The Old America and the New", Chicago, 8 February 1920 in *War-time Addresses,* op cit.

Chapter 3

1. R.K. *A Word to the Legionaries*. Address, Conference of the Agricultural Workers' Association and the Palestine Volunteers, August 1918, in Mauri Samuel ed. *The Ploughwoman*, N.L.Brown Inc.
2. Paul Johnson op cit. refers to Leo Rosen *The Joys of Yiddish*, Harmondsworth 1971
3. Maurice Pearlman, *Collective Adventure*, Heinemann 1938
4. Simha Flapan, *Zionism and the Palestinians*, Croom Helm 1979
5. Yehoshafat Harkabi, *The Bar Kokhba Syndrome: Risk and Realism in International Politics*, Rossel Books NY 1983
6. Hans Köhn, *Living in a World Revolution*, Trident Press N.Y. 1964
7. Letter to Dr. Feival on resignation from *Keren Hayesod*, The Palestine Foundation Fund, 21 November 1929, in Paul Mendes-Flohr ed. *A Land of Two Peoples*, Oxford University Press, New York 1983
8. Hans Köhn, *The Idea of Nationalism*, Macmillan 1944
9. Letter of resignation, 21 November 1929, op cit.
10. William M. Brinner and Moses Rischin eds. *Like All the Nations?* op cit.
11. *Living in a World Revolution*, op cit.
12. Hans Köhn, *Jewish Humanism* (in French), 1931
13. Ahad ha'Am, letter, 18 November 1913, in Mendes-Flohr op cit.
14. Susan Lee Hattis, *The Bi-National Idea in Palestine During Mandate Times*, Shikmona Pub. Haifa. 1970
15. Statutes, reprinted in Mendes-Flohr op cit.
16. Letter of resignation, 21 November 1929, op cit.
17. Hans Köhn, *History of Nationalism in the East*, 1928. English ed 1929
18. *Living in a World Revolution* op cit.
19. See also Hans Köhn, *Force or Reason – Issues of the 20th Century*, 1937
20. 1928, quoted in Arthur Ruppin, ed. Bein, *Memoirs, Diaries and Letters*, Weidenfeld and Nicholson, 1973
21. Ruth Bondy, *The Emissary: A Life of Enzo Sereni*, trans Shlomo Katz. Little, Brown & Co. 1977
22. Enzo Sereni, "Dal Profondo", *Rechovot*, 10 May 1928, in Enzo Sereni, *Vita e Brabi Scelti*, Gruppo Sionistica Milanese, Keren Kajëmeth le Israel, November 1947. Unless attributed to English sources, all Sereni quotations are from the Italian.
23. Quoted in Clara Urquhart and Peter L. Brent, *Enzo Sereni: A Hero of our Times*, Hale 1967
24. Renzo de Felice, *Storia degli Ebrei Italiani sotto il Fascismo*, 1961/1972, or (in English) Susan Zuccotti, *The Italians and the Holocaust: Persecution Rescue and Survival*, Halban / Weidenfeld and Nicholson 1987
25. Quoted in Urquhart and Brent op cit.
26. Enzo Sereni, *Dal Profondo*, op cit.
27. Enzo Sereni, *La Questione Ebraica*, Tel Aviv 1939, *Quaderni di Vita Ebraica* 6, Hechaluz, Rome 1946
28. Enzo Sereni and R.E. Ashery eds. *Jews and Arabs in Palestine*, 1936
29. Ruth Bondy op cit.
30. A useful outline may be found in Peter L. Berger, *Invitation to Sociology*, Penguin 1966

31. "Lettera dal Treno per L'Egitto" (Letter from the Train to Egypt), September 1940, Reprinted in Daniel Carpi, Attilo Milano and Umberto Nahon eds. *Scritti in Memoria di Enzo Sereni*, Jerusalem 1970

32. *Report on the State of Palestine*, Executive Committee of the Palestine Arab Congress, 13 October 1925

33. *Jews and Arabs in Palestine* op cit.

34. Anda Amir, *Enzo Sereni: Ten Dramatic Episodes* (in Hebrew), Gesher Readings in Easy Hebrew, Rabin ed., Vol XII, World Zionist Organisation, Jerusalem 1964

35. "Lettera dal Treno" op cit.

36. Quoted in Brinner et al. op cit from Zeitlin, *Henrietta Szold*

37. Enzo Sereni, Lettera ai figli, 27 December 1942, in *Vita e Brani Scelti* op cit.

38. Golda Meir, Postscript in Bondy op cit.

39. "Lettera dal treno" op cit.

40. *Dal Profondo* op cit.

Chapter 4

1. Rabbeinu Yonah ben Avraham of Gerona *The Gates of Repentance* trans. Shraga Silverstein, Feldheim Publishers, Jerusalem 1976

2. ibid. quoting Bab. Talmud Shabbath 54b.

3. ibid.

4. Deuteronomy XX

5. Deuteronomy XX 10

6. Bab. Talmud Sotah 44b. See also Gendler "War in the Jewish Tradition", in James Finn ed. *A Conflict of Loyalties*, Western Publishing Co 1968, reprinted in M.M. Kellner ed. *Contemporary Jewish Ethics*, Sanhedrin 1978

7. S.Y. Zevin, *L'Or Halakha*, HaMilchama Mosad HaRav Kook, Jerusalem 1946

8. David Biale, *Power and Powerlessness in Jewish History*, Schocken 1986

9. Maimonides, *Mishnah Torah* Book 14, The Laws concerning Kings and Wars, trans. A.M. Hershman, Yale Judaica Vol. III

10. Maimonides, *The Commandments* Vol. 2, Negative Commandments. The 14th Principle, trans. Charles B. Chaval, Soncino Press 1967

11. Millard Lind, *Yahweh is a Warrior, The Theology of Warfare in Ancient Israel*, Herald Press 1971

12. Deuteronomy VII 23, in Jerusalem Talmud, Sotah VIII, tome 6-7 2013c (ed. Schwab in French)

13. Isaiah VI 3 and in the *Amida*, the "standing" prayer whose benedictions are recited by observant Jews three times a day. In the context of Isaiah, *Zvot* (hosts) can be understood to refer to hosts of angels. Since the same word is used in Genesis I, the prayer book of the Reform Synagogues of Great Britain translates it as "all creation".

14. A. Lichtenstein. "Is there an Ethic Independent of Halakha?" in Kellner ed., *Contemporary Jewish Ethics* op cit., also Lichtenstein, "Church and State", in *Judaism* XV 1966

15. Leviticus XIX 2

16. Louis Jacobs, in Moses Cordevero, *The Palm Tree of Deborah*, ed. and trans. Louis Jacobs, Valentine Mitchell 1960. See also David Shapiro, "Doctrine of the Image of God", in *Judaism* XIII 1963

17. Moses Cordevero, *The Palm Tree of Deborah*, ed. Louis Jacobs, Valentine Mitchell 1960
18. ibid.
19. Moses Hyam Luzzatto, *The Path of the Just* (of the Upright), trans. Shraga Silverstein, Feldheim 1966 and 1980
20. ibid.
21. Moses Hyam Luzzatto, *The Way of God*, trans. Kaplan, Feldheim 1978
22. Jerusalem Talmud. Chag 1:7 (see appendix). Norman Lamm, "Ideology of the Neturei Karta according to the Satmerar Version", in *Tradition* 12 Fall 1971
23. Letter 1898, in Emile Marmorstein, *Heaven at Bay: the Jewish Kulturkampf in the Holy Land*, Oxford University Press 1948
24. I. Domb, *The Transformation:The Case of the Neturei Karta*, London 1958
25. Numbers XXIII 9
26. Letter sent at the suggestion of R. Yosef Chaim Sonnenfeld, reprinted *Jewish Guardian* Vol.III No. 2, 5747, Summer '987
27. Aaron Samuel Tamaret, "Politics and Passion" (extracts from *Judaism and Freedom* 1905 and *Knesset Yisrael Umilchamot Ha-Goyim* 1920) trans. Everett Gendler, *Judaism* XII 1 Winter 1963; and "Passover and Non violence", from the Sermon *Liberty* Shabat Hagadol 1906, published in *Musar Hatorah v Hayahadut* Vilna 1912, in English trans. Everett Gendler, *Judaism* XVII 1968. Both articles reprinted in *Roots of Jewish Non-Violence*, JPF reprint 1981
28. *Tosefot* to (Talmud) Baba Kama 23
29. Amrom Blau. Newspaper advertisement, *The Guardian*, London, 28 January 1988, refs to Bab. Talmud Kesubos (Kethubot) 111A and Midrash Genesis Rabbah 93
30. Goan R. Joseph Rosen of Dwinsk, quoted by Domb op cit.
31. Bab. Talmud Kethubot 111a (see appendix)
32. Letter, Goan Rabbi Joseph Rosen of Dwinsk 1903/4 quoted in Domb op cit.
33. Harry M. Rabinowicz, *Hasidism: Its Movement and its Masters*, Aronson 1988
34. *Jewish Guardian* Vol.II No. 7, 5783, Summer '983. Neturei Karta of USA.
35. *Jewish Guardian* Vol.II No. 8, 5784, Spring '984. Neturei Karta of USA.
36. Quoted by John Bulloch, *Independent*, 7 March 1988
37. Manifesto signed by the Guardians of the City, 26 May 1967, quoted in Marmorstein, *Heaven at Bay* op cit.
38. Louis Jacobs, "The Relationship Between Religion and Ethics in Jewish Thought", in Kellner ed. op cit.

Chapter 5

1. Letter to a Dear Friend, New York, May 1920, published in *Dissenter in Zion*, ed. Goren, who suggests it was written to Norman Bentwich. Material published by Magnes in *Like All the Nations*
2. Harkabi, *The Bar Kokhba Syndrome* op cit.
3. S. Zalman Abramov, *The Perpetual Dilemma:Jewish Religion in the Jewish State*, Associated University Presses, Cranbury 1976 also *Encyclopedia Judaica*
4. Magnes, *New York Times*, 24 November 1929, quoted in Goren op cit.
5. Helen Bentwich, *If I forget Thee: some chapters of autobiography 1912-1920*, Elek London 1973

6. *Abraham Isaac Kook*, trans. and ed. Ben Zion. Bokser SPCK Classics of Western Spirituality, 1979

7. Ahad Ha-Am, *The Jewish State and the Jewish problem* trans. in *Ten Essays on Zionism and Judaism*, Routledge 1922

8. Journal, 17 December 1941, in Goren op cit.

9. Quoted in Hattis op cit.

10. 13 September 1929, in Goren op cit.

11. Norman and Helen Bentwich, *Mandate Memories 1918-48*, Hogarth Press 1965

12. Letter to a Dear Friend. New York May 1920, in Goren ed. op cit who suggests it was to Norman Bentwich. Material published by Magnes in *Like All the Nations*, op cit

13. 13 September 1925

14. Letter to Stephen Wise, 6 February 1930, in Goren op cit.

15. Menachem Begin, *The Revolt*, 1952 revised 1979. W.H.Allen, Futura 1980

16. Leo Pinsker, "Auto-Emancipation" from *The Zionist Dream*, ed. Herzberg, from *The Road to Freedom* ed. B. Netanyahu NY 1944

17. Helen and Norman Bentwich op cit.

18. Journal, 4 July 1928, in Goren op cit.

19. Letter, *New York Times*, 18 July 1937 in Goren op cit.

20. 29 October 1939

21. In July 1947 Buber published his solution of the previous year.

22. Minutes of meeting, 26 April 1948, Goren. Islam is as diverse as Judaism in its teaching on war. The Jihad is not endorsed, for example, by Sufi Moslems, or Ahmadi Moslems. see, Hazrat Mirza Tahir Ahmad, *Murder in the Name of Allah*, 1955, English ed. 1989

23. Edward Said, *Orientalism*, Routledge and Kegan Paul 1978

24. From S.Burnshaw, T. Carmi and E.Spicehandler, *The Modern Hebrew Poem Itself*, Holt, Rinehart and Winston 1966

25. Yehuda Amichai, *Selected Poems*, trans. Chana Bloch and Stephen Mitchell, Penguin 1988

26. From T. Carmi ed. *The Penguin Book of Hebrew Verse*, 1981

27. Evidence before the Anglo American enquiry.

28. Norman and Helen Bentwich, *Mandate Memories 1918-48*, 1965

29. Arthur Ruppin, ed. Alex Bein, *Memoirs, Diaries and Letters*, Weidenfeld and Nicholson 1971

30. Paul Mendes-Flohr ed. *A Land of Two Peoples: Martin Buber on Jews and Arabs*, Oxford University Press 1983

31. Martin Buber, *I and Thou*, 1923 trans. Ronald Gregor Smith, T & T Clark 1937

32. "The Demand of the Spirit and Historical Reality", in Martin Buber *Pointing the Way*, Routledge and Kegan Paul 1957

33. Martin Buber, *Israel and the World* (essays), Schocken 1948/1963

34. 1973, originally *Israel and Palestine*, East and West Library 1952

35. Martin Buber, *Paths in Utopia*, 1945, pub Routledge and Kegan Paul 1949

36. Robert Weltsch, "Buber's Political Philosophy", in Schlip and Friedman eds. *The Philosophy of Martin Buber*, Opencourt 1967

37. 18 July 1938, in *The Palestine Post* and *Davar* (in Hebrew)

38. March 1939, in Mendes-Flohr op cit.
39. Martin Buber, *Briefwechsel aus sieben Jahrzehnten*, ed. Grete Schaeder, Heidelberg 1975, quoted as a footnote in Dresner's Introduction to Abraham Heschel, *The Circle of Baal Shem Tov*, University of Chicago Press 1985
40. In Mendes-Flohr op cit.
41. *Paths in Utopia* op cit.
42. "Interpretation and Misinterpretation of Jewish Territorialism", in David Newman ed. *The Impact of Gush Emunim*, Croom Helm 1985. Citing also Richard Hartshorn. "The Functional Approach in Political Geography", *Annals of the Association of American Geographers* Vol. 40, 1950 pp 95-130, David B. Knight, "Identity and territory: Geographical Perspectives on Nationalism and Regionalism", *Annals of the Association of American Geographers* vol. LXXII 1982 pp 514-531
43. Letter fragment, possibly to Felix Warburg, quoted in Mendes-Flohr in Brinner et al. op cit.
44. *The Great Challenge*, N.Y. 1946, in Goren op cit.
45. 15 January 1947, in Goren op cit.

Chapter 6

1. Sermon. Emil G Hirsch, Sinai Temple Chicago, 22 May 1922, published in *Unity*, Chicago, 15 February 1923, in Abraham Cronbach, *The Quest for Peace*, Sinai Press 1937
2. CCAR Yearbook XXXVI, 1926
3. ibid.
4. Address 17 April 1932, in Cronbach, *The Quest for Peace* op cit.
5. Presidential Address, CCAR 1918.
6. Otto Nathan and Heinz Norden eds. *Einstein on Peace*, Simon & Schuster 1960, Methuen 1963
7. Letter to Dr. Eugene Rabinowitch, Editor, *Bulletin of Atomic Scientists*, 5 January 1951, in Nathan op cit.
8. CCAR Yearbook XLI, 1931
9. ibid.
10. CCAR Yearbook XLV, 1935
11. ibid.
12. Abraham Cronbach, *The Quest for Peace*, Sinai Press 1937
13. ibid.
14. CCAR Yearbook XLVI, 1936
15. Abraham Cronbach, "Autobiography", *American Jewish Archives* XI no.1 April 1959, for a biography of Cronbach see also Albert Vorspan, "Abraham Cronbach: Voice in the Wildnerness" in Albert Vorspan, *Giants of Justice*, Union of American Hebrew Congregations 1960
16. Cronbach, "Autobiography" op cit.
17. ibid.
18. "Autobiography" op cit. referring also to Mary Antin, author of the best-seller, *The Promised Land*, Heinemann 1912
19. Abraham Cronbach, "Divine Help as a Social Phenomenon", *Hebrew Union College Annual*, 1928

20. Abraham Cronbach, "Psychoanalysis and Religion", in *The Journal of Religion* (date uncertain, 1919-22)
21. Abraham Cronbach, "The Psychoanalytic Study of Judaism", *Hebrew Union College Annual* VIII-IX, 1932
22. *Quest for Peace* op cit. ref. to Midrash Genesis Rabbah XXIV end
23. "Autobiography" op cit.
24. A. Vorspan *Giants of Justice* op cit.
25. "Autobiography" op cit.
26. Abraham Cronbach, "The Logic of Pacifism", undated. Transcript from personal papers of R. John Rayner.
27. *The Quest for Peace* op cit.
28. 4 May 1939, quoted in Peter Chrisp and David Simkin, *Conscientious Objectors 1916 to the Present Day*, Tressell Publications 1988
29. Rachel Barker, *Conscience, Government and War: Conscientious Objection in Great Britain 1939-45*, Routledge and Kegan Paul 1982, quoting also Alan Bullock, *The Life and Times of Ernest Bevin*, Vol.1 1960
30. Angus Calder, *The People's War: Britain 1939-45*, Cape 1969
31. *Studies in Non-Violence* No.9, Peace Pledge Union 1981
32. Quoted by Hugh Cudlipp, *The Independent*, 15 May 1989
33. *Jewish Chronicle*, 24 November 1939
34. *Quest for Peace* op cit.
35. *Jewish Chronicle*, 29 December 1939
36. *Jewish Chronicle*, 19 January 1940
37. Undated press cutting, Harris archive.
38. *Jewish Chronicle*, 20 October 1939
39. For a full discussion of anti-Semitism see Tony Kushner, *The Persistence of Prejudice: anti-Semitism in Britain during the Second World War*, Manchester University Press 1989
40. *Jewish Chronicle*, 24 November 1939
41. *Jewish Chronicle*, 12 April 1940
42. *Peace News*, 26 April 1940
43. *Jewish Chronicle*, 9 February 1940
44. *Jewish Chronicle*, 29 December 1937
45. *Jewish Chronicle*, 29 March 1940
46. Exodus XIV 14 (see appendix) and Millard C. Lind op cit.
47. Reproduced in Denis Hayes, *Challenge of Conscience*, Routledge and Kegan Paul 1949
48. Geoffrey S. Smith, *To Save a Nation: American countersubversives, the New Deal and the coming of World War II*, Basic Books NY 1973
49. *Tidings* II, February 1944, quoted by Michael Young, "Facing a Test of Faith: Jewish pacifists during the Second World War", *Peace and Change* III Nos 2 and 3, Summer/Fall 1975
50. CCAR Yearbook Vol L, 1940
51. Open letter, Rabbinical Assembly, October 1940, Hoffman papers, quoted in Michael Young, "Facing a Test of Faith: Jewish Pacifists during the Second World War" op cit.
52. CCAR Yearbook LI, 1941

53. *Tidings* 1, February 1943, quoted by Michael Young op cit.
54. Louis Jacobs, *A Tree of Life, Diversity, Flexibility and Creativity in Jewish Law*, Oxford University Press 1984
55. CCAR Yearbook LII, 1942
56. *Biographical Encyclopedia of American Jews*, 1935
57. Quoted by Michael Young op cit.
58. Peter Mayer ed. *The Pacifist Conscience*, Hart Davis 1966
59. Michael Young, "Facing a Test of Faith: Jewish pacifists during the Second World War", *Peace and Change* III Nos 2 and 3, Summer/Fall 1975
60. June Stillman, "The Jewish Peace Fellowship", *Fellowship*, 1976
61. Quoted in Murray Polner, "Isidor Hoffman", in Harold Josephson ed. *Dictionary of Peace Leaders*, Greenwood Press 1985

Chapter 7

1. Eyewitness 10, recorded by Mikhl Zylberberg, Prague, published in Isaiah Trunk, *Jewish Responses to Nazi Persecution*, Stein and Day 1979
2. Apenszlak ed. *Black Book of Polish Jewry: An Account of the Martyrdom of Polish Jewry under the Nazi Occupation*, NY American Federation for Polish Jews 1943
3. Inge Scholl, *The White Rose: Munich 1942-1943*, trans. A Schultz, Wesleyan University Press, Connecticut 1970, German ed., Frankfurt 1952
4. From a Kibbutz Haggadah, in Avshalom Reich, *Changes and Development in the Passover Haggadot of the Kibbutz Movement*, Ph.D. Univ. of Texas 1972, quoted in C.Liebman and E.Don Yehiya, *Civil Religion in Israel*, Univ. of California Press 1983
5. M.R.D. Foot, *Resistance*, Eyre Methuen 1976
6. Viktor Frankl, *Man's Search for Meaning*, Hodder 1959/62 (German edition 1946)
7. Mishneh Torah, Hil Yesode Ha Torah V, quoted in H.J. Zimmels, *The Echo of the Nazi Holocaust in Rabbinic Literature*, 1975
8. Joseph Friedenson in *The Jewish Observer*, September 1963, quoted in R. Wolpin ed. *A Path through the Ashes*, Mesorah Publications NY / Agudath Israel of America, 1986
9. M.K. Gandhi, "The Jews", *Harijan*, 26 November 1938, for text see Mendes-Flohr op cit. for a full discussion, Gideon Shimoni, *Gandhi, Satyagraha and the Jews*, Davis Institute, Jerusalem 1977
10. Final Statement of the Accused, published in Inge Scholl, *The White Rose* op cit.
11. ibid. 3rd leaflet
12. Isaiah Trunk, *Jewish Responses to Nazi Persecution*, Stein and Day 1979
13. 1st Leaflet published in Inge Scholl, *The White Rose* op cit.
14. Joshua Sobol, lecture at Yakar, London. Source, un-named surviving Jewish doctor then living in Australia.
15. Valentine Senger, *The Invisible Jew*, Sidgewick and Jackson 1980, *Kaiserstrasse 12*, 1978
16. Evidence printed by Trunk op cit.
17. Wilfred Harrison, BBC Everyman Film *Rescuers Speaking*, based on the research of Samuel and Pearl Oliner of Humboldt State University, California, broadcast 11 June 1989. See also Samuel and Pearl Oliner, *The Altruistic Personality: Rescuers of Jews in Nazi Europe*, Free Press 1988

18. Kurt Hiller, *Das recht auf Leben*, 1924
19. Wolfgang Benz ed. *Pazifismus in Deutschland*, Fischer 1988
20. Bruno Bettelheim, *Surviving and Other Essays*, Thames and Hudson 1979. *Surviving the Holocaust*, Flamingo 1986
21. Anonymous, Oliner op cit.
22. Lamentations III 30-31
23. Enc. Judaica vol. XIII, 1972
24. Bab Talmud Gittin 57b. London 1948. quoted Spiro op cit.
25 Raul Hilberg, *The Destruction of the European Jews*, Quadrangle 1961
26. ibid.
27. Trunk, 1979 op cit. and Isaiah Trunk, *Judenrat: The Jewish Councils in Eastern Europe under Nazi Occupation*, Macmillan 1972
28. Trunk, 1979 op cit.
29. Adam Barkai, "German Jews in Lódz Ghetto", *Yad v Shem Studies* XVI, 1984
30. Jean Jacqumain, *The Occupation of the Channel Islands 1940-45, a counter example of nonviolent civilian defence*, in *Studies in Nonviolence* 9, PPU 1981, referring also to Charles Cruickshank, *The German Occupation of the Channel Islands*, 1975
31. Apenszlak ed. 1943 op cit.
32. YVA 01/52, quoted in A. Barkai, "German Jews in Lódz Ghetto", *Yad v Shem Studies* XVI, 1984
33. Evidence of Nahum Hoch, Eichmann Trial, session 71, 8 June 1961
34. Elie A Cohen, *Human Behaviour in the Concentration Camp*, 1954, Free Association Books 1988
35. Victor Frankl op cit.
36. Primo Levi, *The Drowned and the Saved*, Michael Joseph 1988
37. Jack Kugelmass and Jonathan Boyarin trans. *From a Ruined Garden, The memorial books of Polish Jewry*, Schocken 1983
38. ibid.
39. Nitza Spiro op cit.
40. *Jewish Guardian* Vol. 2 No. 8, 5784, Spring '984.
41. "Who is a Hero?" in Albert Axelrad, *Meditations of a Maverick Rabbi*, Rossel Books 1985
42. *Jewish Guardian* Vol. 2 No 8, 5784, Spring '984. op cit.
43. Rabbi Moshe Sherer's comments, appended to the Report of the American Jewish Commission on the Holocaust, quoted in R. Wolpin ed. *A Path through the Ashes*, collected from the *Jewish Observer*, Mesorah Publications NY 1986
44. Adam Czerniakow, *Warsaw Ghetto Diary*, Warsaw 1983
45. Apenszlak ed. op cit.
46. Shimon Huberband, *Kiddush Hashem*, op cit., quoted in Trunk op cit.
47. Yaffa Eliach, *Hasidic Tales of the Holocaust*, Oxford University Press 1982
48. ibid.
49. Marie Durand, a Protestant girl, was incarcerated at Aigues Mortes when she was fifteen years old and endured 38 years in appalling conditions rather than convert to Catholicism. Many of her fellow-prisoners died. Anne Danclos, *Marie Durand et Les Captives d'Aigues-Mortes*, Favre 1983
50. Lucien Simon, *Les Juifs à Nimes et dans La Gard durant La Deuzième Guerre Mondiale*, Lacour 1985/7

51. Aimé Bonifas, *Détenu 20801 Dans les Bagnes Nazis*, Fédération Nationale des Déportés et Internés Résistants et Patriotes 1985

52. Central Historical Committee of Liberated Jews in the American Zone 1947 No 6 pp 44-7, in Yiddish, quoted by Trunk op cit.

53. Trunk op cit. See also Moshe Prager, *Sparks of Glory*, Shengold NY 1974

54. Evidence of Joseph Zalman Kleinman, The Eichmann Trial. See also Moshe Pearlman, *The Capture and Trial of Adolph Eichman*, Weidenfeld and Nicholson 1963

55. R. Wolpin ed. *A Path through the Ashes*, 1986

56. Shimon Huberband, *Kiddush Hashem, Jewish Religious and cultural life in Poland during the Holocaust*, KTAV 1987

57. Irving Halperin, "Spiritual Resistance in Holocaust Literature", *Yad v Shem Studies* VII

58. Kugelmass and Boyarin eds op cit.

59. Shimon Huberband, *Kiddush Hashem, Jewish Religious and cultural life in Poland during the Holocaust*, KTAV 1987

60. Robert Brenner Reeve, *The Faith and Doubt of Holocaust Survivors*, Free Press NY 1980

61. Quoted in Robert Brenner Reeve op cit.

62. Zdena Berger, *Tell me another morning* (a novel), quoted by Irving Halperin, "Spiritual Resistance in Holocaust Literature", *Yad v Shem Studies* VII

63. Retold by Rabbi Shmuel Unsdorfer in Wolpin ed. op cit.

Chapter 8

1. Abraham Heschel, in Robert McAfee Brown, Abraham Heschel and Michael Novak, *Vietnam: Crisis of Conscience*, Association Press, Herder and Herder, and Behrman House, New York 1967

2. Balfour Brickner, *Abraham Joshua Heschel, Chasid*, quoted in John C.Merkle, *The Genesis of Faith, the Depth Theology of Abraham Joshua Heschel*, Macmillan 1985

3. Abraham Heschel, *The Sabbath: Its meaning for modern man*, Farrar Straus & Young 1951

4. Abraham Heschel, "In Search of Exaltation", *Jewish Heritage* 13 No 3, 1971, quoted in Samuel Dresner, introduction to A. Heschel, *The Circle of Baal Shem Tov: Studies in Hasidism*, Univ. of Chicago Press 1985

5. Abraham Heschel, *God in Search of Man: A Philosophy of Judaism*, Farrar, Straus & Cudahy 1955

6. Abraham Heschel, *Man is not alone: A Philosophy of Religion*, Farrar, Straus & Young 1951

7. A. Heschel, *In Search of Exaltation*, op cit.

8. R. McAfee Brown, quoted in John C. Merkle, *The Genesis of Faith: The Depth Theology of Abraham Joshua Heschel*, Macmillan 1985

9. Unpublished talk, John C. Merkle, *The Genesis of Faith* op cit.

10. Allan Solomonow ed. *Roots of Jewish Non-Violence*, JPF 1981

11. Heschel, *Man's Quest for God: Studies in Prayer and Symbolism*, 1954

12. Heschel, *The Sabbath*, op cit.

13. Heschel et al. *Vietnam* op cit.

14. ibid.

15. Will Herberg, *Protestant, Catholic, Jew: An Essay in American Religious Sociology*, Doubleday 1960

16. Robert Bellah, "Civil Religion in America", *Daedalus* XCVI, Winter 1967 and *The Broken Covenant: American Civil Religion in Time of Trial*, Seabury Press, NY 1975

17. Frances Fitzgerald, *Fire in the Lake: The Vietnamese and Americans in Vietnam*, Little, Brown 1972

18. Irwin Zeplowitz, *Jewish Attitudes to the Vietnam War*, HUC Rabbinic Thesis 1984

19. CCAR Yearbook LXXVI, 1966

20. Michael Meyer, *Response to Modernity: A History of the Reform Movement in Judaism*, Oxford University Press 1988

21. Irwin Zeplowitz op cit.

22. Maurice N. Eisendrath, Conference Lecture. CCAR Yearbook LXXVI, 1966

23. Seeger decision of March 1965. Charles C. Walker, *Quakers and the Draft*, Friends' Co-ordinating Committee on Peace, Philadelphia 1968

24. Charles Walker, *Quakers and the Draft*, Friends' Co-ordinating Committee on Peace, Philadelphia 1968

25. Diana Francis, International Secretary, IFOR, conversation with the author, September 1989

26. Zeplowitz, *Jewish Attitudes to the Vietnam War* op cit.

27. June Stillman, "The Jewish Peace Fellowship", *Fellowship* op cit.

28. Frances Fitzgerald 1972 op cit.

29. Religion's Responsibility to the Human Race, from Homer A. Jack ed. *Religion and Peace*, Papers from the National Inter-religious Conference on Peace USA, 1966

30. Michael Meyer, *Response to Modernity* op cit.

31. Report of the Committee on Chaplaincy, CCAR Yearbook LXXVIII, 1968

32. Michael Herr, *Dispatches*, Alfred A. Knopf 1977

33. CCAR Yearbook LXXVIII, 1968

34. Michael Le Burkien, CCAR Yearbook LXXIX, 1969

35. *Army Field Manual*, Chapter 58 Section 109a. Religious Service and Religious Education, cited by Rabbi Michael A. Robinson, CCAR Yearbook LXXIX, 1969

36. Gabriel Kolko, *Vietnam, Anatomy of War 1940-75*, Unwin 1985/6

37. Zeplowitz, *Jewish Attitudes to the Vietnam War* op cit.

38. Charles Walker, *Quakers and the Draft* op cit.

39. Zeplowitz, op cit.

40. Tatum and Tuchinsky, *Guide to the Draft*, 3rd ed. 1970, (1st ed. 1969)

41. ibid., for Jewish objection procedures see also Albert Axelrad, *Call to Conscience: Jews, Judaism and Conscientious Objection*, KTAV 1986

42. Michael Zigmond A.J.A., cited in Zeplowitz op cit.

43. F. Raphael, "Les Juifs d'Alsace et La Conscription au Dix-Neuvième Siècle", in Bulmenkranz and Soboul eds, *Les Juifs et la Révolution Française*, privately printed, Toulouse 1976

44. Michael Herr, *Dispatches* op cit.

45. CCAR Yearbook LXXVI, 1966

46. Charles Walker, *Quakers and the Draft*, op cit.

47. Figures from Lawrence M. Baskir and Wm. A Strauss, *Chance and Circumstance*, quoted in Michael Maclear, *Vietnam: The Ten Thousand Day War*, Methuen 1981

48. Aaron Samuel Tamaret, "Passover and Nonviolence", 1906/1912, translated by Everett Gendler in *Roots of Jewish Nonviolence*, Jewish Peace Fellowship, reprinted New York 1981

49. Ba. Talmud Berakhot 10a, in Everett Gendler, "Judaism and Nonviolence", in *Fellowship*, January/February 1976, quoting Reuven Kimelman, "Nonviolence in the Talmud", reprinted in *Roots of Jewish Nonviolence*, op cit. For feminist insight into the character of Beruriah, I am indebted to a lecture by Rabbi Elizabeth Sarah, 1989

50. Albert Axelrad, *Meditations of a Maverick Rabbi*, Rossel Books NY 1985

51. Norma Sue Woodstone, *Up Against the War*, Tower Publications NY 1970

52. Zeplowitz op cit.

53. C. Louis Heath ed. *Mutiny Does not Happen Lightly: The Literature of the American resistance to the Vietnam War*, Scarecrow Press Inc. 1976. See also Sheldon Zimmerman, "Confronting the Halakha on Military Service", *Judaism* XX, 1971

54. Albert Axelrad, *Meditations of a Maverick Rabbi*, op cit.

55. Leo Landman, "Law and Conscience in Judaism", *Judaism* XVIII 1. Winter 69. quoted in Zeplowitz op cit.

56. Quoted in Zeplowitz op cit.

57. Gabriel Kolko, *Vietnam, Anatomy of War 1940-75*, Unwin 1985/6

58. Zeplowitz op cit.

59. Zeplowitz op cit.

60. Heschel et al. *Vietnam* op cit.

61. Paul Johnson, *A History of the Jews*, 1987

62. Maimonides, *The Book of Judges* Kings and Wars, Ch. 5 para 1. (see appendix)

63. CCAR Yearbook LXXVII, 1967

64. Gillette v. U.S. (U.S.33 SSLR 3741,1971) cited in Tatum and Tuchinsky 1980

65. Emil Fackenheimn, *Quest for Past and Future*, Indiana University Press 1968, also *The Jewish Return into History: Reflections in the Age of Auschwitz and a New Jerusalem*, Schocken 1978

66. Peter Brock, *Pacifism in the United States: Colonial Era to the First World War*, Princeton University Press 1968

67. Arthur Cohen, *The Natural and Supernatural Jew*, Valentine Mitchell 1967

68. e.g. David Bleich, "Pre-emptive War", *Tradition* XXI No 1, Spring 1983

69. Michael Walzer, *Just and Unjust Wars: a moral argument with historical illustrations*, Basic Books 1977

70. Steven Schwarzschild, "The Religious Demand for Peace", delivered 16 March 1966

71. For the work of Steven Schwarzschild see Menachem Kellner ed. *The Pursuit of the Ideal: Jewish Writings of Steven Schwarzschild*, State University of NY Press 1990. For an outline of modern Jewish thought, without coverage of pacifism, see Eugene Borowitz, *Choices in Modern Jewish Thought: A Partisan Guide*, Behrman House 1983

72. "The Prevention of War", report of conference address by Steven Schwarzschild, World Union for Progressive Judaism, London, July 1949

73. Steven Schwarzschild, "Theologians and the Bomb", in William Clancy ed. *The Moral Dilemma of Nuclear Weapons, Essays from World View*, The Church Peace Union 1961
74. Deuteronomy XX 19, and Maimonides, *The Book of Judges* op cit.
75. Steven Schwarzschild, "The Necessity of the Lone Man", *Fellowship*, May 1965, Fellowship of Reconciliation
76. Julius Guttmann, *Philosophies of Judaism*, 1933 trans. D.Silverman, Holt, Rinehart & Winston 1964
77. Steven Schwarzschild, "To Recast Rationalism", in Arthur Cohen ed. *Arguments and Doctrines*, Harper and Row 1970
78. from Homer A Jack ed. *Religion and Peace*, op cit.
79. *Religion and Peace* op cit., for Isaiah II, see appendix
80. Steven Schwartzschild, "Theologians and the Bomb" op cit.
81. Steven Schwartzschild, "Towards Jewish Arab Co-operation", from *Subject to Change*, October 1979, reprinted by the Middle East Peace Project
82. Steven Schwartzschild, "Shalom", in *Holy Land*, quarterly of the Franciscan Custody of the Holy Land, VII No.4, Winter 1987, based on a paper prepared for a conference on The Quest for Peace Beyond Ideology, September 1980
83. Steven Schwartzschild, "The Radical Imperatives of Judaism", *Judaism* Vol. 21 No 1, Winter 1972

Chapter 9

1. Enzo Sereni, *La Questione Ebraica*, 1939 op cit.
2. Uri Davis, *Israel: An Apartheid State*, Zed Books 1987
3. Letter 28 June 1972, in Martin Blatt, Uri Davis, and Paul Kleinbaum eds, *Dissent and Ideology in Israel, Resistance to the Draft 1948-73*, Ithaca Press 1975
4. All quotations from Hofshi are from Natan Hofshi, *With Heart and Soul, A presentation from his friends on his 75th birthday* (Hebr.), privately printed 1964
5. Interview in Martin Blatt, Uri Davis and Paul Kleinbaum eds. op cit.
6. Joseph Abileah speaking at a meeting, Jerusalem, November 1987, quoting Konrad Lorenz, *On Aggression*, Methuen 1966
7. Joseph Abileah, "Judaïsme et Non-Violence", in *Cahiers de la Réconciliation* No 2, February 1982, IFOR France
8. Anthony Storr, *Human Aggression*, Allen Lane 1968
9. Quotes the Bab. Talmud Shabat 31a (see Appendix)
10. Natan Hofshi, *Looking Inwards*
11. Blatt et al. op cit.
12. Natan Hofshi, *Looking Inwards*
13. Christopher Sykes, *Crossroads to Israel: Palestine from Balfour to Bevin*, Collins 1965
14. Conversation with author 1987; see also Axelrad, *Call to Conscience* op cit.
15. Natan Hofshi, *Letter to a Soldier*, 1955
16. Quoted from the Hebrew in Liebman and Don Yehiya op cit.
17. Natan Hofshi, 17 October 1938
18. C. Liebman and E. Don Yehiya op cit.
19. Kenneth Thompson, *Beliefs and Ideology*, Ellis Horwood/Tavistock Publications 1986

20. Natan Hofshi, *The Sin and Its Causes*, October/November 1958
21. Zechariah IV 6
22. Quoted by Hofshi op cit.
23. Amos Elon, *The Israelis, Founders and Sons*, 1971 2nd ed. Penguin 1981. Moshe Greenberg, "Rabbinic Reflections on Defying Orders", *Judaism* XIX, 1970
24. G.W. Hunt, 1878
25. *A Land for Two Peoples* op cit. reference to *New Outlook* IX No.8, October – November 1966
26. Natan Hofshi, November 1939
27. Michael Jansen, *Dissonance in Zion*, Zed 1987
28. Marc H. Ellis, *Towards a Jewish Theology of Liberation*, Orbis Books 1987/8
29. Muki Tzur, from Avraham Shapira et al. eds, *The Seventh Day: Soldiers Talk about the Six Day War*, Deutsch 1970
30. Dom Helder Câmara, *Le Désert est Fertile*, De Brouwer 1971
31. Tamar Mossinson, in *The Seventh Day* op cit.
32. ibid.
33. Amos Gvirtz, conversation with author, 1987
34. Uri Davis, *Israel an Apartheid State*, op cit.
35. Natan Hofshi, from *Hallal*, 5 July 1941
36. Appeal to the High Court of Justice by Gady Al. Gazy, 27 September 1980, reported in Amnesty International, *Israel and the Occupied Territories, Conscientious Objection in Israel*, MDE/15/40/88
37. Interview in Carol Birkland, *Unified in Hope: Arabs and Jews talks about Peace*, World Council of Churches 1987
38. Natan Hofshi, letter to Jacov Fishman, 25 February 1940
39. Natan Hofshi, to his friend.
40. Storr op cit. quoting Peter Matthiessen, *Under the Mountain Wall*, Heinemann 1963
41. Jeremy Milgrom, "Tear gas, Flying Rocks and Rabbi Meet in Arab Village", *Manna*, Spring 1985
42. Natan Hofshi, 1955
43. Simon Glustrom, *The Language of Judaism*, KTAV 1966/73. See also Appendix for other sources on the sword as incongruous to religion.
44. Midrash Rabba Deuteronomy (Re'eh) IV 2
45. Hans Mommsen, *From Weimar to Auschwitz: Essays in German History*, trans. Philip O'Connor, Polity Press 1991

Index

If you have difficulty ordering this book from a bookshop, please order direct from Hawthorn Press, Hawthorn House, 1 Lansdown Lane, Lansdown, Stroud, Gloucestershire, U.K. GL5 1BJ. Fax 0453 757040.